AN UNEASY EQUILIBRIUM:

The African Revolution versus Parasitic Capitalism

The Political Report to the Sixth Congress of the
African People's Socialist Party

Chairman Omali Yeshitela

Commemorative Edition
Foreword by Luwezi Kinshasa

CONGRESS OF THE
AFRICAN PEOPLE'S SOCIALIST PARTY

African People's Socialist Party USA
1245 18th Avenue South
St. Petersburg, FL 33705
727-821-6620
info@apspuhuru.org

Published by Burning Spear Publications
1245 18th Avenue South
St. Petersburg, FL 33705
www.burningspearmarketplace.com

Dedication

To the toiling masses of the world, backs stooped, bodies misshapen, spirits crushed from producing for others food, clothing, shelter and happiness that we seldom share;

*To Katura Carey and Lawrence Mann,
two co-founders of the
African People's Socialist Party;*

To my dear comrades of the African People's Socialist Party and the Uhuru Movement throughout the world who have boldly and arrogantly assumed the responsibility to overturn a social system born of our oppressive exploitation;

To the women, men and children committed to building a new world free of the oppressed-oppressor nation dialectic that has defined our existence for the last five centuries;

*To all those who have refused to surrender:
We will win! We are winning!*

Lawrence Mann
February 29, 1944 - January 10, 1973

Katura Carey
November 30, 1947 - April 17, 1997

Contents

Part I: Political Report to the Sixth Congress
By Chairman Omali Yeshitela

Part II: Resolutions

Part III: Solidarity Statements

Part IV: Photos

Foreword

Now is the time for the
Final Offensive against Imperialism!

The Vietnamese revolutionaries called it *thoi co,* translated roughly as the "opportune or critical moment." The Black Revolution of the 1960s mobilized around the same principle with its cry to "Seize the Time!"

There is a precise and fleeting moment in the history of every struggle when the balance of power has shifted, a moment ripe for revolutionary action and victory, when the dying-but-not-yet-dead imperialism has no more legitimacy in the eyes of the oppressed, and no capacity to rule in the same old way.

All around us, in every headline and news report, we see the death crisis of imperialism playing out before our eyes, day by day. Global resistance of oppressed peoples, generalized social volatility and rising anti-U.S.-European-imperialist sentiments abound.

These conditions are responsible for imperialism's economic crisis, which the imperialists are powerless to turn around. For the first time ever, North Americans and Europeans look to the future with fear and despair while the traditional victims of their countries' policies are marching ahead with increasing confidence.

The urgency of understanding that we are facing a *thoi co* moment right now permeates the pages of *An Uneasy Equilibrium: The African Revolution versus Parasitic Capitalism* written by Omali Yeshitela, who characterizes the present era as the "Final Offensive against Imperialism."

As Chairman of the African People's Socialist Party and leader of the African Socialist International, Omali Yeshitela presides over the fastest growing African revolutionary movement in the world today. With Party organizations or influence throughout Africa, Europe, the Caribbean, Canada and the U.S., the Chairman's message of One Africa! One Nation! resonates across the African world.

This is the Party of workers who have never been paid for centuries of forced, stolen labor, workers who produced the cotton, sugar, coltan, gold, oil, diamonds, tin and bauxite for others' enjoyment. This is the Party of workers forced to live on 50 cents a day, many of whom have never seen a dentist or an electric stove; of young men stuffed into the prison camps. This is the Party of women who walk miles to get water unfit for human consumption or bury their loved ones who are shot down by police every 28 hours.

In *An Uneasy Equilibrium,* the Political Report to the Sixth Congress of the African People's Socialist Party held in St. Petersburg, FL in December 2013, Chairman Omali takes us on an incredible journey from the viewpoint and experience of the African working class.

This journey is informed by the certainty of the fall of this parasitic capitalist social system now resting tenuously on the backs of African and Indigenous peoples whose centuries of blood and sweat, enslavement and genocide fertilized the ground on which capitalism was born and grew. It is we who are now rocking imperialism's pedestal with resistance and struggle in every corner of the planet.

With an arrogance that flows from confidence in the people's victory, Chairman Omali shows us that while this crisis offers dismal prospects for all who have hooked their destinies to imperialism, for those of us fighting to free ourselves from imperialism's long and bloody grip, this is a time pregnant with unlimited possibility for our collective future.

With his forward vision, Chairman Omali cautions against being "stuck in a time warp, locked in the past at that point in time when our revolution was militarily defeated and the many political and ideological contradictions thrust upon us were left unresolved."

Systematically and with great ease, Chairman Omali destroys every theoretical, political and practical barrier standing in the path of our people's centuries-long struggle for the total liberation and unification of Africa and African people everywhere. Each unresolved question lingering from the '60s—or otherwise—is studied under the microscope of the theory of African Internationalism where it is scientifically dissected and resolved.

To anyone mired in nostalgia about the past era, the Chairman points out that the decade of the 1960s is a half-century behind us. The responsibility of the revolutionary is to lead us into the future.

As the only African working class-based revolutionary organization that successfully bridged the gap between that period and this one, the African People's Socialist Party has indeed led during all its four decades of existence, boldly and with revolutionary swagger.

The Chairman takes us through the current crisis of imperialism and shows us its profound significance. As far back as 1981 Chairman Omali analyzed this crisis in the Political Report to the Party's First Congress, noting that "imperialism is not accommodating us by committing suicide."

Built and sustained from the land, labor and resources stolen from the oppressed peoples of the world, the current parasitic social system, the Chairman wrote, "is being shaken by the continuous struggles of the people to reverse the verdict of imperialism, to take back what is ours and to use it for our own benefit."

"Never," remarks Chairman Omali, "has the decline of imperialism exposed itself in such absolute terms. Never has the future been so bleak for imperialism...and so bright for the struggling and oppressed peoples of the world."

Delving into his theory of African Internationalism, the Chairman gets to the essence of the most critical questions of our times, providing an understanding of the "material forces at work in the movement of history."

We learn that capitalism was *born* parasitic through the European assault on Africa and the world. "Rapes, massacres, occupations, genocides, colonialism and every despicable act humans are capable of inflicting" make up the DNA of capitalism, writes the Chairman.

The same process that results in "progress" for white people, elevating them out of poverty, disease and oppression, has pushed Africans and the rest of us backwards into the most base and repressive subsistence, ending *our* progress and forward motion as nations and peoples.

These opposing realities are two poles of the same capitalist process. Without this parasitic relationship, Yeshitela asserts, there could be no capitalism, no America, no imperialism as we know it today.

As a historical materialist and African Internationalist, Yeshitela is not a Marxist, but uses his critique of the works of Karl Marx as a building block for the theory of African Internationalism. Chairman Omali quotes Marx to show that, limited by his own European viewpoint on the pedestal of colonialism and slavery, Marx was not capable of understanding the significance of his own words.

Marx summed up the ruthless and bloody enslavement of African people, genocide of the Indigenous people, the conquest and looting of India with the term "primitive accumulation" of capital.

If Marx had comprehended his own words, he would have "been forced to declare that the road to socialism is painted black," the Chairman argues.

One of the most outstanding sections of the book is the chapter on the African nation. The Chairman thoroughly establishes that African people wherever we are located around the world, in Africa, the U.S. or elsewhere, are one people, one African nation oppressed by imperialism and colonialism.

"We are not a race," the Chairman asserts, "but a nation of people forcibly dispersed across the globe." He makes it clear: Africans are a colonized people struggling against imperialist state power for the liberation of our national homeland, Africa. We are fighting for political power in our own hands, not against racism and the perverted, narcissistic and self-adulatory ideas in white people's heads, an effort that the Chairman calls a "self-defeating waste of time."

The Chairman crushes the petty bourgeois philosophy of Pan-Africanism and defines the qualities and national sense of sameness shared by African people everywhere.

The struggle for the African nation represented in this book cuts through every obstacle used by the imperialists and the African petty bourgeoisie. Africa's borders are neocolonial creations, which only facilitate exploitation by the imperialists and all those who serve them.

The building of one, united, liberated African nation under the leadership of the African working class forever resolves the plague of tribalism, which is used to entrap and fragment Africa, maintaining the violent control of imperialism and the neocolonial class.

Chairman Yeshitela's visionary leadership lays out the foundation of a liberated political and economic revolutionary project that ties every single African located in every part of the world to the struggle to free Africa and African people everywhere.

The amazing history of the African People's Socialist Party and its political and practical impact on the world and on the consciousness of African and oppressed peoples everywhere is also chronicled in this book.

Founded in 1972, in the wake of the U.S. government's COINTELPRO and other assaults on the African Revolution and on anti-colonial movements around the world, the Party was the only force that correctly summed up that an imperialist counterinsurgency was waged to defeat the U.S. Front of the African Revolution.

The Party's early years were characterized by non-stop political motion and mass struggle aimed to advance the African Revolution, accompanied by bursts of rapid theoretical development on the part of the Chairman.

Throughout its history the Party has been on the front lines of every political question. It has built campaigns and espoused positions far ahead of its time that have defined for generations of Africans and the world at large how to understand events and issues through a revolutionary perspective.

From the victorious campaign to free Dessie Woods in the 1970s, to the First Tribunal on Reparations to African People making reparations a household word in 1982; from the relentless exposure of neocolonialism, to the formation of the African People's Solidarity Committee; from the building of the African Socialist International, to the continuous publication of *The Burning Spear* newspaper since 1968; from the creation of numerous economic institutions and the building of Black Star Industries as dual and contending African power, its fighting history has poised the Party—more than any other organization on the planet—to lead the revolutionary period before us.

It is a testimony to the fact that a few dedicated cadres informed by the correct theory and tireless practice, under the leadership of the bold and brilliant Chairman Omali Yeshitela, can and have forever changed the world.

Now with the presence of an organized African working class, armed with our own programs, strategy and political theory, with African Internationalist members in key locations around the world, based in imperialist centers and oppressed territories alike, the African Socialist International represents a new paradigm from which imperialism cannot escape.

An Uneasy Equilibrium shows us that the vision of Marcus Garvey and his worldwide African movement a century ago based on "Africa for the Africans, those at home and those abroad" is in the process of becoming a reality.

Our time is now. We must seize it.

African independence in our lifetime!

Luwezi Kinshasa,

Secretary General
African Socialist International

Preface

Sixth Congress Political Report: the way forward for Africans everywhere

With magnificent pageantry, beautiful decor and powerful cultural performances, the Sixth Congress of the African People's Socialist Party convened on Saturday, December 7, 2013 at the Catherine Hickman Theater in Gulfport, Florida, a small beach town next to St. Petersburg.

Africans and our allies converged for our five-day Congress from all over the world—from North, East and West Africa; from Sweden and England in Europe; from The Bahamas in the Caribbean, as well as from Canada and the U.S.

For two days, Gulfport was headquarters to the African Socialist International and the African Revolution. For the remaining three days—December 9 through 11—the Congress was held at Akwaaba Hall in our own Uhuru House in St. Petersburg.

Under the slogan "One Africa! One Nation! One Party!" the Congress brought Party members together to unite on our upcoming plans and strategy for building the African Revolution in this period that we have named the "Final Offensive."

On the opening day, the large stage at the Hickman Theater was set off by a large banner with the Congress logo hanging from the ceiling: red, black and green stripes in the shape of Africa resting on a golden symbol of the sun with a red star in its center. Bright red lighting drenched the back curtain creating a dramatic aura that highlighted the significance of the event.

The electricity in the room was tangible. It wasn't just the energy of the participants, many of whom would be meeting each other for the first time. Nor was it the black-clad Uhuru security forces whose serious visage allowed others to comfortably engage in discussion and ceremony designed to forward our struggle.

More than anything, it was the fact that we were all there at our own Congress where ordinary working class Africans and our guests and allies would discuss the pressing issues of the day on our own terms and through our own worldview. There was a palpable sense of excitement and unity among comrades who had come together to set the course of history that will make Africans, Africa and the world free!

Tammy Harris, Administrative Assistant to Chairman Omali Yeshitela, opened the ceremonies and greeted the constituency. Anticipation filled the audience as the curtains parted and renowned actor Ron Bobb-Semple dressed as Marcus Garvey in full regalia stepped to the front of the stage. To enthusiastic applause Bobb-Semple brought Garvey to life with words from Garvey's speech, "Look for me in the whirlwind!"

As the lights faded on Marcus Garvey, the sound of African drums filled the hall announcing the dynamic procession of flag-bearing National Central Committee (NCC) members slowly moving to the front from the rear doors. Each NCC member carried the Party's flag to the stage where she or he was introduced to the audience. Chairman Omali Yeshitela was the last in the procession and was greeted with cheers and extended applause.

Gaida Kambon, Secretary General of the African People's Socialist Party, then formally convened the Sixth Congress of the African People's Socialist Party with three dramatic strikes of the gavel.

As soon as the Central Committee returned to their seats, the stage curtains opened again to the sight and sound of Carolyn Lake at her piano. Her imploring and melodic voice hovered soulfully over the auditorium, plaintively asking the question in song, "What does it mean to be free?"

Immediately after Lake's much appreciated performance, the youthful energy of the hip-hop group People's Vanguard from St. Mary's, Georgia had the Congress participants on their feet, fists pumping in the air, calling for the African Revolution.

Then came the popular Princess Williams from St. Petersburg who gave a beautiful rendition of the Staple Singers song, "When Will We Be Paid?"

Chimurenga Waller, Director of the Party's National Office of Recruitment and Membership presented plaques to relatives of victims of police violence, including Ms. Pearlie McCullough whose grandson Marquell was brutally murdered by Pinellas County Sheriffs.

Recognition was given to special guests followed by messages of solidarity and congratulation given by comrades, friends and fraternal organizations from around the world. Statements of solidarity came from Chokwe Lumumba, leader of the New Afrikan People's Organization and recently elected mayor of Jackson, Mississippi, and from Mafundi Lake, political prisoner in Alabama and husband to Carolyn Lake.

Other notables whose congratulatory statements were presented to the Congress included the S.H.A.P.E. organization in Houston, Texas; the People's Organization for Progress in Newark, New Jersey; Emma Khadija Jones, mother of Malik Jones, murdered by police in Connecticut; and Nkwame Cedile from Enkangala Kwantu Embo in Occupied Azania (South Africa).

Statements of unity also came from Amaru Pachacutec, a representative of Tawantinsuyu Nation, an Indigenous group of the Americas, and Marcos Garcia, Labor Attaché of the Venezuelan embassy in Washington, DC.

Compañero Benjamin Prado, a member of the Central Committee of Unión del Barrio, a Mexican national liberation organization based in San Diego, gave a profound statement acknowledging the decades-long unity of the two organizations and of the Mexican and African peoples.

Comrades Filiz Demirova and Georgel Caldararu, representatives of the Roma people, presented a moving and strong statement via video expressing unity with the politics of African Internationalism and describing the conditions of the Roma in Europe who live under conditions similar to Africans inside the U.S.

These profound messages best reflected the Party's ideology of African Internationalism as a worldview addressing the struggles and future of Africa as one with the struggling oppressed peoples of the world.

When the delegation from Unión del Barrio was called to the stage the comrades were greeted by thunderous applause from the Congress participants. They marched from the back of the auditorium to the stage carrying both the Mexican flag and their organizational flag.

The Party has always understood that the relationship between Unión del Barrio and ourselves represents the highest interests of our two oppressed peoples, both made landless and shorn of our freedom by U.S. imperialist white power.

The Roma or Romani people, located primarily in Europe but dispersed throughout the world, are a stateless and landless people who suffer brutal exploitation, oppression and slander. Derogatorily referred to as Gypsies, a name they despise, the Roma are thought to have originated in India. In parts of Europe they are regularly killed by state organizations and white mobs with impunity.

During the Nazi era in Germany, up to a half million Romani were murdered by the German state. Unlike the Jews, however, who were recognized as "white," neither reparations nor recognition of their victimization has ever been granted to the Romani.

The Sixth Party Congress resolved to help end the isolation of the Romani people and to provide assistance to their efforts to organize themselves in defense of their lives and in promotion of their self-defined interests in opposition to imperialist white power.

Congress revolved around the Political Report

The most important event of the first day—the event that had implications for the entire Congress—was the presentation of the Political Report or Main Resolution by Chairman Omali as mandated by our Constitution.

The 250-plus-page Political Report had been publicly available for three months prior to the Congress, during which time it had been studied and discussed widely within the ranks of the Party and in the world. This process facilitated the rapid, unanimous adoption of the report on the opening day.

Divided into nine chapters, the Political Report covers a wide spectrum of political, theoretical, practical and organizational questions tied to the struggle to overturn imperialism and build a new world.

The most comprehensive presentation of African Internationalism to date, the Chairman's brilliant and groundbreaking Report analyzes the current irreversible crisis of imperialism and its implications for the growing resistance of the oppressed peoples of the world.

A highlight of the Report is the chapter defining the African nation and the issue of our national identity. The Chairman irrefutably proves the long-debated theory that black people everywhere are one African people whose birthright is a united and liberated Africa.

The Political Report also ideologically defeats the superstition that is the basis of the concept of racism and "race" nationalism that has dominated our struggle since the defeat of the Black Revolution of the 1960s. The Report shows conclusively that Africans, wherever we are located in the world, are fighting against colonial domination and for national liberation of Africa and African people everywhere.

Another key accomplishment of the Political Report is its thorough elaboration on the question of "parasitism" as the key component of capitalism.

Parasitism explains how capitalism was built and is maintained on a pedestal of stolen labor and stolen resources of African people and the exploitation and colonial dispossession of most of the world. The Chairman shows how the struggle of Africans and other historical imperialist victims are responsible for the current economic and political crisis roiling the entire imperialist system.

Following a deep and thoughtful discussion of the Political Report from the floor, followed by its enthusiastic adoption, the Congress broke for lunch.

The afternoon session opened with Comrade Deputy Chair Ona Zené Yeshitela, under whose authority the Office of Economic Development and Finance now functions. Yeshitela led her team in a lively workshop that included handing out gifts to all Party donors and supporters, showing a multimedia presentation that emphasized the enormous scope of the Party's work around the world as well as the Party's main accomplishments since the last Congress in 2010.

Deputy Chair Ona put on her red boxing gloves and called on Africans and our allies to support the Party as an investment in our future and our liberation. The moving appeal resulted in direct contributions from attendees in the hall and online of more than $93,000!

The spectacular opening day of the Congress continued with an evening celebration, the One Africa! One Nation! Freedom Ball. Many local people joined the Congress participants dressed to the nines for a night of great food, entertainment and dancing at the Gulfport Casino where Ron Bobb-Semple and Princess Williams hosted the gala event.

Comedian John X and the young African dancers known as Reality DC got the audience out of their chairs. The political highlight of the banquet was a presentation by Chairman Omali Yeshitela that brought the packed hall to its feet in appreciation for his vision of a free and liberated Africa and African people in our lifetime.

The second day of the Congress featured a presentation by Glen Ford, the courageous Executive Editor of Black Agenda Report who lived up to his reputation for sharp, uncompromising analysis. Ford's presentation on the long history of U.S. surveillance of the African community was set in the context of the current belated concern by Americans following the revelations of the U.S. government's massive data collection targeting U.S. citizens and everyone else on the planet.

African Socialist International (ASI) Secretary General Luwezi Kinshasa provided a resolution on building a united Africa as the way forward for the liberation of our people. This was discussed and adopted by unanimous vote.

A special presentation by Unión del Barrio given by Compañeros Benjamin Prado and Ron Gochez on Day Two included a resolution on the unity of our organizations and peoples. This was discussed and adopted unanimously and enthusiastically by the Congress.

Cultural presentations by Kazoots, a Miami-based Haitian musical group, People's Vanguard and spoken word artist Mona Leza kept the energy and spirits in the room high.

Charo Walker-Morley unveiled the launching of the Party's travel agency and announced that the movement's annual fundraiser, the Marcus Garvey Legacy Cruise will sail on December 14, 2014 taking Party members and friends to Jamaica and The Bahamas.

Party direction and leadership voted on

One of the most important sessions of the Congress took place on Day Three. Following reports from the leaders of Party departments and organizations and the adoption of the Political Report as our strategic direction, Party members adopted resolutions, voted to revise the Party's Constitution and elected the Party's leadership, the National Central Committee.

Comrade Waleeah Brooks from Newark, New Jersey stepped forward to give the report from the International People's Democratic Uhuru Movement (InPDUM). Brooks's report served as her first official act as the newly appointed President of the International People's Democratic Uhuru Movement (InPDUM), following the removal of Diop Olugbala from that post.

Sister Waleeah's enthusiastic unity with her new assignment is an example of our dynamic Party cadres who are ambitious to take on every challenge in this era of a mortally wounded imperialism when African people are ready to get organized to fight for our liberation.

An outstanding report was given by Deputy Chair Ona Zené Yeshitela, who laid out the amazing accomplishments of her department in the development of the Party's economic work since our last Congress. Her report featured a multimedia presentation showcasing such victories as the completion of the Uhuru Jiko commercial kitchen at the St. Petersburg Uhuru House as well as the work being done at our Oakland Uhuru House that will result in a commercial kitchen being opened there as well.

The ongoing development of our long-standing Uhuru Furniture stores in Oakland and Philadelphia were also showcased in the presentation. Deputy Chair Ona went on to elaborate on the significance of the creation of Black Star Industries, the limited liability company (LLC) that is the umbrella for existing and future economic ventures by the Party as part of the process of establishing the economic base for a liberated African nation.

All the Party members and observers took the election and voting process very seriously. Some commented that while the tedious discussions concerning resolutions, reports, constitutional revisions and elections were things they might have thought would be boring, they actually found this to be one of the most exciting parts of the Congress. It was an exercise in the democratic process of the African working class.

The new National Central Committee of the Party included Comrades Omali Yeshitela, Chairman; Ona Zené Yeshitela, Deputy Chair; Gaida Kambon, Secretary General; Dedan Sankara, Director of Agitation and Propaganda; Chimurenga Waller, Director of the National Office of Recruitment and Membership; and Luwezi Kinshasa, Director of International Affairs.

Others elected to national leadership offices included Ushindi Watu, Northeast Regional Leader and Kobina Bantushango, Southeast Regional Leader.

The appointed positions of the Director of the All African People's Development and Empowerment Project (AAPDEP) and the President of the International People's Democratic Uhuru Movement will be represented on the NCC by Comrades Aisha Fields and Waleeah Brooks, respectively.

During a side meeting on Day Two representatives of the African Socialist International determined the ASI leadership body that would assume the responsibility to advance the important work of the International.

Continuing in the posts of ASI Chair and Secretary General are Omali Yeshitela and Luwezi Kinshasa, respectively. Comrade Charo Walker-Morley assumed the role of Director of Economic Development and Sabrin Ibrahim became ASI Secretary. Alex Morley, Chair of the APSP Bahamas, continued in his role as ASI Caribbean Regional Representative and Ka Meritah, based in Egypt and Kenya, became North and East Africa Regional Representative. Fenty Tholley, our leader in Sierra Leone, was given the responsibility of West Africa Regional Representative, and Makda Yohannes, based in Sweden, became leader of the European region.

Concrete visions for Party work

One of the great highlights of the Congress came on Day Four with the powerful workshop on the theoretical basis for the advent of the nation in history and the specific role of the African nation as key to our struggle for liberation.

Who is part of the African nation? What is a nation? How was the white nation created at the expense of African people and what are the implications of the consolidation of the African nation? These were some of the profound questions answered by and discussed during this workshop.

Led by Chairman Omali Yeshitela, this discussion also included insightful participation from ASI Secretary General Luwezi Kinshasa and Omowale Kefing, Political Editor of *The Burning Spear* newspaper.

Day Four also featured exciting reports from representatives of the African Socialist International, including Fenty Tholley from Sierra Leone, Alex Morley from The Bahamas, Patricia Lumumba from the United Kingdom, Gaida Kambon from the U.S. and Makda Yohannes from Sweden. Ka Meritah also presented reports from Egypt and Kenya.

The extremely talented Krown, a popular St. Petersburg-based hip-hop artist offered a blistering revolutionary cultural presentation.

Ralph Poynter, husband of political prisoner Lynne Stewart, was warmly received when he presented a resolution calling for redoubled efforts to free Stewart. This resolution was resoundingly and unanimously adopted by the Congress just weeks before worldwide political pressure—including mobilizing efforts by our Party—forced the U.S. government to release her.

A report from the Department of Agitation and Propaganda on its work since the last Congress was adopted, as well as the plan of action for the development of the department by Agit-Prop Director Dedan Sankara.

Following the Agit-Prop report, Sankara was joined by Deputy Chair Ona Zené Yeshitela in a presentation on joint plans for building economic self-sufficiency for Agit-Prop.

The report from the African People's Solidarity Committee, given by APSC Chairwoman Penny Hess, laid out the political basis for the Party's formation of the organization of white people under the Party's direct leadership whose role is to be the face of black power inside of the white communities. Hess's report also laid out the various fronts of APSC work and the plans for the upcoming period, including the campaign to win North Americans to a stand of reparations to African people.

Recruitment and cadre building key to Party's development

The last day of the Congress was dedicated primarily to moving the work forward. This day featured an inspiring presentation by Chairman Omali on cadre development as critical to the success of all our Party goals. This presentation was based on an elaboration of the Political Report, which laid out the qualities of cadres who put the interests of the African Revolution before their personal needs.

Chimurenga Waller of the National Office of Recruitment and Membership and Fenty Tholley led a workshop on political action which laid out the 10-10-10 method for block organizing. The comrades presented tactics and strategies for organizing the African community as a process of building dual power by occupying actual territory—organizationally, politically and ideologically.

The Congress closed with a performance by Comrade Tammy Harris who took a song by Donny Hathaway—"Some Day We'll All Be Free"—and made it her own, proving that there is a difference between someone who is simply singing the words and someone who is engaged in changing the world.

Harris's wrenching performance brought the Congress to its feet. There was not a dry eye in the auditorium at the conclusion of the song that ended the Congress.

After five days of being together with our comrades and allies from throughout the world and strategizing about winning African independence in our lifetime, all participants were filled with a new determination. Everyone was ready to go out into the world to arm the African masses with the theory of African Internationalism. This is our time! African workers, unite to build our own African People's Socialist Party!

Take the Congress to the streets!

Uhuru!

Part I

Political Report to the Sixth Congress of the African People's Socialist Party

I. Challenging the time warp

The extraordinary journey of the African People's Socialist Party began nearly 42 years ago in St. Petersburg, Florida. It is fitting that this journey, celebrated with our Party's Sixth Congress, was launched during the process of building the first African Liberation Day mobilization in Washington, DC held on May 27, 1972.

Throughout our history we have often emphasized the significance of the African People's Socialist Party, but today we are clear that at no time has the existence of our Party been more important and urgently needed than it is now.

Not only is building the Party a crucial task of our organization, it is also *the* fundamental task of the African Revolution as a whole at this critical historical juncture.

Our Party was begun by a mere handful of us at a time when U.S. imperialism was gloating about its victory over many of the forces of liberation that defined the spirit of the 1950s and '60s when revolution was the main trend in the whole world, including inside the borders of the U.S.

The African People's Socialist Party was founded in the wake of the crushing military defeat of the African Revolution in Africa, within the U.S. and worldwide. It was a period when the U.S. government was confident its years-long efforts to wipe out our struggle for liberation had been successful.

The U.S. government's bloody wave of political repression in the '60s left some of our most outstanding leaders imprisoned, overthrown or murdered. As a result, our movement's most significant organizations were enfeebled or destroyed.

Nevertheless, even as an era of struggle was being brutally brought to a close and the dreams of freedom and happiness of millions of our people were being subordinated to the whims of imperialism, another era was being born with the founding of our Party. That era is now fully upon us. We have defined this era as the Final Offensive against Imperialism.

Although a final offensive is generally considered to be the strategic culmination of a military engagement, we are speaking here of the Final Offensive in historical terms. We are talking about the fact that current conditions have resulted in the emergence of oppressed peoples as the determinant social force, actively reversing the verdict of an imperialism built on our backs.

The tables have turned and the U.S. is now attempting to stave off the growing global threats to imperialism as it currently exists, desperately fighting to regain its preeminence in the tottering imperialist system.

Today, there is an uneasy equilibrium between the past and the future and much anxiety abounds throughout the world. Every individual, every social force that perceives its future attached to the existing imperialist social system is experiencing severe distress.

With the initiation of the Sixth Congress, our Party stands on the heights established by our 41-year history of struggle. This is the metaphorical mountain top from which we can see a future of Our Africa and our people, liberated and united, propelling all oppressed humanity, all the workers and toiling masses of the world into a future of peace, prosperity and eternal social justice.

We know that the imperialist ideologues—philosophers, politicians and economists alike—have no answers to the pressing issues of our times. Every day there is a new lamentation by one or another thinking representative of the white ruling class that the latest proffered solution to imperialism's unending crisis has proved to be illusory.

At the same time, the defeat of our movement of the 1960s has resulted in more than two generations of Africans with no revolutionary practice or points of reference that can be relied on for direction.

As the sole force that has kept alive the revolutionary aims of the African Liberation Movement over this period, it has always been up to the Party to lead the way forward out of the morass of defeat.

Many militants are stuck in a time warp. They are locked in the period of our military defeat, when the many political and ideological contradictions thrust upon us by the African Revolution were left unresolved. That era is now nearly a half-century behind us.

We learn from Malcolm X and the Black Panther Party, for example, but we do so while recognizing that we must build for the present and future off the platform they provided us from the past.

Too often attempts are being made to base struggle on what others did in the 1960s as opposed to what is needed to advance the struggle of African workers and the African nation today. To do this is to emulate imperialists who are always unsuccessful, trapped in the past because they are fighting the last war.

Our Party prevailed in the face of defeat

Since the defeat of the Black Revolution of the Sixties the masses of the people have been sidelined, pushed out of political life. What passes for struggle is relegated most often to single-issue activism that is nothing but an appendage to social media militancy or liberal and other bourgeois schemes.

The significance of our Party lies in the fact that we have never surrendered or deviated from the path of the same African Revolution that motivated the imperialist white power attacks in the 20th century. We continue to lead despite the general setbacks suffered by our movement as a whole.

We are the only organization that correctly analyzed the fact that the Black Revolution of the '60s was defeated by imperialist counterinsurgency—a military attack intended to keep our people and our movement from ever rising up again.

Our Party's summation of this defeat has informed our work and our mission to complete the Black Revolution instead of settling for the limitations of the present. This has been a necessary recognition that has prevented us from confusing events subsequent to the defeat of our revolution with events of our actual revolutionary movement that shook imperialism to its foundations.

This recognition is what helped us to understand that much of what has transpired since then in the name of the Black Revolution has often been merely the activities of the African petty bourgeoisie functioning to hijack the consciousness of the masses.

This false "revolution" or "liberation" advanced by the colonized petty bourgeoisie was addressed in our book *Izwe Lethu i Afrika! Africa is Our Land!*, the Political Report to our Third Party Congress held in 1990. We made it clear that the liberation of the petty bourgeoisie can never meet the needs and aspirations of the colonized working class. These words remain relevant:

> The "national liberation" of the aspiring black petty bourgeoisie is a "liberation" from the limitations of its development into a full-blown bourgeoisie, [limitations] which are imposed on it by domestic colonialism, the imperialist rule by foreign gangsters. Within this concept of "national liberation" is the germ of a future continuing exploitation of the African working class by a black bourgeoisie that has been liberated from the "national" oppression which prevented the emergence of a free, independent black boss. Such

a "national liberation" is not in the interests of the colonized African working class.

The national liberation of the working class is a liberation which will sweep away all forms of oppression and exploitation. The national liberation of the domestically colonized African working class is not only interested in removing the oppression of foreign rule, it is also interested in destroying the class rule which exploits the workers and toiling masses of all countries where the capitalist system prevails. The national liberation of the working class is explicitly anti-capitalist and consciously a part of the worldwide socialist movement.

Written nearly a quarter of a century ago, this is a position from which we have never retreated. This is the position that informs how we lead today and by which we measure the state of the movement at any given time.

Throughout our entire history all our work has been designed to solve the problems of the revolution, not to find a way to get along within the circumstances provided us by our imperialist enemies and their servile lackeys in our midst. Our commitment to continue to forge ahead with the African Revolution has not been without consequences, however.

From the Party's beginning in 1972 we worked to rebuild our entire movement with various campaigns including attempts to give African Liberation Day a revolutionary character. From its very inception, as our Party aimed to unite the anti-colonial tendency—the primary target of the U.S. counterinsurgency of the 1960s—around a collective movement to liberate Africans imprisoned in the U.S. colonial prison system, we had to combat sundry political opponents that were incapable of venturing beyond the quagmire of defeat.

In the 1980s we were attacked for correctly identifying the presidential campaign of Jesse Jackson as a diversionary move to draw the African masses back into the safe embrace of the imperialist Democratic party, instead of into the ranks of their own independent revolutionary organization. The Party stood alone as most of the so-called revolutionary organizations of the time attempted to build themselves on the Jackson presidential campaign coattails.

Today more and more people are capable of recognizing the complicity of the African National Congress (ANC), if not Nelson Mandela, in the attempt to rescue imperialist interests in South Africa. More than thirty years ago, however, in the 1970s and '80s, the African People's Socialist Party stood alone in correctly identifying and struggling against the ANC as the mass organization of the opportunist, nearly lily-white Communist Party of South Africa and as petty bourgeois neocolonialists in waiting.

We have not changed. Our Party, as the advanced detachment of the African working class, continues to uphold the responsibility to show the way forward, especially when the way forward is murkiest. This is why we were first out of the gate to criticize Barack Hussein Obama, the current, most insidious face of U.S. imperialism.

It is understandable that the masses of Africans worldwide would grasp at the slightest perceived chance of advancing from the crucible of colonial hell by embracing Obama's imperialist presidency. From liberal democrats, to black nationalists and Marxists, so-called African leaders were delirious in their salivating embrace of Obama. This opportunism kept in front of us the requirement of the Party of the African working class to lead at all times.

Our Party's responsibility to lead the masses

So must we lead today, at this moment. This is the meaning of all our work. This is why we organized the International People's Democratic Uhuru Movement (InPDUM) in 1991 as one of our organizational and political strategies to lead. It is the primary organization we have created to help bring the masses back into active, independent political life.

InPDUM represents our recognition that a revolutionary period is characterized not by Negroes running for president or any political office for that matter, but by the masses fully participating in political life on their own terms and under the leadership and influence of their own revolutionary Party.

This does not mean that we confuse the Party with the masses. We are not the masses; we are the advanced detachment, the general staff of the African working class. We do not bury or liquidate the Party among the masses; we lead, always.

Sometimes our positions are unpopular in the short term, even among the masses, only to be vindicated as events unfold to reveal a truth that was obscured by the faulty analysis of the prevailing common perception. On such occasions we must move in opposition to the direction the masses are attempting to go. Otherwise, what is the meaning of leadership?

When a representative of our Party and movement stood up in an Obama campaign meeting in St. Petersburg, Florida in August of 2008, our challenge to Obama met a fierce, solid wall of vocal rejection and opposition from the African masses themselves. Even some members of our movement and Party fell under the sway of liberal imperialism after being intimidated by the delirious mass response to the Obama candidacy and presidency.

It was our responsibility to provide leadership around this question. Otherwise the people would have been left absolutely defenseless in the face of this most insidious imperialist attack. Whatever the initial negative response of the masses, our continued leadership among the people and the ruthless policies of U.S. imperialism in crisis with Obama at its helm will ultimately contribute to the ability of the people to rise up against imperialism from a stronger position than before.

The tradition of organized, practical resistance that characterized the last magnificent period of struggle in the 1960s has been relegated to a past only conjured up for the purpose of abstract celebrations of poorly recorded, seldom correctly analyzed and understood, now long-gone glories. Aside from the leadership of the Party, what remains of the African Liberation Movement has succumbed to the political and ideological stagnation that often follows the defeat of a revolution.

When repression sets in and crushes the revolutionary trajectory, what is left is often a caricature of revolution—simple careerism on the part of those happily occupying space in the movement without an agenda for the revolutionary capture of power. The revolutionary essence has been removed or diluted to meet the legal requirements of the day. Many would-be revolutionaries have learned to speak this new language of non-struggle struggle and muted revolution. This has become a fundamental weakness, making it difficult to recognize, respond to and participate in genuine revolutionary politics.

We of the African People's Socialist Party are confident that we know the way forward. Our organizational capacity is growing and we are capable of answering the questions confounding both the imperialist ruling class and the revolutionaries struggling to advance during this imperialist crisis.

The Sixth Congress of the African People's Socialist Party is occurring at a time that the presence of our Party is sorely needed by Africans and the laboring masses across the globe. It is a time when the world seems to be adrift and in turmoil, unleashed from its political, ideological and economic moorings.

The 2010 Fifth Congress of our Party, with its slogan "One People! One Party! One Destiny!" laid a solid foundation for this period, focusing on organization and capacity-building. Our last Congress has guided our subsequent work to this point and gives us the confidence with which we enter our Sixth Congress and this historical moment.

Following the days of democratic discussion and resolutions at the Fifth Party Congress we temporarily brought all Party organizations and offices under the direct leadership of the Office of the Chairman through the creation of the One People! One Party! One Destiny! Committee. With this ad hoc committee we initiated a Party and movement-wide campaign under the same title that created protocols for the implementation of the Fifth Congress resolutions and mandates for rapid recruitment and organization-building in this ripe and urgent period of imperialist crisis.

As a result our Party today is one of the fastest growing, most effective revolutionary organizations in the world. We are grounded in England as well as in several cities in Germany, France, Sweden and Belgium in Europe. We are actively working in West Africa, particularly in Sierra Leone, and we have growing ideological and political influence and bases in Northern, Southern and Eastern Africa.

Party organizers are active in The Bahamas in the Caribbean and we are growing within the U.S., with political and ideological influence among Africans and others in Canada. The growth of our Party will contribute to the definition of revolution during this period.

For the past 30 years, with the failure of the Chinese and Soviet Marxist models, it has been the specter of Islam that by default unites millions of the oppressed in general opposition to imperialism.

This is because Islam is most concentrated in the areas of the world where impoverished masses suffer from imperialist domination that, since the time of the so-called Christian Holy Wars or Crusades of the Middle Ages, has been understood and defined in religious terms.

Now, through the Party's increasingly global presence and growth, our theory of African Internationalism gives us the opportunity to provide scientific, materialist-based leadership to the African Revolution and the oppressed peoples everywhere. The existence and work of the African People's Socialist Party and all that we do stemming from our Sixth Congress, spell death to imperialism, something we can say with sublime confidence.

II. The crisis of imperialism

The crisis of imperialism is deepening before our eyes. Every day that passes exposes more stench and rot of this dying social system. One of the benefits of the Party's longevity has been our ability to witness the evolution of this crisis in which imperialism's death rattle is becoming increasingly audible.

In *A New Beginning: The Road to Black Freedom and Socialism,* the Main Resolution of our Party's First Congress held in September 1981, we defined the imperialist crisis as it was unfolding at that moment:

> *The U.S. is the sharpest manifestation of "dying imperialism" in the world today. But any discussion of the weakness of U.S. and Western imperialism must be taken out of the abstract. Its metaphysical, one-sided character must be destroyed if this discussion is going to serve us, if it is going to deepen our understanding of the world and inform our practice.*
>
> *In the first place, U.S. and Western imperialism is not simply dying or weakening on its own accord. It is not accommodating us by committing suicide. U.S. and Western imperialism is BEING weakened; it is BEING killed.*
>
> *The present world situation ought to be enough to convince the most opportunist doubting Thomas of the centrality of the struggle for national liberation to the destruction of imperialism. For it is clear that the present crisis of imperialism, as in the past, is being caused by the defeat of imperialism by the struggles for national liberation and independence.*

The U.S. and Western imperialist empire, built and sustained even now by "the primitive accumulation of capital," the theft of land and resources from the oppressed peoples of the world, is being shaken by the continuous struggles of the people to reverse the verdict of imperialism, to take back what is ours and to use it for our own benefit.

From our perspective it is not enough to simply state that imperialism is dying, that U.S. world power is declining. We must understand that we are winning; we must convey this understanding to the masses of our people, and we must escalate the process.

The present crisis of imperialism that reveals U.S. weaknesses was brought on by the success of the Iranian people in casting out the Shah of Iran. Before that, it was the victory of the Ethiopian people which caused the crisis; before that, the victories in Angola and Mozambique. In addition, there have been the victories of Viet Nam and Kampuchea; the OPEC [the Organization of Petroleum Exporting Countries] alignment which challenged the U.S. and Western imperialist energy monopoly, [along with] Cuba and Chile, Korea and China, Afghanistan and Laos and Nicaragua, etc., etc., etc.

The U.S. empire, its strength and muscle, are built on the oppression and enslavement of the oppressed peoples of the world. The same can be said of Western civilization and U.S. society. And the empire is shaken; the society is challenged on every occasion the oppressed peoples and subject nations win an aspect of our liberty and resources back.

The present attempt by the U.S. imperialists to recover from this crisis is an attempt to place the chains back on the unchained, and to build better padlocks for the chains of those of us still struggling for liberation. This is the only context within which it is permissible to view the present world situation that is characterized by desperate and frenzied U.S. and Western imperialism in the face of the freedom blows thrown by the oppressed.

This passage resonates 32 years after it was written because this is the same crisis of imperialism, except that it has become deeper and more generalized, with fewer avenues of relief available to imperialists.

Permanent warfare has become the order of the day. For more than ten years, the U.S. and other imperialist forces have waged wars against the people of Iraq and Afghanistan that have implications for the entire Middle East.

Desperate imperialism's permanent war

We see this playing out today as the U.S. and other imperialist forces threaten to invade Syria in a U.S.-CIA fomented war that is now spilling over into Lebanon with the possibility of drawing in Russia, Iran and other forces from around the world. Egypt continues to be volatile while the people of Occupied Palestine struggle against near genocidal Israeli oppression and the entire Middle East region is on the brink of upheaval.

For nearly a decade, the U.S. has been threatening overt war against the government of Iran. Simultaneously, it has bombarded Iran with undeclared, low intensity warfare, including economic starvation, U.S. and Israeli cyber warfare, sabotage and assassinations and kidnappings of Iranian scientists associated with the country's development of its nuclear capacity.

The situation in North Africa is unpredictable. The aftermath of the "Arab Spring" has erupted in violent instability. The current U.S.-dependent, U.S.-trained and U.S.-funded military, that was left in power after mass political intervention by the people of Egypt ousted president Hosni Mubarak, recently murdered more than a thousand protesters, pushing the country close to civil war.

The popular uprisings leading to the fall of the Mubarak government in 2011 were impressive. However, our Party always recognized the limitations of that movement, which was without revolutionary leadership that acknowledged the Egyptian struggle as part of the overall struggle for the liberation and unification of Africa and that recognized the Egyptian army as an instrument of U.S. imperialist state power.

The anti-Mubarak movement was infatuated with the U.S.-backed Egyptian army, believing it to be a defender of the peoples' interests, unlike the police, which were seen as oppressive. The movement was thus incapable of projecting a general program reflecting the interests of the people beyond the removal of Mubarak and the obvious representatives of his regime.

Because of the repressive nature of the Egyptian regime, the only organized sectors in the country were the U.S.-funded and U.S.-trained state apparatus—especially the military—and the Muslim Brotherhood, an organization that had been under severe repression for generations. Over the years the Muslim Brotherhood became adept in underground organizing and through its social programs developed as a major influence in working class and poor communities.

The influence of the Muslim Brotherhood led to concerns by the U.S., Israel and all the imperialists with interests in maintaining the status quo in Egypt about the ongoing access to the Suez Canal for U.S. warships. The imperialists were also concerned about anti-Israel, pro-Palestinian movements, especially in the Sinai region, as well as threats to the Egyptian-Israeli alliance that protected U.S. and imperialist interests from challenges by the Arab masses.

Because of this, there was a reluctance by the Egyptian military along with the U.S. and Israel to allow the participation of the Muslim Brotherhood in "free" elections to establish a post-Mubarak government.

Unable to block Muslim Brotherhood participation in the elections without exposing the military's repressive character, however, the Egyptian military brokered a deal with the Brotherhood. With approval from the U.S. and Israeli governments, elections were allowed to go forward with Brotherhood participation. This resulted in the election of Brotherhood representative Mohamed Morsi as president of Egypt.

The outcome of a post-Mubarak, Muslim Brotherhood-dominated government proved unacceptable. Moving beyond the constraints expected to be imposed by the Egyptian middle class liberals in the government and the implicit if not explicit threat of Egyptian military intervention, the Muslim Brotherhood acted swiftly to shore up its power once in government.

While this thrilled both Hamas, the militant Muslim organization in power in the Gaza Strip of Palestine, and the government of Turkey, where a Muslim-led regime is vying for regional leadership, the U.S., Israel and the Egyptian military found this shift in the balance of power intolerable.

This resulted in a formal or informal coalition made up of the Egyptian military, the U.S., Israel, other imperialist governments as well as the mass movement led by the Egyptian liberal petty bourgeoisie to oust Morsi. During this process the number of people who came out to demonstrate against

Morsi was always exaggerated by the Egyptian military and U.S. media.

These classic elements of imperialist "regime change" poorly cloaked the Egyptian military's function as U.S. extended state power. The military coup was designed to appear to be a response to popular demands for a restoration of democracy that supposedly had been snatched from the Egyptian people by the democratically elected Muslim Brotherhood.

But there will be no putting the genie back into the bottle. The military coup overthrowing the Egyptian government has resulted in the blatant murder of thousands of Egyptians and the wounding of many thousands more. Hamas, Turkey and millions of Muslims worldwide were outraged by these imperialist machinations.

The reactionary Arab governments of Saudi Arabia, the United Arab Emirates and Kuwait are further exposing themselves to public scrutiny by the Arab and Muslim masses for their naked alliance with Israel and their contribution of $12 billion to support the Egyptian military coup makers.

The only thing certain about the Egyptian situation today is that its impact will linger far longer than the U.S. anticipates and its implications for the future continue to develop for an imperialism fighting for its very life.

Elsewhere in the region, imperialist plans for a quick overthrow of the Syrian regime failed to materialize. The opportunists, murderers and other imperialist hirelings promoted as the "rebels" have proven incapable of carrying out their task of regime change without assistance. France and other imperial white powers that initiated the Syrian crisis clearly made the same mistake that the U.S. made when it went into Iraq with the expectation of being welcomed with open arms by the Iraqi people.

The opposite has been the case. Now, the U.S. finds itself having to fend off criticism from reactionaries within its government and media, as well as from imperialist allies for not more aggressively and openly participating in the efforts to topple the administration of Syrian president Bashar al-Assad by providing more weapons and possibly open, as opposed to covert military assistance on the ground.

These are critics from another era who do not respect the changing balance of power that restricts U.S. actions that could unleash an avalanche of contradictions that would further erode U.S. power and influence.

Not the least of U.S. problems with the Syrian conflagration is the influence of the "Jihadists" who have entered the fray among the hundreds of various, sometimes contending rebel groups attempting to overthrow the Assad regime. Proving to be the best trained and most committed fighters—and also drawing hundreds of recruits from the U.S. and Canada—a Jihadist victory over the secular Assad forces could result in the creation of another anti-Israeli regime. The Jihadists could usher in a government that is virulently opposed to everything the U.S. and white power stands for and the very presence of Europe and the U.S. in the region.

In both Egypt and Syria we are witnessing a major confrontation between an array of national petty bourgeois forces. Some of these forces are patriotic; some are wedded to liberal imperialism; some are uneasy combinations of the two; while others are tied to clan and contending ethnic loyalties subject to manipulation by imperialists.

While this situation has made the Obama regime cautious, some sectors of the U.S. government and France, driven into a frenzy by economic desperation, have no such inhibitions. In the final analysis it will be the workers and not the petty bourgeoisie that will resolve this crisis that dominates the political terrain in the Arab, African and Muslim world.

This is why our responsibility continues to be to expose and exploit the contradictions driving imperialism's attempts to rescue itself from crisis. We continue to organize the African working class while supporting the workers of all countries who will be awakening and achieving organizational strength and traction as the contradictions continue to unfurl and our Party continues to provide analysis and leadership.

Pakistan, Palestine and Iran contribute to the instability of imperialist—especially U.S.—hegemony in the region. These places and others must be understood in the context of the vortex of a region undergoing the tremendous and—for liberals—unsettling and abrupt changes that accompany the weakening of a defining political and economic power such as the U.S. and its junior imperialist partners.

The overthrow and brutal murder of Mu'ummar Qaddafi in Libya in 2011, and the murderous imperialist-created, led and funded war in Syria are further evidence of general instability lending to the anxiety of many in the U.S. and Europe.

Europe continues to stagger from one unity-fracturing economic crisis to another. As the declining dominant imperialist state, the U.S. is still unsuccessful in maneuvering a face-saving retreat from their bloody military engagements in Afghanistan and Iraq. At the same time it is spreading carnage throughout Africa and intrigue in South America and other areas in an attempt to forestall its inevitable downfall.

After a decade of costly colonial expeditions in Afghanistan and Iraq that were designed to remake the Middle East in the image of the U.S. and establish the U.S. as the permanent global imperial power, an unintended political reconfiguration of the area has resulted in the opposite.

Developments in the Middle East have contributed to the growing isolation of Israel, the U.S. strategic military outpost and white cop on the regional block. U.S. satellites that include Tunisia, Egypt, Bahrain, Saudi Arabia and Yemen have been severely undermined by mass uprisings while anti-imperialist opponents of the U.S. have grown in strength and influence.

Iran is now a burgeoning force in the region despite U.S. attempts at destabilization and regime change, and notwithstanding the immediate success of the U.S. and European imperialists in overthrowing the Libyan Arab Jamahiriya and sowing havoc in Syria.

In addition, Turkey, perennially struggling to be accepted as a part of the white world or European nation by its ruling elite and consistently willing to function as a pawn of Euro-American geopolitical strategic interests, has now set out to forge its own path to regional power, without entirely relinquishing its white aspirations.

With the U.S. and Europe experiencing obvious decline and the fate of Israel increasingly challenged by the consequences of the "Arab Spring," Turkey has been seeking its regional credentials as a Muslim leader. Turkey was the first Muslim country to recognize the Jewish, white nationalist settler state of Israel in 1949 and has been linked to the West thereafter by NATO, trade, secret treaties and a strategic U.S.-dominated partnership.

Despite the fact that Turkey's current support for the U.S.-led attempt to overthrow the Syrian government is in objective unity with Israel, in the recent period Turkey has had public spats with Israel over such issues as natural gas discoveries in the Mediterranean.

The 2010 Israeli attack on a peace flotilla of ships involved in an attempt to take resources to the Israeli-blockaded Palestinian Gaza Strip resulted in the deaths of eight Turkish citizens. There was general outrage in Turkey, something that helped to establish it as a legitimate Muslim, anti-Israeli force in the minds of some. We are witnessing an apparent stance of Turkish independence that would have been unthinkable just a few years ago.

World resistance deepens imperialism's crisis

Another example of the inability of imperialism to rule in the same old way is the fact that U.S. troops that entered Iraq with great fanfare and bombast were forced to sneak out like thieves in the dead of night. Author Tom Engelhardt wrote on the website *TomDispatch.com* of the U.S. withdrawal in 2012 in "Debacle! How Two Wars in the Greater Middle East Revealed the Weakness of the Global Superpower":

> *[S]et aside the euphemisms and the soaring rhetoric, and if you want a simple gauge of the depths of America's debacle in the oil heartlands of the planet, consider just how the final unit of American troops left Iraq. According to Tim Arango and Michael Schmidt of* The New York Times, *they pulled out at 2:30 a.m. in the dead of night. No helicopters off rooftops, but 110 vehicles setting out in the dark from Contingency Operating Base Adder. The day before they left, according to* The Times *reporters, the unit's interpreters were ordered to call local Iraqi officials and sheiks with whom the Americans had close relations and make future plans, as if everything would continue in the usual way in the week to come.*
>
> *In other words, the Iraqis were meant to wake up the morning after to find their foreign comrades gone, without so much as a goodbye. This is how much the last American unit trusted its closest local allies. After shock and awe, the taking of Baghdad, the mission-accomplished moment, the capture, trial, and execution of Saddam Hussein, after Abu Ghraib and the bloodletting of the civil war, after the surge and the Sunni Awakening movement, after the purple fingers and the reconstruction*

funds gone awry, after all the killing and dying, the U.S. military slipped into the night without a word.

If, however, you did happen to be looking for a word or two to capture the whole affair, something less polite than those presently circulating, "debacle" and "defeat" might fit the bill. The military of the self-proclaimed single greatest power on planet Earth, whose leaders once considered the occupation of the Middle East the key to future global policy and planned for a multi-generational garrisoning of Iraq, had been sent packing. That should have been considered little short of stunning.

Face what happened in Iraq directly and you know that you're on a new planet.

The "new planet" is actually a new day, a new era, one that our Party has participated in creating for 41 years. It is our day, our era. It is the era of the Final Offensive against Imperialism!

However, the full measure of the shifting balance of geopolitical power cannot be fully understood without considering other areas of the world where U.S. imperialism is experiencing a tucked-tail retreat. In South America, the advent of the government of the late Hugo Chavez of Venezuela, as well as the governments of Evo Morales of Bolivia and Daniel Ortega of Nicaragua among others, is representative of dwindling U.S. influence on that continent, derisively considered the U.S. "backyard" in the past.

The death of Hugo Chavez in March of 2013 will not change that reality. Proven to have been an extremely important figure in the development of the struggles against imperialism, Chavez was representative of the sea of change occurring in the world. This is something the U.S. and other imperialists are forced to accept or to defend themselves against.

There is currently an escalation of intrigue and interference in the political situation in Venezuela and the region with the goal of intensifying political and social instability that will support and justify U.S. efforts to isolate the Venezuelan government of Chavez's successor Nicolás Maduro and replace it with a puppet regime. This represents a typical imperialist misunderstanding reflecting an inability and unwillingness to see the generalized historical trend manifested in specific events.

Barack Hussein Obama's military maneuvering and warlike bluster permeating the Asia-Pacific basin revolves around the Democratic People's Republic of Korea, but is clearly reflective of a U.S. attempt to stem the hemorrhaging of its economic and political influence in that area of the world. This is the explanation for the strategic shift or "pivot" of the U.S. military concentration to Asia last year designed to counter China's emerging and contending world influence.

U.S. claims of a nuclear-armed North Korea are partially intended to obscure U.S. moves in the Asia-Pacific basin to contain the rise of China as the most obvious challenge to the political, economic and strategic hegemony of U.S. and European imperialism.

War games initiated by the U.S. with its puppet regime recognized as South Korea were meant to provoke and intimidate the Democratic People's Republic of Korea, once characterized as part of an "Axis of Evil" by the past U.S. regime of George W. Bush.

Despite the fact that North Korea since its founding has always been in the crosshairs of U.S. aggression, the December 2011 death of its leader and head of state, Kim Jong-il, was met with a dangerous escalation. U.S. military flyovers in the spring of 2013 using sophisticated war planes capable of delivering nuclear bombs were planned to provoke a militant response from Kim Jong-un, the new young leader of the government.

The U.S. and its proxies used the reasonable response from the Democratic People's Republic of Korea to U.S. provocations to justify the increased militarization of the Asia-Pacific basin. Again, this is a thinly veiled attempt to exert political and economic containment of China in the region.

The U.S. has been the reigning world hegemon since the collapse of the Soviet Union in the 1980s. U.S. domination has been an accepted fact in the Asia-Pacific basin since the U.S. conquest of Japan during the Second Imperialist World War.

The first big challenge to this hegemony was the successful Chinese Revolution of 1949. This was followed quickly by the efforts of the Democratic People's Republic of Korea to liberate "South Korea" and unite the Korean people who had been forcibly divided by Western imperialist powers since the end of Japanese colonial rule in 1945. Korea's reunification efforts were met with the U.S. invasion known as the "Korean war."

The Vietnamese Revolution and resulting "domino" effect throughout the Southeast Asian region where more than half the world's 50 busiest container ports are located and where most of the world's illegal heroin trade was concentrated at the time, drove U.S. and Western imperialism into paroxysms of fear that they would lose their access to imperialist exploitation and strategic geopolitical control in the area.

Threatened by China's rising challenge to U.S. economic supremacy in the region, the U.S. has incited and exacerbated contradictions between China and several of its neighbors. Old territorial disputes between China and Japan and between China, Viet Nam and the Philippines, pushed to the forefront by U.S. presence as a bullying big brother, flared up this year.

This is not only an attempt to contain China militarily and politically, it is also a move to divert China's economy into its military instead of other sectors that would contribute to raising the overall economic capacity of China and further its drive to replace the U.S. as the largest, most influential economy in the world.

Significantly, China's emergence as the fastest and most significant external economic force in Africa is squeezing the U.S. and Europe's capacity to continue hegemonic extraction of economic and political resources. It removes Africa as a guaranteed strategic U.S. geopolitical resource.

Russia—once thought to be dead in the water—is also flexing its muscles with growing effectiveness, sometimes in alliance with China in areas where their interests converge in opposition to the U.S. and Europe. Russia's current relationship with Syria and Iran appears to be a case in point.

Imperialist pundits alarmed by imperialism's decline

Today's reality clearly shows an imperialism in deep crisis. Even the thinking representatives of the imperialists are beginning to say so.

Former National Security Advisor for U.S. president James Earl Carter and current advisor for U.S. president Barack Hussein Obama, Zbigniew Brzezinski felt it necessary to alert the U.S. bourgeoisie of impending peril for an America that refuses to recognize the shifting balance of power in a world that now favors the rise of the oppressed.

In his 2007 book, *Second Chance: Three Presidents and the Crisis of American Superpower,* Brzezinski tutored the U.S. ruling class:

> *Global political awakening is historically anti-imperial, politically anti-Western, and emotionally increasingly anti-American. In the process, it is setting in motion a major shift in the global center of gravity. That in turn is altering the global distribution*

of power, with major implications for America's role in the world.

The foremost geopolitical effect of global political awakening is the demise of the imperial age. Empires have existed throughout history, and in recent times American paramountcy has often been described as a new global empire....

Imperial stability has historically depended on skilled domination, superior military organization and—ultimately most important—political passivity on the part of dominated peoples... The more recent Western European empires grew predominantly through superior transoceanic navigational capabilities motivated by trade and greed for valuable minerals. Modern imperialism is thus largely a Western emanation.

In any case, the combined impact of global political awakening and modern technology contributes to the acceleration of political history. What once took centuries now takes a decade; what took a decade now happens in a single year....

Anti-Westernism is...more than a populist attitude. It is an integral part of the shifting global demographic, economic, and political balance.

Patrick Buchanan, an imperialist ideologue, opponent of Brzezinski and former speechwriter for U.S. president Ronald Wilson Reagan, is even more pessimistic and alarmist in his assessment. In his 2011 book, *Suicide of a Superpower: Will America Survive to 2025?*, Buchanan laments:

Not one nation of Europe or North America, save Iceland, has a birth rate sufficient to replace its population. All have been below zero population growth (2.1 children per woman) for decades. Who will inherit the Western estate? Between now and

2050, Africa's population will double to 2 billion and Latin America and Asia will add another 1.25 billion people....

The great European powers fought two great wars. All lost their empires. All saw their armies and navies melt away...All are undergoing invasions from formerly subject peoples coming to the mother country to dispossess their grandchildren. All of their welfare states face retrenchment even as they face tribal decline and death....

The conquest of Europe by peoples of color from the old colonies is well advanced. The numbers of those lined up waiting to come, and of those lined up behind them, stagger the mind....

People of European descent are not only in a relative but a real decline. They are aging, dying, disappearing. This is the existential crisis of the West.

Certainly this is *an* existential crisis of the West. However, long ago we discovered *the* existential crisis of the West. That crisis is one that both Buchanan and Brzezinski refuse to understand. It is a crisis born of the very foundation of the imperialist West. Put another way, it is the pedestal upon which the fortunes of the West have rested since its cankerous emergence on the body of humanity.

The "West" achieved its significance in modern history through the advent of capitalism as a unifying, defining social system. Capitalism's foundation was characterized as "primitive accumulation" by Karl Marx who declared its function as playing "in political economy about the same part as original sin in theology..."

We refer to this statement by Marx from his book, *Capital*, published in 1867, clearly one of the most influential political works in history. We find it necessary to come back to this segment repeatedly in the discussion of our theory of African Internationalism:

> *The discovery of gold and silver in America, the extirpation, enslavement and entombment in mines of the aboriginal population, the turning of Africa into a warren for the commercial hunting of black skins, signalized the rosy dawn of the era of capitalist production....*
>
> *Whilst the cotton industry introduced child slavery in England, it gave in the United States a stimulus to the transformation of the earlier, more or less patriarchal slavery, into a system of commercial exploitation. In fact, the veiled slavery of the wage workers in Europe needed, for its pedestal, slavery pure and simple in the new world.*

Herein lies the basis of *the* existential crisis. The motion of the oppressed peoples of the world is fast snatching the pedestal out from underneath the "Western" or white parasite that has feasted off the life and blood of much of the world for the past few centuries.

Europe exists as a parasite upon the body of the rest of humanity. What Buchanan and Brzezinski do not want to understand and what Marx did not anticipate is that we are now facing a world system in existential crisis because the parasite is losing its host due to the growing resistance of the world's peoples and the unexpected economic competition from some of those who previously functioned as hosts to this parasite.

Today's world is characterized by turbulence. While there is a continuing discussion among the thinking representatives of the white ruling class about the perceived shift of global power, even they do not know exactly what this means.

Conditions for Africans worsen in imperialist crisis

The white ruling class selection of Barack Hussein Obama as U.S. president has served to neutralize various Africans in the U.S. that have been traditional critics of U.S. domestic and foreign policies. Even some who were previously considered critics of U.S. imperialism overall have exposed themselves as white nationalists in black face: U.S. patriots who through their support for Obama are endorsing every crime committed against our people and the world by the U.S. government.

For the most part, these U.S. patriots offer up the argument that things would be much worse if one of the white candidates had become president, or they say that Obama is being unfairly blamed by white "racists" and by Africans motivated by self-hatred.

However, the conditions faced by Africans in the U.S. clearly repudiate this line. The same reality that has driven most of the world to crisis-creating resistance has resulted in a smoldering tinderbox in the U.S. African community awaiting the spark to set it off and for our Party to organize and direct its rage. Here is a look at the conditions faced by the African population colonized within current U.S. borders.

More than five years into the economic crisis that came to a head in 2008, things are generally very bad economically for a large sector of the U.S. population. For example, even though the U.S. population grows at the rate of about three million people a year, the number of people in the U.S. with full-time jobs currently is the same as in 2001 at only 115 million people, reports *Examiner.com* in "As U.S. Workforce Shrinks, Disability Claims Skyrocket," April 9, 2013.

A reported 663,000 people left the workforce in March of 2013 alone. Those without jobs and those who have given up looking for work total a record 90 million people out of a total U.S. population of 315 million, according to the website *Zerohedge.com,* April 5, 2013. The number of people relying on food stamps and other social programs has skyrocketed. According to the website of *The Fiscal Times,* nearly 50 million people or 15 percent of the U.S. population are receiving food stamps.

While things are bad in general within the U.S., the conditions for Africans can only be explained by our status as colonial subjects. This oppression continues just as starkly under the Obama regime as under any previous U.S. president, except that there is less political struggle against these conditions under Obama than against white imperialist representatives that preceded him in the White House.

On April 1, 2013, the *Atlanta Daily World* reported that more than half of African men without high school diplomas are unemployed while those with high school diplomas are facing an unemployment rate at 26 percent—four times the U.S.-wide average. National Public Radio reported in July of 2013 that African *teen-aged* high school dropouts are experiencing a 95 percent unemployment rate! African male college graduates are unemployed at a rate of 6.2 percent as opposed to white males who are only 2.9 percent unemployed.

And if this were not bad enough, a study by the University of Wisconsin-Milwaukee revealed that in the 25 largest U.S. cities, fewer than 55 percent of African men overall are employed. The same study shows that in Milwaukee only 44.7 percent of African males between the ages of 16 and 64 held jobs in 2010, the lowest rate ever recorded, with Detroit and Buffalo showing roughly the same rates.

Similar figures can be found in virtually every city and state in the U.S. Even during this so-called economic recession in the U.S., white household wealth is 22 times greater than that of African households. According to the website *CNN Money,* the average white family holds $110,729 in assets compared to the average African family in the U.S., which has only $4,955.

All of this is compounded by other profound differences in the conditions of existence for U.S. North American citizens and domestically colonized African subjects. When these differences are examined, we clearly see that we are talking about African national oppression rather than racism, as the source of our condition is erroneously called.

This is a difference that exists between colonial subjects and U.S. citizens, even though some of them may also experience economic exploitation and some forms of social oppression. Even exploited or oppressed white people live on the pedestal of the national oppression of Africans and others whose lives and resources have gone to create the capitalist social system that provides general benefit for all Europeans, including those Euro-Americans inside the U.S.

With more than 2.2 million people behind bars in 2012 and nearly 7 million under "correctional supervision," including probation, parole, jail or prison, the U.S. has by far the largest prison population in the world, according to the website of The Sentencing Project. The states of Texas and California alone, with nearly 150,000 prisoners each, have incarcerated populations comparable to those in countries such as Ukraine and South Africa.

The state of Louisiana has the highest per capita prison population in the world with more than 1,600 per 100,000 of its population locked up. The U.S. as a whole has 743 per 100,000 people in prison. By comparison China has only 122 per 100,000 incarcerated, according to the web page, "United States Incarceration Rate" on *Wikipedia.org.*

The number of imprisoned people within the U.S. quadrupled from 1980 to 2008. In that 28-year period the prison population grew from roughly 500,000 to 2.3 million. With five percent of the world's population, the U.S. has 25 percent of the world's prisoners according to the American Civil Liberties Union.

According to "The Criminal Justice Fact Sheet" of the NAACP, Africans are incarcerated at nearly six times the rate of whites and now constitute nearly 1 million of the total 2.2 million behind bars. When the numbers of Africans and "Latinos" are combined, we make up 58 percent of the prison population of the U.S. There are 1.2 million African children in the U.S. with a parent in prison. One out of every 8 persons in prison in the entire world is an African locked up in the United States!

"Unlocking America," a report on the U.S. prison system written by academics, estimates that if Africans and Latinos were arrested at the same rate as whites in the U.S., the prison population would drop by roughly 50 percent.

One in six African men had been imprisoned by 2001 and it is estimated that current trends would result in one in three African men born today spending some time in prison in his lifetime. One in 100 African women is also in prison.

We are not about to debate the question of whether these figures represent a greater penchant for crime by Africans as some do contend. "Crime" is the opinion of the ruling class and anything that challenges the monopoly of power and property by the ruling class is defined as crime.

It is impossible to ignore the fact that the majority of the prison population here consists of those whose general conditions of existence derive from our oppressors' historical crimes of forced labor and land expropriation resulting in what is currently known as the U.S.

Obama is the face of imperialism in crisis

This Sixth Congress and the existence of our Party are informed by this national oppression of our people on this U.S. Front of the African Revolution. This Congress and every move we make in response to the national oppression of African people in our struggle for the total liberation and socialist unification of Africa and African people under the leadership of the African working class are also part of the deep, irreversible crisis of imperialism that is roiling the world.

U.S. president Barack Hussein Obama did not create the current manifestation of imperialist crisis. His presidency is an attempted solution to the crisis put forward by a sector of U.S. imperialism following the dismal failure of the George W. Bush regime to quiet the storm of resistance and change the course of history at gunpoint—the traditional and familiar method of U.S. imperialism.

Bush was the white man imposing white power on recalcitrant and backward dark peoples of the world who had forgotten our places. Not only was Bush the white man, he was also the *American* white man who was not satisfied with the simple reassertion of white power over the ignorant colonial masses. The intent of the Bush regime was clearly to re-establish global white power under the undisputed imperial leadership of the U.S.

The outcome was a disaster from which the U.S. and general imperialist white power are still attempting to recover in this period when other imperialist powers and contenders are fighting for a redefinition of the relationship between imperialist thieves—a redefinition that challenges absolute U.S. hegemony.

The selection of Barack Hussein Obama was seen as a solution by at least a sector of the white ruling class that grew in influence following the Bush regime. Through Obama this sector opted to *seduce* the world into imperialist compliance as opposed to Bush's failed attempt to bomb it into compliance.

Rather than the obvious manifestation of imperialist white power that the Bush regime did little to disguise, Obama's face of imperialism is one of the oppressed. On a mission to calm Muslim sensibilities about U.S. intent, Obama went to Egypt in 2009, making a speech at Cairo University entitled,

"A New Beginning." To great applause Obama addressed the audience within the first paragraph of his speech with the Muslim greeting of "Assalamu alaikum."

Obama also moved quickly to convince Europe and others that the U.S. hegemon was being reigned in. More and more the word "partnership" was used to describe the relationship between the U.S., Europe and others that were needed to facilitate the U.S. agenda for pushing back the crisis engulfing the imperialist world and threatening the economic future and strategic interests of the U.S.

Domestically, Obama is useful as a cathartic relief to pent-up white anxiety in the wake of the history of white oppression of Africans in the U.S. at a time of growing generalization of resistance by the oppressed of the world. He represents a safe, white conscience-salving solution that also serves as a template by which the behavior and general stance of the African working class is measured and judged.

Despite the fact that Obama's foreign and domestic policies are far more draconian and repressive than Bush's were, Obama has served as the vehicle through which the political motion of the African population in the U.S. has been contained within the safe embrace of the imperialist Democratic party. His presidency has provided a diversion for Africans who might otherwise be inclined to turn to our Party to fight for solutions to the escalating contradictions threatening our nominal freedom and security.

Obama is a global, imperialist, neocolonial solution to an imperialist problem with the masses of the colonized oppressed who inevitably rise up to resist the foreign oppressive interloper. Obama is a means by which colonialism attempts to disguise its presence by pretending to be the people.

Kwame Nkrumah referred to neocolonialism as the last stage of imperialism. It is telling that a sector of the imperialist white ruling class recognizes that the depth of the crisis of imperialist rule requires Obama as a stand-in. He is a sign of the overall weakness of imperialism and certainly not a solution for Africans in our struggle for the future. While appearing to many as a success for imperialism—true for the short term—Obama is, in fact, the *face* of imperialist crisis.

The understanding of neocolonialism has become more generalized. It has been 50 years or so since Nkrumah coined the term to define indirect imperialist rule, made necessary for continuing trans-colonial control of African economies by the colonial powers.

Neocolonialism is fraud. It is a form of political sleight of hand that provides cover for the ongoing treacherous expropriation of land, labor, resources and life itself from Africans and others of the world's oppressed.

In many ways the imperialists are being confronted with a crisis of neocolonialism, where their puppets are increasingly unable to carry out their roles without growing interference by the masses of the oppressed.

This can lead and, indeed, has led to mass opposition that destabilizes regimes and makes it necessary for U.S. or other imperialist intervention to rectify the situation, sometimes to the disadvantage and dismay of loyal native sycophants. The mass uprisings against the Tunisian, Egyptian and Yemeni regimes that came to be identified as the "Arab Spring" are examples. And sometimes otherwise loyal neocolonialists are forced to heed some of the demands of their people who oppose the role of the U.S. in their countries.

The crisis of imperialism is real and powerful. Although "crisis" is a term often used to describe imperialist difficulties at different times, the situation is different today. Today's crisis is a generalized one that makes it impossible for imperialism to rebound. In the past, the imperialists have been able to rescue themselves by transferring the burden of crisis to other oppressed peoples and countries.

However, today, part of the crisis is defined by the turbulence stemming from oppressed peoples and countries becoming the defining event in history. It is an imperialism that is running out of space and authority throughout the world—in South America, Asia, the Middle East and elsewhere.

While all the imperialist forces, old and new, are seeking to rescue themselves in Africa, our Party and the contradictions among the imperialists themselves constitute impediments that they will find insurmountable there.

Never has the decline of imperialism exposed itself in such absolute terms. Never has the future been so bleak for imperialism and so bright for the struggling and oppressed peoples of the world.

III. The theory of African Internationalism

The science of African Internationalism enabled our Party to avoid the ideological pitfalls that validate the assumption of the superiority of white people. Thus, we have never been diverted from our mission of capturing power and uniting Africa and our nation under the leadership of the African working class.

Our Party brought science to our defeated African Liberation Movement at a time when it was generally bogged down in racial and cultural nationalism that indulged in candlelit ceremonies, religious obscurantism and nostalgia for an often imaginary African past. Through African Internationalism we were able to discover the material basis for the exploitation and oppression of Africans and others in this world.

With African Internationalism we can understand the material forces at work in the movement of history. We can clearly see the current shift in the balance of power between the oppressor and the oppressed, between Europe and the rest of us, between the "white man" and the "black man."

We determined long ago that characterizing our movement as a struggle against racism was a self-defeating waste of time. What is called racism is simply the ideological foundation of capitalist imperialism. Racism is a concept that denies Africans our national identity and dignity, rather than defining the system of our oppression. It relegates us to the Sisyphean task of winning acceptance from, and often of becoming one with, our oppressors.

With African Internationalism we have proven that race is simply a colonial invention originating from the enslavement and colonization of Africans and Africa that gave birth to capitalism and, simultaneously, the European nation. Our struggle has always been for *power,* not against racism. To the extent that we win power, the "racism" of others becomes irrelevant. Power is the great equalizer, the fundamental "aphrodisiac" that is capable of turning a racist of today into a fawning sycophant of tomorrow.

The struggle against "racism" is the struggle of the petty bourgeoisie fighting to integrate into the white capitalist world, to board the sinking ship of white power. It is a diversionary struggle reliant on failed philosophical assumptions that must be cast aside as a precondition for moving forward.

This is not an innocent issue of semantics. The way this is understood informs our practice. The struggle against "racism" presupposes one approach and the struggle against imperialist colonialism another.

Africans are not a race but a nation of people, forcibly dispersed across the globe. We have been pushed out of history by our imperialist oppressors, partially through the concept of "race." Our national homeland has been occupied in various ways for millennia. Our people have been captured and shipped around the world as capitalist commodities. Our labor and land have been violently extracted to build the European nation and the international capitalist system. This is what determines our reality and the contours of the struggle in which we have been engaged for more than 500 years.

The fight against AFRICOM[1] cannot be characterized as a struggle against "racism" any more than the liberation of our people in Haiti from France in 1804 or the necessary unification of Africa to stop the rape of our Motherland and the theft of its resources.

---

1 *The United States Africa Command with U.S. military involvement in at least 49 African countries.*

The material conditions Africans suffer worldwide have their origin in the attack on Africa that led to the capture of our national homeland and our people. Our poverty and susceptibility to ignorance, violence and material want throughout the world—including in the U.S., UK and the rest of Europe—result from the material conditions of existence in Africa since its capture and partition!

Are the Iraqis and Afghans fighting against racism? What about all the people of South America and the Caribbean? Certainly, the bourgeois ideology of "racism" serves to unite the vast majority of whites and even some Africans in support of the imperialist agenda.

Increasingly though, this ideology is running up against the material reality of a global power shift, where the oppressed are clearly the locomotive of history. More and more whites are themselves running from their own "racial" designation.

Patrick Buchanan, whose worldview is informed by assumptions of white superiority that we recognize as racism, is himself alarmed by the growing evidence that shifting power relations are chasing whites away from solidarity with their "racial" identity. Apparently this phenomenon has achieved such significance that Buchanan has conceptualized it as "ethnomasochism." In his book *Suicide of a Superpower*, Buchanan laments,

> *Questions about the future arise. If the end of white America is a cultural and demographic inevitability, what will the new mainstream of America look like—and what ideas or values might it rally around? What will it mean to be white after "whiteness" no longer defines the mainstream? Will anyone mourn the end of white America? Will anyone try to preserve it?*
>
> *One reaction professor Hsu reports is that, among cultural elites, some are shedding their*

white identity. "[I]f white America is 'losing control,' and the future will belong to people who can successfully navigate a post-white, multicultural landscape—then it's no surprise that many white Americans are eager to divest themselves of their whiteness entirely..."

The day after Obama's inaugural, television host Larry King blurted out to an uneasy Bob Woodward a secret desire of his son. "My younger son Cannon...is eight. And he now says that he would like to be black. I'm not kidding. He said there's a lot of advantages. Black is in. Is this a turning of the tide?"

Indeed, black *is* in. The tide has turned; black is the future—not because of some defeat of "racism" but because Africans are a part of the dispossessed, the Wretched of the Earth that are overturning a world social system whose ideological foundation is racism. This system is no longer able to withstand the tide of history sweeping all forms of capitalist parasitism into the proverbial dustbin of history.

The anti-racists would have us fight for a place in the dying system by fighting against its ideology instead of the system itself. In this way they would have us objectively uniting with our oppressors. Anti-racists would transform us into "house Negroes," fighting to save the master's burning mansion, to paraphrase Malcolm X.

Parasitism is the essential question

Up to now, since the successful rise of imperialism some 500 years ago, Europe and white people have been the subjects and Africans and others have been the objects of imperialist history.

We have been voiceless and reduced to invisibility in stature and significance. Karl Marx characterized the slavery, rape, pillage and genocide associated with the emergence of white power and our current status as "primitive accumulation." In another instance, he referred to slavery as "an economic category of the greatest importance."

In the book *One People! One Party! One Destiny!*, the Political Report to our Fifth Congress, I commented on what that meant:

> *Here the relationship between peoples and countries is...obscured and mystified. Marx attributes European "development" solely to the "genius" and productive forces inside of Europe. He is thereby covering over or liquidating the fact that this so-called development for Europe requires the parasitic impairment of the capacity for independent development in Africa and other places victimized by Europe.*

In another place in the Political Report this rhetorical question was raised:

> *Would capitalism and the resultant European wealth and African impoverishment have occurred without the European attack on Africa, its division, African slavery and dispersal, colonialism and neocolonialism?*

The answer is obvious to anyone with even a smattering of historical knowledge: No! No! No! and a thousand times no!

But Marx didn't get it. Most of our movement still doesn't get it. Revolutionaries around the world have missed this crucial understanding of the foundation of imperialist existence.

The most erudite practitioners of the superstition called capitalist economics don't get it. This is one of the reasons nothing they say about the extant economic crisis of the imperialist world makes any sense.

Our summation of this imperialist dilemma is reflected in this quote from *One People! One Party! One Destiny!*:

> *The North Americans, like most Europeans, assume they have some idea of the basis of the contradictions because of the fantasies passed on to them historically about the source of their comparative wealth and "good fortune."...*
>
> *Nevertheless, those are resources stolen from others that have become increasingly difficult for them to afford in their malls and supermarkets. It is somebody else's oil, wrenched from the earth with bloody consequences, for which they now have to pay more.*
>
> *The bauxite, coltan, gold and diamonds along with the cocoa beans, cotton and cheaply produced clothing have cost the rest of us dearly and our combined struggles to seize control of our lives and resources are affecting the ability of North Americans and other Europeans to enjoy a parasitic economy that requires global misery for an oasis of white happiness.*

In reality the essential feature of capitalism is parasitism.

The inconsistent materialism of Patrick Buchanan as well as Zbigniew Brzezinski, cited in Chapter I, allows them to recognize some relationship between the decline of imperialism and the rise of formerly subject peoples.

Yet their overarching philosophical idealism, a worldview stemming from white assumptions of superiority, blinds them to the dialectic between Western or "white" success and African impoverishment. They cannot accept that the changing relations of power are exposing the real dependency—the dependency of the colonizer upon the colonized and of whites on Africans.

This is as true for the capitalism of Adam Smith, the 18th century free market proponent, as it is of the capitalism of Karl Marx, the 19th century scientific socialist. Wage labor, commodity production, private ownership and control of the means of production are features of capitalism that function on the foundation of parasitism, the "primitive accumulation," that Marx correctly identified as the equivalent of "original sin." This is the starting point of capitalist accumulation and production, of the capitalist system itself.

This is not to say that everything that Marx said was wrong, but it is to say that everything he said must be re-evaluated based on a materialist appreciation of the centrality of capitalist parasitism, what he called the primitive accumulation of capital. Otherwise we will continue to be duped by those who verbally claim to oppose capitalism, but who cannot oppose *parasitic* capitalism—the reality that capitalism rests on the backs of African, Indigenous and oppressed peoples everywhere.

We are not Marxists. We are historical materialists. We have used the historical materialism of Marx, the science of investigating and analyzing society, to investigate and analyze our reality as Africans. Our findings prove that we are a part of the "primitive accumulation" mentioned by Marx in his works.

Malcolm X, a materialist of sorts in his own right, has been quoted as saying that a person watching someone sitting on a hot stove would describe the experience differently from the person actually sitting on the stove. This is true. The spectator is not required to have a full understanding of the experience. The victim of the hot stove is provoked by his reality; it becomes a historical necessity to understand the question.

Using the collective experience of African people as a starting place, we were able to use the science of dialectical and historical materialism, cleansing it of its Marxist metaphysics and idealism, to investigate and analyze our relationship to the world.

For us, the rise of capitalism in the world is not based on some purely abstract Marxist theory about the development of human society. It is not a theoretical question. *"Primitive accumulation" is not a theory.* The rape of Africa, the enslavement of our Continent and our people, the forcible dispersal of Africans throughout the world as a means of rescuing Europe from disease and poverty—the process that gave rise to capitalism—is a matter of historical record.

Marx, the spectator, did not have to understand this. The person sitting on the hot stove—the living, breathing, thinking "primitive accumulation"—would either understand this question or perish. We chose to understand. More than that, we chose to develop a worldview stemming from this understanding. This is the origin of African Internationalism.

African Internationalism is simply the worldview stemming from a historical materialist investigation and analysis of the world with its starting point being the experience and role of Africans and Africa in the advent of capitalist-imperialism as the rise of white power.

Parasitic capitalism is the real issue. It is this reality that ultimately distinguishes African Internationalist socialism from the struggle for "white rights" that usually characterizes most movements of Europeans worldwide. It is the difference in socialism resulting from overturning the pedestal upon which all capitalist activity occurs and some variation of the national socialism achieved by the infamous Nazis of Germany.

In the past few years the crisis of imperialism has thrust a number of North Americans and Europeans into motion, from Tea Partiers and Wall Street Occupiers in the U.S. to thousands of militants in Greece, Spain, Brazil and other crisis-ridden countries.

White people have been mobilized by the inability of capitalism to live up to their expectations. They are demanding to be restored to their "rightful" place atop the pedestal of capitalist prosperity, sharing in the stolen loot of colonial plunder.

The problem is that this can only happen at the *expense* of the well-being of the historical victims of capitalist prosperity— the subject and colonial peoples of the world, whose exploited labor and resources create the pedestal upon which all white people sit. Europe's economic uncertainty has been brought about by oppressed peoples who are currently fomenting the crisis with our struggle for the recapture of our resources, our sovereignty, dignity and our history.

It is an error to assume that "primitive accumulation" is dead history, something that happened a long time ago with no implications for today. The truth is that today's capitalist-imperialist structures, the ones being challenged in a thousand different ways, are structures that originated in the very genesis of capitalism as it emerged through the assault on Africa and the majority of humanity from the primordial sludge of backward and disease-ridden Europe.

These understandings of African Internationalism *require* action. They are not for consumers of information. Our Party's theory is the only body of political understanding that can make sense of what is happening in the world today.

Our African Internationalist theoretical contributions serve to break the shackles historically imposed on revolutionary theory as perceived through the lens of oppressor nation intellectuals whose worldview was determined by their existence on the pedestal of our oppression.

African Internationalism for the first time allows for Africans and the oppressed of the world to become the subjects of history, defining our own destiny, something not possible with the theory of Marx or his contemporaries and followers.

Today the conditions of the real world manifested by the crisis of imperialism are beginning to confirm what African Internationalism has so long predicted.

The reality of primitive accumulation of capital and the fact that capitalism was born at the expense of the suffering of African and Indigenous peoples and is therefore parasitic; the reality of Africans as one people dispersed around the world who are colonized wherever we may be located; the understanding that African people live under a policy of U.S. counterinsurgency in the U.S.—these are some African Internationalist understandings whose significance is becoming recognized by the world.

Seeing the world as it is, not as we wish it were

African people, like all of humanity have always been motivated by the struggle to understand our place and destiny in the world. We, like others, have through our collective life experiences been compelled to find answers to the fundamental philosophical questions revolving around the primacy of the spiritual versus the material world.

What is the basis of our oppression? Can the answer be found in religious scripture? Are we oppressed because we have offended the gods or perhaps sought solace from the wrong gods? Are the white colonial oppressors and some of the African petty bourgeoisie correct when they say we are experiencing the consequence of insufficient civilization or inadequate education or that we are morally depraved?

Those who see the spiritual as primary are philosophical idealists. For them the idea of reality is greater than reality itself. For idealists, the real, material world is dependent on the spiritual. Philosophical idealists do not look for answers about the nature of the world by examining the world itself.

They see the world as the creation of an external force that is incapable of standing up to scientific investigation.

This is a ruling class worldview that is funneled into the consciousness of the working masses through the African petty bourgeoisie as well as other petty bourgeois and bourgeois mediums. Philosophical idealism assumes that there are things that humans are unable to comprehend. It claims that the hand of the mysterious is somehow responsible for what we perceive as reality.

During the historical period when our Party was founded, philosophical idealism was central to the worldview of the Black Liberation Movement which relied mainly on religious, moral and colonial explanations to understand and analyze our situation.

African philosophical idealists of that period sought explanations for our conditions of existence and our future in the articulations of great leaders or simply in the consciousness of the Black Liberation Movement itself.

In other words, the idealists accepted the movement's and its leaders' own self-definition as primary, rather than fundamentally examining the actual material conditions that *gave rise* to the movement and its leaders.

Other philosophical idealists with whom our movement had to contend were the various white liberals including those who defined themselves as "leftists."

Many of the white leftists relied on religious and moral explanations for their analysis, attributing our oppression to the flawed character of our oppressors. According to these idealists our oppressors were people who had strayed from the American or European moral ideal. In this way the white liberals were not that different from the petty bourgeois leaders of the Black Liberation Movement.

White leftist ideological intervention usually represents itself in the paternalistic, condescending tendency to approach the issue of the oppression of African people from a predetermined assumption of the universality of the white experience. This Eurocentric viewpoint shows that the leftists have pretty much the same viewpoint as all other whites.

Often influenced by Karl Marx, many "leftists" deny being philosophical idealists. Their idealism, nevertheless, is reflected in their demand that Africans, the Indigenous of the Americas and the majority of the world's peoples understand our struggle as objects of European-defined and experienced history.

From their perspective, Africans and others are relegated to the position of auxiliary forces whose ultimate unhappy destiny, independent of our will, history and experience, is to facilitate the emergence of the industrial or white working class as the new ruling class in a utopian post-capitalist world.

The African People's Socialist Party sprang from the very bowels of the remorseless reality and struggles of our people. As we developed, we were increasingly forced to shed all reliance on religion, other forms of superstition and the good will or moral epiphany of our oppressors.

Our struggles to understand our reality, while occasionally encumbered and influenced by the worldview of the educated and upper classes, were rooted in attempts to solve the real problems of the concrete contradictions in which our people are embroiled.

We were forced to learn that our preconceived notions gleaned through colonial civics books, preachers and liberal white friends only helped to obscure the real contradictions with which our people are confronted. We came to recognize that we must understand the world just as it is, not as we would wish it to be.

We were forced to become philosophical materialists.

Materialism teaches us that the world is tangible, knowable and can be experienced through the senses. It teaches us that all existing phenomena result from material causes that come into being, develop and pass away according to the laws of the motion of matter. Materialism informs us that the material world is primary. It is objective reality that exists independently of the mind and will of individuals. It does not require the permission of gods or important persons for its existence.

The development of the African People's Socialist Party during our historical 41-year trajectory in the midst of intense struggle compelled us to understand that the savage and genocidal brutality inflicted upon our people and the world by Europeans or whites has a material basis. It is not due to the will of the gods or simply some moral deficiency on the part of whites.

While the humanity of Europeans was clearly open to suspicion (the original Nation of Islam, for example, declared the white man to be the "devil"), the answer to the avaricious motivation of white people is not to be found in an examination of morality, religion or genetics.

Our Party and movement were forced to conclude that all humans, including Europeans, are trapped by an absolute necessity to secure and develop the means of subsistence. In other words, the primary motivating factor in human society is the production and reproduction of life. Without life, all other questions—religion, culture, genetics, etc.—are moot, meaningless. Indeed, culture is a byproduct of the process of producing and reproducing life.

However, the process of Africans producing and reproducing life was drastically disrupted and altered by the European attack that resulted in the capture and colonial enslavement of Africa and Africans. This attack by Europeans on Africa also resulted in the imposition of artificial borders that separate the dispersed African nation from our human and material resources and from a meaningful relationship among ourselves and with the peoples of the world.

The material *and* human resources of Africa have gone to satisfy the requirements of life for Europeans at the expense of Africa and Africans. The process of Africans producing and reproducing life has not been primarily for Africa and Africans—it has been primarily for Europe and the white world at our expense.

This progenitor of world capitalism—the attack on Africa and Africans, along with the European assault on Asia and the Americas—rescued Europe and Europeans from an oppressive, thousand-year-long, disease-ridden, impoverished existence known as feudalism. This was the genesis of the capitalist system as a world economy, created on a base of the enslavement of Africans and others.

A scientific analysis of human society requires that we take a dialectical approach. We cannot see the world as static and ready-made. Society has to be analyzed as a process that is in a constant state of motion, change and development. There is always something new arising to replace the old and all social motion occurs in relationship to this process of coming into existence and dying away.

Europe's attack on Africa was effectively an assault on Africa's ability to produce life for itself. This assault has had the effect of pushing Africa and Africans out of history—history being the summation of the ongoing struggle to produce and reproduce life.

Slavery, genocide and colonialism are the stuff of which capitalism was born. African enslavement was the *first capital* in the development of capitalism. The prevailing legal system, culture, religion and general philosophical outlook or worldview constitute the superstructure of capitalism thus conceived. This superstructure is a natural product and reflection of this economic base of colonial slavery.

Slavery and colonialism gave rise not only to capitalism but also to the capitalist and working classes alike of Europe and North America. The workers and the bourgeoisie, the two primary capitalism-defining classes, have occasionally fought great battles with each other since their inception as contending social forces.

Nevertheless both were born and developed on a platform of slavery and colonialism. Consequently, what is often called "class struggle" inside the U.S. and Europe is actually contention among the workers and the ruling class for control of the parasitic capitalist pedestal and its stolen resources.

The parasitic foundation of world capitalism continues to exist up to now as the true economic base upon which the entire superstructure of the capitalist-defined, capitalist-dominated world rests.

The total existence of "white" people and their ability to produce and reproduce life is dependent on this parasitic relationship that came into being with the attack by feudal Europe on Africa and the world.

Instead of separate, more or less self-contained worlds existing in casual relationship to each other, *there is one capitalist world system united by a parasitic economic relationship imposed by Europe upon the rest of us.*

There is, therefore, no European reality separate from that of Africa and the rest of the world. The entire world is now locked into a single dialectical process, a unity of opposites, whereupon the gruesome extraction of life and resources from Africa and the rest of the world is a condition for the life and "development" of what we now know as Europe, "white people" and the capitalist system to which we have been forcibly affixed.

The legal system, culture, white sense of sameness and political institutions are reflections of this parasitic economic base. Every white aspiration and dream, every expectation for happiness and a good life—from a successful marriage to a secure future for their children—requires drone strikes in Pakistan, police murders and mass imprisonment in the African colonies and barrios of the U.S., and starvation and forced displacement of the oppressed throughout the world.

Our theory, practical struggle prepared Party to lead

While not fully appreciative of the parasitic foundation of the entire capitalist system resting on the brutal oppression of Africans and others, Karl Marx nevertheless recognized the relationship between the economic foundation of society and the resultant institutions and ideas.

In his preface to *A Contribution to the Critique of Political Economy,* published in 1859, Marx expounds on this relationship between the economic base and superstructure that defines society:

> In the social production of their existence, men inevitably enter into definite relations, which are independent of their will, namely [the] relations of production appropriate to a given stage in the development of their material forces of production. The totality of these relations of production constitutes the economic structure of society, the real foundation, on which arises a legal and political superstructure, and to which correspond definite forms of consciousness. The mode of production of material life conditions the general process of social, political and intellectual life. It is not the consciousness of men that determines their existence, but their social existence that determines their consciousness...The changes in the economic

foundation lead, sooner or later, to the transformation
of the whole, immense superstructure. In studying
such transformations, it is always necessary to
distinguish between the material transformation
of the economic conditions of production, which
can be determined with the precision of natural
science, and the legal, political, religious, artistic,
or philosophic—in short, ideological forms in which
men become conscious of this conflict and fight it out.
Just as one does not judge an individual by what
he thinks about himself, so one cannot judge such
a period of transformation by its consciousness,
but, on the contrary, this consciousness must be
explained from the contradictions of material life,
from the conflict existing between the social forces
of production and the relations of production.

The era of struggle and resistance within which our Party
was born was an era of ebb and flow in the challenge to
this parasitic relationship. The survival and longevity of the
African People's Socialist Party, our persistent involvement
in and learning from the practical struggles of the African
working class and the fighting and oppressed peoples of the
world, are among the things that prepared us more than any
other political formation for the tasks that confront Africa,
Africans and the world today.

The birth of capitalism did not simply involve the
replacement of the old feudal economic system in Europe with
a new system. The death of European feudalism threw the
entire European world into turmoil. All the institutions and
ideas that held feudal society together were challenged and
sometimes cast aside, leaving Europeans with the frightening
experience of ideological drift, foundering without a stable
belief system.

This is because capitalism required a different set of values and beliefs than feudal society. In feudal society the Church had been a powerful presence in the life of Europeans for a thousand years. The Divine Right of Kings functioned as a key belief of feudal society that tied the peasant serfs to the land and to service to the lords and nobility, fettering every aspect of their lives.

In addition to the social chaos that befell Europe with the arrival of capitalism, the existing philosophical coherence was also a casualty. It was the end of one world and with it the end of the effectiveness of a worldview.

Karl Marx was one of the many who vigorously sought to explain the world and Europe's destiny in that world, although generally the Europeans saw the destiny of Europe and the world as being the same thing—and still do.

Marx's *Capital* and other works were products of this effort to explain the world and Europe's destiny. Moreover, Marx sought to distinguish himself and his works not simply as attempts to explain the world, but as agents for changing the world.

Today the people of the world find ourselves very much in the same situation as the Europeans of dying feudal society. We are watching and experiencing the world changing beneath our very feet.

The old world is gone. The white ruling class is busily, frantically, attempting to explain the world and humanity's destiny in it while refusing to recognize that the social system is irreversibly broken. It cannot be fixed. No explanation based on an assumption of the continued domination of white power, whether by socialist workers or the capitalist bourgeoisie, will suffice.

This is the significance of African Internationalism at this historical moment. African Internationalists understand that what is required is the ideological leadership to show the way forward. Only we are able to explain the crisis of the old, dying capitalist system.

Only we can predict the unfolding future shaped by the oppressed masses of the people, whose resistance deprives the capitalist parasite of access to the resources, life and blood of the colonized, subject and dominated peoples whose conditions of existence represent the foundation of capitalist white power and imperialism as we know it today.

Unlike Marxism and the bourgeois philosophers that have been blinded by their relationship with the world, African Internationalism gives Africans and the oppressed our own voices and our own brains, capable of investigating the world from our reality and making an analysis stemming from that investigation.

Africans *are* "primitive accumulation"

We recognize that capitalism has always rested and depended on a parasitic foundation. As a part of the "primitive accumulation" that Marx spoke of as a function of capitalist development, we are *key to capitalism's destruction*. Indeed, the historical basis for the advent of socialism lies in the struggles of the colonized and dominated oppressed of the world coming to power under the revolutionary leadership of our own workers and laboring masses in all countries.

Marx was unable to fully understand the importance of this question. Marx was able to declare that this "primitive accumulation" is the historic equivalent of "original sin" in theology. He was able to characterize the earth-shaking events that resulted in the theft, sale, forced labor and enslavement of hundreds of millions of African human beings. Nevertheless, Marx's position on the pedestal of our oppression prevented him from seeing the centrality of African and oppressed peoples in the struggle to overturn capitalism.

What Marx termed primitive accumulation was in fact the deadly European assault on Africa, North and South America and Australia, and the extinction and the near decimation of whole peoples. It was the brutal rape of much of Asia and the Middle East, and the numerous internecine wars between European states battling for control of the slave trade and the colonies. It was the resultant growth in wealth that overturned European feudalism and ushered forth capitalism and the European nation.

A real understanding of "primitive accumulation" would have required Marx to center most of his work on an examination stemming from this reality and to look to Africa, Asia and the Americas for the leading forces against capitalism.

But, objectively Marx was himself a beneficiary of "primitive accumulation." Like others, his consciousness was shaped by this material relationship to imperialism during his lifetime. The libraries and universities he used for his research were filled with books and philosophy that were informed by this parasitic relationship. Historical necessity did not require Marx to understand and center his work on this reality.

However, the African working class is required by history to understand this parasitic historical process that has from the beginning linked Europe, capitalism and the rest of us in the embrace of death from which we are now disengaging.

This is why Buchanan and Brzezinski are crying copious intellectual tears! Understanding the reality of parasitic capitalism and drawing the correct conclusions from this understanding is the task that our Party willingly undertook. To the dismay of the Buchanans, Brzezinskis and all the defenders of the imperialist status quo, our success in this area constitutes a fundamental component of the existential crisis of imperialism.

For centuries, the advent of capitalism has been shrouded in mystery and superstition. Every explanation, whether by capitalists or anti-capitalists, has overlooked the source of capitalism's emergence as the dominant world economy and its implications for the present. This has happened despite the fact that the truth has been hidden in plain sight.

The problem is that the arrival of capitalism marks the emergence of Europe and white people as the driving economic and political force in the world. It marks a signal moment, a turning point, in the fortunes of white people and the world. It is the beginning of an era from which the progressive material development of the white world would henceforth be measured.

This is an issue that is increasingly being forced into the public domain. In 2012, *The New York Times* carried an article by Harvard professor Walter Johnson entitled, "King Cotton's Long Shadow."

The premise of the article, excerpted here, is that African enslavement was crucial to the development of global capitalism.

Johnson wrote:

> *It is not simply that the labor of enslaved people underwrote 19th century capitalism. Enslaved people were the capital: four million people worth at least $3 billion in 1860, which was more than all the capital invested in railroads and factories in the United States combined. Seen in this light, the conventional distinction between slavery and capitalism fades into meaninglessness.*

Capitalism born of imperialism–not other way around

Certainly slavery was the main contributor to the emergence of capitalism, not only in the U.S., but in the world. However, while slavery was the main contributor to capitalism it was not the only contributing factor.

In the early 20th century, Vladimir Lenin, a Russian revolutionary of profound significance, struggled with other socialists of the era to come up with a definition of imperialism at a critical time in the anti-capitalist struggle in Europe.

Lenin defined imperialism as capitalism developed to its highest stage. Imperialism, Lenin liked to say, is capitalism that has become "rotten ripe."

The term "imperialism" comes from the word "empire," which can be defined as the complete domination of territories and peoples by foreign state power. During the era of the First Imperialist World War that was fought to divide the world among several European bandits, the term "imperialism" was used to define political and economic features of capitalist-dominated European social behavior and reality.

Lenin's definition of imperialism was one of several at the time, but it has come to dominate the understanding of politically active European and other anti-imperialists to this day.

According to Lenin's *Imperialism, the Highest Stage of Capitalism:*

> *Imperialism is capitalism at that stage of development at which the dominance of monopolies and finance capital is established; in which the export of capital has acquired pronounced importance; in which the division of the world among the international trusts has begun, in which the division of all territories of the globe among the biggest capitalist powers has been completed.*

In *Imperialism and the Split in Socialism,* Lenin declares,

> *We have to begin with as precise and full a definition of imperialism as possible. Imperialism is a specific historical stage of capitalism. Its specific character is threefold: imperialism is (1) monopoly*

capitalism; (2) parasitic, or decaying capitalism; (3)
moribund capitalism.

Indeed, it is certainly true that Lenin has described certain features of capitalism. However, Lenin is wrong about imperialism being the highest stage of capitalism.

The discussion of imperialism in Europe was a response to contradictions being experienced primarily by Europeans in Europe itself. The foray into an inclusion of the partitioning of the world and the intensification of colonization was to contribute to the definition of European reality. It was not a discussion of the reality of Africans and the colonized.

Lenin characterized himself as a Marxist, a revolutionary whose worldview was fashioned by his acceptance of revolutionary theory and conclusions advanced by Karl Marx. We African Internationalists have found particular interest in a critical insight of Marx that was clearly not understood as such by Marx's followers or by Marx himself.

Again we return to the brilliant insight of this quote that we often cite from *Capital*—the quote that Marx himself did not recognize the significance of:

> *The discovery of gold and silver in America, the*
> *extirpation, enslavement and entombment in mines*
> *of the aboriginal population, the beginning of the*
> *conquest and looting of the East Indies, the turning*
> *of Africa into a warren for the commercial hunting of*
> *black skins, signalized the rosy dawn of the era of*
> *capitalist production. These idyllic proceedings are*
> *the chief momenta of primitive accumulation.*

In the same work Marx also explains, though not intentionally, the obvious contradiction impacting the relationship between white people, including "workers," and Africans and other oppressed peoples. This is the contradiction that is responsible for a commonality of cross-class or national interests within European society, and one of Marx's most important statements:

> *Whilst the cotton industry introduced child slavery in England, it gave in the United States a stimulus to transformation of the earlier, more or less patriarchal slavery, into a system of commercial exploitation. In fact the veiled slavery of the wage workers in Europe needed, for its pedestal, slavery pure and simple in the new world.*

There is no little irony attached to the fact that Karl Marx wrote much of *Capital* while being supported financially by his friend and collaborator, Friedrich Engels. Engels received his income from his father, a bourgeois factory owner whose wealth was derived from cotton and textile mills supplied by plantations in the Caribbean.

Stated simply, Marx's work on the plight of the working class that promised the future to the white workers of the world was financed by the labor of enslaved Africans who constituted what Marx would refer to as the primitive accumulation of capital, the beginning of the process, equivalent in political economy to "original sin" in theology.

African Internationalists are historical materialists whose investigation and analysis of the world has its starting point in an examination of the capitalist-dominated world from the objective reality and experiences of Africans and the vast majority of the peoples on the planet, including "white" or European people.

It is clear to us that imperialism is not a product of capitalism; it is not capitalism developed to its highest stage. Instead, capitalism is a product of imperialism.

If anything, capitalism is imperialism developed to its highest stage, not the other way around.

The imperialism defined by Lenin has as its foundation the "primitive accumulation" spoken of by Marx. Finance capital, the export of capital, monopoly, etc., are all articulations of a political economy rooted in parasitism and based on the historically savage subjugation of most of humanity.

Road to socialism is painted black

Unlike Marx and Lenin, we African Internationalists deny that there has ever been anything progressive about capitalism.

Capitalism was born in disrepute, of the rapes, massacres, occupations, genocides, colonialism and every despicable act humans are capable of inflicting.

Capitalism was *not* responsible for some great, otherwise unimaginable leap in production, which "despite its contradictions" resulted in human progress and enlightenment.

What capitalism did was to rip the vast majority of humanity out of the productive process—in Africa, Asia, the Middle East, Australia and what has come to be known as the Americas.

The hundreds of millions dead due to the slave trade and slavery itself; the millions exterminated everywhere Europeans ventured—these are people whose hands were forever removed from a relationship with nature that would result in "production."

Europeans achieved their national identity by way of this bloody process. This is not something that only happened a long time ago. The world's peoples are suffering the consequences of capitalism's emergence right now.

Locked in colonies and the indirect rule of neocolonialism; restricted to lives characterized by brutality, ignorance and violence in the barrios of the Americas; in other internal colonies characterized as Indian reservations and black ghettos; kept under the paranoiac, nuclear-backed, armed-to-the-teeth watch of military forces born of a state power that has its origins in protecting the relationship between capitalism and its imperial pedestal, capitalism has been the absolute factor in *restricting* our production and development.

It has concentrated productive capacity in the hands of the world's minority European population that sits atop the pedestal of our oppressive reality.

Capitalism was not the good, "progressive" force that is the precursor to something better for "humanity." Capitalism was a disaster that rescued Europe from a diseased, feudal existence at the expense of the Africans and the rest of world.

In the 17th century, Galileo, an Italian scientist, ran afoul of the Catholic church with his claim that the Earth circumnavigated the sun, as opposed to the prevailing view in feudal Europe, supported by the church, that the Earth was the center of the universe.

The white Left has always been locked into a worldview that places the location of Europeans at the center of the universe.

If this were not the case, Marx would have been forced to declare that the road to socialism is painted black. The destruction of the "pedestal" upon which all capitalist activity occurs, not some maturation of contradictions within European capitalist society resting upon the pedestal, is the key to overturning imperialist capitalism.

In an earlier work entitled *The Poverty of Philosophy*, Marx made this startling admission:

> *Direct slavery is just as much the pivot of bourgeois industry as machinery, credits, etc. Without slavery you have no cotton; without cotton you have no modern industry. It is slavery that gave the colonies their value; it is the colonies that created world trade, and it is world trade that is the pre-condition of large-scale industry....*

> *Without slavery, North America, the most*
> *progressive of countries, would be transformed*
> *into a patriarchal country. Wipe North America off*
> *the map of the world, and you will have anarchy—*
> *the complete decay of modern commerce and*
> *civilization. Cause slavery to disappear, and you*
> *will have wiped America off the map of nations.*

What an excellent formula for the overthrow of capitalism!

The "slavery" of today is comprised of the colonial, subject and oppressed peoples of the world. The existence of our Party and the convening of our Sixth Congress are part of the trajectory to cause slavery to disappear and, objectively, to achieve the consequence predicted by Marx.

African Internationalism is the way forward

African Internationalism has brought us to a different understanding than that held by Marx and Lenin regarding the way forward in the struggle against capitalism. It is rooted in our recognition, supported by the quotes from Marx above, that it was imperialism that gave birth to capitalism and not the other way around.

Lenin stated that imperialism is capitalism that is characterized in part by parasitism. But from what we have already seen from the pen of Marx, and what we know from our own experiences and historical investigation, capitalism was born parasitic. That is the meaning of the enslavement, colonization and annexation of other countries and peoples by Europe.

A direct line of connection, a unity of opposites, a dialectical relationship exists between the vast majority of the planet and Europe and Europeans. There is no other explanation for the vast differences in the conditions of existence of Europeans and the rest of us.

The original peoples of the Americas, Australia, Canada, the Caribbean, much of Asia, the Middle East and everywhere the U.S. and Europe are currently engaged in bloody wars and intrigues, represent what Marx has objectified with the term "primitive accumulation."

Indeed, the current irreversible crisis of imperialism is the result of the imperialist "pedestal," the very foundation of capitalism, freeing itself from its supporting role of the capitalist edifice.

Objectively, this is the meaning of Afghanistan, Iraq, Palestine, Venezuela, Bolivia and other countries where the people are attempting to liberate themselves from the yoke of empire. It is in self-defense that the U.S. and its partners are engaged in every effort, no matter how brutal or duplicitous, to protect the capitalist status quo.

This is the meaning of AFRICOM, the U.S. military project created to ensnare the entire African Continent in the permanent embrace of U.S. imperial domination to the exclusion of other avaricious imperialist contenders and African people ourselves.

The future of capitalism also rests on the continued subjugation of Mexicans and Indigenous people within current U.S. borders, and especially of internally colonized Africans whose conditions of existence demand a permanent state of often spontaneous and unorganized but ever-present resistance.

The enduring impact of Marx's theory is the fact that it was a response to a desperately needed explanation of the world and the way forward during a time when the thousand-year reign of European feudalism was colliding with the emergence of capitalism, a time when the existing European superstructure was incapable of representing the transforming economic base of society. The established political, legal and cultural institutions and philosophy were incapable of representing the emerging capitalist social system that was ruthlessly uprooting feudalism.

The similarity to today's world is obvious to African Internationalists. Confusion abounds in every arena. Prior explanations fail to satisfy the test of reality. The U.S. popular culture is replete with examples of decadence and philosophical inadequacy. The most oft-viewed movies and TV shows in the U.S. include those of white super heroes, mostly from a past era of imperialist strength and ghoulish vampires and zombies of today.

In other words, one is offered a thrill of nostalgic, vicarious super strength reflecting the imperialist past or the "walking dead," representative of the imperialist socio-political purgatory of today. A superstructure resting on the shaky foundation of a terminally ill imperialism is incapable of seeing the future.

Nor are Buchanan and Brzezinski the only ones confused by how imperialist crisis expresses itself today. The special 90th anniversary issue of *Foreign Affairs,* the political journal of the Council on Foreign Relations, a bourgeois entity historically associated with the Trilateral Commission and the Rockefellers, is dedicated to scrambling for an ideological grasp of this era of imperialism in crisis.

The January/February 2012 anniversary issue is entitled, "The Clash of Ideas, the Ideological Battles that Made the Modern World–And Will Shape the Future."

Among the submissions to this journal is one by Francis Fukuyama. With the implosion of the Soviet Union and the capitulation of China to the capitalist model, Fukuyama popularized the term "End of History" to suggest the U.S. Western imperialist model represents the extent to which human society would develop.

Today Fukuyama is one of the many who have had to reconsider outdated notions of imperialist permanency. In his submission to *Foreign Affairs*, "The Future of History," Fukuyama is now advancing a modified outdated defense of imperialism, in which he asks the question in the subtitle, "Can liberal democracy survive the decline of the middle class?"

Interestingly, Fukuyama addresses what is for him, one of the "most puzzling features of the world in the aftermath of the financial crisis," the fact "that so far, populism has taken primarily a right-wing form, not a left-wing one..."

Fukuyama continues:

> The main trends in left-wing thought in the last two generations have been, frankly, disastrous as either conceptual frameworks or tools for mobilization. Marxism died many years ago, and the few old believers still around are ready for nursing homes. The academic Left replaced it with postmodernism, multiculturalism, feminism, critical theory, and a host of other fragmented intellectual trends that are more cultural than economic in focus.

The 41-year history of the African People's Socialist Party is clear evidence that history did not end. In anticipation of Fukuyama's current intellectual dilemma, the Main Resolution of our First Congress, held in Oakland, California, all the way back in 1981, laid out direction and leadership for our struggle. Its revealing title is, *A New Beginning: The Road to Black Freedom and Socialism.* Indeed, Fukuyama's end *is* our beginning!

This Sixth Party Congress and the theory of African Internationalism represent the "future of history" that Fukuyama is searching for.

The emphasis on African Internationalist theory in this Political Report to the Congress is a refutation of Fukuyama's outdated assumptions. The slave, previously brutalized into silence, has found a voice, and we do understand the world and the future. Our Sixth Party Congress is living testimony to that reality.

We are not the "Left" that Fukuyama speaks of. We are not some radical, loyal opposition. We are African Internationalists, committed to the overthrow of the entire system of empire that has feasted off the blood and resources of Africans and others around the world. We are the African People's Socialist Party that survived the war without terms unleashed against our revolution of the sixties.

Indeed, what is reflected in the popular culture of vampires and geriatric superheroes is the end of history that Fukuyama presumed to see with the failure of the Soviet Union. Were it not for the seriousness of the occasion of our Sixth Congress, I would be tempted here to say to Fukuyama, not without some element of smug satisfaction, "Be careful what you ask for!"

Class question found in the colonial contradiction

It is the liberty of the oppressed, the colonized and enslaved laboring masses of the world currently involved in a massive attempted jailbreak, that will destroy capitalism, the prevailing dominant social system that has the world in lockdown.

Therefore the crisis of capitalism does not cause us anxiety. We know that this is the crisis of the parasite that has, since its historical emergence, required the lives and resources of Africans and others for its success and survival.

While this is not a new position of our Party, confusion on this question has led to profound errors within the African liberation and socialist movements. *Izwe Lethu i Afrika*, the 1990 Political Report to the Third Congress of our Party, attempted to bring clarity and leadership to this crucial issue. In that report we stated:

We have always said that those who saw the fundamental struggle in the world as existing between the minority white workers and bosses of the world were mistaken. We have always said that the essential class struggle in the world does not exist between the white workers and the white ruling class but is actually concentrated in the struggle against colonialism and economic dependency. Indeed whether he knew it or not, Marx inferred as much himself when in Part VIII of Capital he wrote [in a quote that we find so important that we use it for the third time in this current report]:

"In fact, the veiled slavery of the wage workers in Europe needed for its pedestal slavery pure and simple in the new world."

This statement by Marx is simply another way of saying that capitalism, the entire basis and superstructure of white power as it exists, has its origin in and rests upon a pedestal of African oppression.

This point is further elaborated in *Izwe Lethu i Afrika*:

The significance of this research is its usefulness in exposing that the fundamental contradiction, the resolution of which would result in the historically based advent of socialism, has never existed between the industrial (white) working class and ruling class. The real locus of the class contradiction in the real world exists in the contest between capitalism born as a world system, and the "pedestal" upon which it rests.

Hence the 1917 revolution in Russia was not a true socialist revolution since the real historical basis of socialism, which is the destruction of the pedestal upon which capitalism rests and which is required for its existence, had not occurred. What happened in Russia in 1917 was the emergence of conditions that constituted the political basis for socialists to seize power.

However, this seizure of state power by socialists did not change the reality that the world economy, even the world economy within which Russia existed, was and continues to be, a capitalist world economy. It is the same world economy created by the slave trade and augmented by other facets of parasitic or "primitive accumulation" that transformed the vast majority of the peoples and countries of the world into great reservoirs of human and material resources largely for European and North American exploitation.

This is why the presence of our Party is so important. We are the living custodians of the history of struggle and the political, ideological and organizational bridge from the last era of struggle up to now. We are the organization whose every action is guided by our political theory and whose political theory always has been tested and deepened by our action.

Some stuck in last period of struggle

Many of the African liberation organizations of the past period no longer exist, and most that do have lost all semblance of revolutionary content. Though some forces act as if the Black Panther Party (BPP) still exists, there has been no functioning BPP in the U.S. for nearly 40 years. The race nationalist hybrid that calls itself the "New Black Panther Party" has absolutely nothing in common with the Black Panther Party of the 1960s except for appropriating the name and the fact that its members wear berets.

The New Black Panther Party is a caricature of the original Black Panther Party, whose founding was tied to the historical process in which the questions of class struggle and nonviolence were being hotly debated throughout the African Liberation Movement in the U.S. and by diverse liberation movements in contests with colonialism and their own petty bourgeoisie around the world.

Unlike the New Black Panther Party the original Black Panther Party was not a race nationalist organization that perceived a race-based society locked in a Manichean battle between evil whites and good blacks. And, while for much of its short, effective existence, the Black Panther Party was ideologically eclectic, it was, unlike the New Black Panther Party, never religiously based and almost always consistently socialist.

Today, some forces formerly associated with the original Black Panther Party consider themselves a kind of post-revolutionary alumni functioning primarily as guardians and beneficiaries of the legacy of the long dead entity. For them the struggle is over. Through their actions they have either declared victory or conceded defeat.

The original Nation of Islam, through which the world came to know Malcolm X, does not exist. The original organization was, in fact, slipping into *revolutionary* irrelevance, despite the best efforts of Malcolm X when he split with the organization prior to his assassination.

Philosophical idealism, which prohibited the organization from actively engaging in political life during the heat of the African Liberation Movement of the 1960s, was one of the factors leading to Malcolm X's departure from the Nation of Islam.

Malcolm's continuous move into secular politics, embracing some of the civil rights activists and offering scientific, revolutionary analysis for the most important events of his times, endeared him to Africans and oppressed peoples throughout the world. At the same time it created friction between him and leaders of the Nation of Islam who thought Malcolm was straying too far from the religious idealism around which much of the Nation of Islam was defined.

Even so, the leader of the existing Nation of Islam rides the coattails of Malcolm X's legacy. It was Malcolm X who, to his personal detriment, raised the Nation of Islam from relative obscurity as a religious organization to the most influential black nationalist political organization of that era. It was Malcolm X who gave revolutionary legitimacy to the Nation of Islam in a period when the oppressed of the world sought revolutionary direction for ending the colonial domination of Africans and the world's oppressed.

The Provisional Government of the Republic of New Afrika (RNA) was an organization that from its inception in 1968 considered itself the political heir to Malcolm X. The RNA was a militant organization that held up the principle of self-determination that included a real struggle to capture five geographically contiguous states of the southern U.S. as a national homeland for Africans whom the RNA called "New Afrikans."

The RNA experienced years of U.S. government repression. This included military assaults on their meetings and headquarters and jailings of their members and leaders. While the organization continues to exist, it appears to be merely a shell of its earlier self, despite the ongoing political activism of some militants that continue to identify with the organization's aims.

Of the Civil Rights organizations of the era, only the NAACP continues more or less unchanged. It continues to be a shameless expression of African petty bourgeois opportunism. It is essentially a wing of the bourgeois Democratic party and functions mainly as a pipeline through which the liberal white ruling class imposes informal, indirect, neocolonial authority over the colonized African community of the U.S.

The situation is no better on the Continent of Africa. The African National Congress (ANC) is probably the best known of the liberation organizations of the sixties. This is mainly because the struggle against the South African Apartheid regime succeeded in winning support from much of the world, and its leader, Nelson Mandela, became the world's most recognized political prisoner.

The ANC was initially recognized due to the former Soviet Union's designation of the organization as one of its "Authentic Six" revolutionary groups on the Continent during that period. The politically influential Soviet Union did much to win support for the ANC throughout the world.

Later, in 1994, when Apartheid was no longer viable because of mass resistance, and the Soviet Union no longer existed, Mandela was released from prison through pressure from the liberal bourgeoisie of the world. Because a black face was necessary to represent white imperialist interests in South Africa, the U.S. took the lead in world sponsorship of the ANC.

In the 1960s the African National Congress was recognized along with the Pan-Africanist Congress of Azania (PAC) as one of the two legitimate liberation organizations in South Africa. The ANC was for all practical purposes the mass organization of the South African Communist Party, a mainly white political formation that could not fight for control of a black African movement and government with its own white face.

Today it is clear to most of the world that the ANC is not fundamentally different from the white nationalist regime it replaced. At the time, however, our Party was the only force that was clear and outspoken on this question as documented in articles from *The Burning Spear* from the 1970s and '80s. As we predicted, the only thing that has transpired since ANC's rise to power is that a sector of the African petty bourgeoisie or middle class has been recruited to administer the white capitalist state after direct white rule became untenable.

Now in South Africa there is *settler* neocolonialism. Now it is the "black" government that protects the interests of international capital and the white minority that still owns more than 80 percent of the land, an area four times larger than England and Northern Ireland combined. Today the ANC government orders police murders of protesting African miners.

The ANC presides over a regime under which more than 40 percent of African workers are unemployed in steadily deteriorating conditions, while the conditions of the whites have improved considerably.

APSP represents interests, aspirations of African working class

In Zimbabwe, Algeria, Egypt, Angola, Kenya, Guinea Bissau, Mozambique, Democratic Republic of Congo and other places where armed organizations led struggles against the prevailing forms of colonial white domination, there is no forward motion. In most instances there has only been a replacement of white oppression by imperialist-backed black oppression of the masses of our people.

However, we are here—the African Socialist International, the global expression of the African People's Socialist Party. We are here, forged and prepared over the last 41 years for the tasks confronting Africa, Africans and the toiling masses of the world.

We represent historical continuity, the ongoing development of a revolutionary process guided by our ever-developing revolutionary theory, despite the shortcomings and failures of various expressions of our Revolution at particular moments in history.

Our Party has become the custodian of the interests and aspirations of the oppressed and dispersed African nation. It is our existence that represents the dynamic future of Africa and the African Revolution, despite the setbacks experienced by the limitations and/or abandonment of particular African personalities or organizations of the past period.

Political parties are always organizations that represent the interests of particular classes, although efforts are often made to disguise this fact. In so-called democratic capitalist societies, political parties often obscure their class character. This is especially true in the United States, where the main ruling class parties are the Democrats and Republicans.

These two parties most often share political power in a number of ways, including elected offices, as well as appointments to posts within the administrations of either or both parties in government.

Regardless of the capitalist political party in power, each party looks out for the interests of capitalism in general, even as it pursues the specific interests of the specific sector of the bourgeoisie that is responsible for its elevation to power.

The African People's Socialist Party is also the Party of a class, the African working class. Our work is responsive to the interests of our class, interests that distinguish it from other social forces, whether those of the oppressor nation capitalists or the oppressed nation, neocolonial-aspiring African petty bourgeoisie.

Our objective is to provide the political leadership for the African working class in its pursuit of political power, the power to govern, the power to become the new ruling class of a liberated, united Africa and African population whose conditions of existence worldwide are a reflection of the rape and colonization of Africa.

African Internationalism is our scientifically based, ideological guide that informs our actions and keeps us on the right track. It keeps us away from the lures of race nationalism, superstition and other toxins that attempt to divert the masses and us from our historical mission of African liberation, unification and socialism.

What we are currently experiencing, sometimes in the name of revolution, is the consequence of revolutionary defeat. This is what has contributed to the stupefication of the masses of our people and the peoples of the world. This is why our Party and African Internationalism are so important.

Our Party represents the clearest evidence of revolutionary continuum in the world. And it is revolution that continues to be necessary; not prayer to the "right" god while turned in the correct direction. It is not that we need cultural enrichment, nor is social media militancy—audacity in front of a computer screen—the missing element.

It was revolution that won the hearts of masses of Africans and other oppressed peoples around the world. It was revolution that was defeated and counterrevolution that succeeded almost absolutely, except for the presence and work of the African People's Socialist Party.

Material basis of white terror

One of the issues that has served to befuddle sectors of the African Liberation Movement in the U.S. and elsewhere is the definition of "white people," their role in history and their place, if any, in the struggle to end oppression and exploitation.

This is an issue that has been complicated by the fact that for centuries, race-based biological definitions have been used by European oppressors as justification for the horrors they have inflicted on most of the world and especially on Africans.

To justify the colonial enslavement and brutal oppression of Africans, Europeans concocted pseudo-scientific biological "evidence" purporting the inherent inferiority and bestiality of the colonized. Africans and other oppressed peoples were the primary victims of the violent oppression that accompanied the ruthless exploitation used to create the capitalist system and the sense of sameness necessary for the consolidation of the European nation.

Capitalism entered the historical scene as a world system stemming from slavery and colonialism, and its power to define reality was nearly absolute. What is known as "racism" is a consequence of the power of capital built on the backs of Africans and Indigenous peoples. In fact, racism, as we discussed earlier in this chapter, is the ideological foundation of the global capitalist social system. Racism is a component of the superstructure spawned by the process of capitalism's conception. Therefore it is nearly impossible to exaggerate the extent of its intellectual influence in the U.S., Europe and the world.

What is called racism is a biological analysis. It is reinforced by the creation of such things as the discipline of anthropology, used for the express purpose of proving the superiority of whites or Europeans over Africans and all others. This analysis had an understandable influence over how Africans would begin to explain "white people" as oppressors in the struggle to recapture our humanity, resources and freedom.

Victimized by this pseudo-scientific approach Africans adopted a competing biological analysis to explain the evil nature of the white man.

One result of this has been a hodgepodge of theories that spanned the genetic gamut. This included assertions that the white man is a mutation; the white man's depravities are expressions of melanin deficits; and finally, from the Nation of Islam, the white man was created by an evil black genius named Yakub through a selective breeding process.

Contributing to the complexity of the issue has been the perennial willingness of the white majority to suffer voluntary isolation from the majority of humanity in exchange for the material benefits of imperialist colonialism, as well as the extraordinary, irrationally based spiritual or ideological rewards of "whiteness."

As long ago as 1858, in a letter to Karl Marx, his comrade and collaborator, Friedrich Engels, offered this materialist observation about the ability of the whites to unite with their ruling class in the exploitation of the colonial world: "For a nation which exploits the whole world this is of course to a certain extent justifiable."

Later, in 1882, in a letter on the same subject, Engels would comment to Karl Kautsky: "You ask me what the English workers think about colonial policy. Well, exactly the same as they think about politics in general...the workers gaily share the feast of England's monopoly of the world market and the colonies."

What Engels has begun to do here is attempt a scientific, materialist-based explanation for white behavior. We have spoken to this issue earlier in our description of the economic foundation of capitalism and the resultant superstructure. However, our Party has much more to say on this issue that has provided such a Gordian knot until cut asunder by the incisive blade of African Internationalism.

Writing in *A History of Africa*, a book we have often quoted, Hosea Jaffe makes another important contribution to a materialist explanation for the emergence and behavior of Europe or the "white man," declaring:

> *Europe was born out of colonialism, as the exploiting, oppressing, negating pole that tried always to destroy and assimilate its opposite pole: the rest of the world....*

It was out of this process that the very idea of a European man arose, an idea that did not exist even in etymology before the 17ʰ century. Before the slave trade in Africa there was neither a Europe nor a European. Finally, with the European arose the myth of European superiority and separate existence as a special species or "race"; there arose indeed the myth of race in general, unknown to mankind before—even the word did not exist before the lingua franca of the Crusades—the particular myth that there was a creature called a European, which implied, from the beginning a "white man." Colonialism, especially in Africa, created the concept and ideology of race. Before capitalist-colonialism there were no races; but now, suddenly and increasingly, there were races: once born, the myth grew into a reality.

Clearly this and other African Internationalist philosophical materialist analyses offer a correct explanation for the "creation," power and influence of the "white man."

This is the same explanation provided by our book *A New Beginning:*

Living in a country built and sustained off slavery, colonialism, and neocolonialism, the impact of victorious revolutionary struggles reaches down into the gas tanks, shopping centers and tax brackets of the North American population. There is an objective relationship between world slavery and U.S. affluence, and up to now the North American population, opportunistically and demagogically led by their stomachs, pocketbooks and corrupt leadership, have chosen the continued enslavement of the world.

In the U.S., imperialism was constructed off the enslavement of African people and the near-decimation of the Native population. This system has been the cornerstone of world capitalism since the Second Imperialist War, which means among other things, that the resources, the wealth, the near-slave labor of the vast majority of the peoples of the world have been the basis for the development, not only of the wealth of the ruling class, but of the entire North American society.

African Internationalism helps us to understand that white people are just that, people. And, like all people their actions can be explained by material causes. African Internationalism teaches us that key to the actions of white people is the fact that they have lived on the pedestal of the oppression of most of the world since the advent of capitalism as a social system.

White people: join humanity; commit national suicide!

This is not to state that white people are not beset with various contradictions with their own ruling class within the capitalist system. Certainly they are. However, these contradictions require for their existence the primary contradiction—the parasitic extraction of value from Africans and others that constitute the foundation of the entire capitalist social system that has been generally beneficial to Europe and white people at our expense.

For white people to overturn the contradictions with the white ruling class they find themselves contending with from time to time they must end their voluntary exile from the rest of the toiling masses of the world and their parasitic relationship to us. They cannot simply claim to be a part of the "99 percent," as the Occupy Movement proclaimed, when it suits them to suddenly identify with the oppressive circumstances of the rest of us. They are not a part of the 99 percent and it is dishonest for them to make such a statement.

However, this is not simply a complaint about the capacity of white people for truth and veracity. The problem is that the claim by whites to be part of the rest of us is an attempt to use the energy of Africans and the oppressed of the world, whose exploitation facilitates the extraction of value that feeds the white population, as a means of remedying white people's problems on the pedestal. The problems of white people are the direct result of the struggles of the oppressed to take back our resources and our future.

In other words, the contradictions faced by many white people today are the result of the crisis of imperialism brought about by the resistance of oppressed peoples who are struggling against the imperialist theft of their oil, minerals, land and resources.

It is insane for Europeans or whites to assume that the 80 percent of the world that attempts to survive on $10 or less a day would be a willing part of a struggle defined and designed for reinstatement of white student loans or retirement guarantees for the white elderly.

The real, legitimate struggle for white people is to commit national suicide by joining in the struggle for black power and against the white power that is representative of the oppressor nation relationship with the rest of us. The various contradictions plaguing the world are contradictions born of the ascent of white power.

Like Africans, Mexicans, Arabs, Iranians, Roma, South Americans, etc., white women, white homosexuals and white workers are all victims of capitalism that was born as white power at the expense of everybody else in the world. Yet, white people have always attempted to solve their contradictions with capitalism at our expense rather than in solidarity with us.

Progressive, forward-looking whites who are committed to the creation of a new world without war and exploitation have to join in this struggle by the world's majority against white power instead of using inane slogans and opportunistic subterfuge to attempt to win world participation in solving their perceived problems at our expense.

We have already discussed the opportunism of the Euro-North American Left. It is real, historical and universal. In *Izwe Lethu i Afrika* we quoted from the 1907 congress of the Second Communist International, held in Stuttgart, Germany and attended by more than 800 delegates. This piece was cited in *Lenin's Struggle for a Revolutionary International*, edited by John Riddell.

The crux of the quote revolves around a majority resolution at that congress that, "Under a socialist regime, colonization could be a force for civilization." While today most opportunists attempt to disguise the self-serving basis for their opportunism, the "99 percenters" at this congress were refreshingly and unreservedly open in their intent to preserve white power on the backs of the rest of us.

Let us listen in to the debate on the question. This statement by Hendrick van Kol of the Netherlands is in support of the majority socialist colonization resolution:

> *The minority resolution also denies that the productive forces of the colonies can be developed through the capitalist policy. I do not understand at all how a thinking person can say that. Simply consider the colonization of the United States of North America. Without it the native peoples there would today still be living in the most backward social conditions.*
>
> *Does Ledebour want to take away the raw materials, indispensable for modern society, which the colonies can offer? Does he want to give up*

the vast resources of the colonies even if only for the present? Do those German, French, and Polish delegates who signed the minority resolution want to accept responsibility for simply abolishing the present colonial system?...Surely there are few Socialists who think that colonies will be unnecessary in the future social order. Although we do not need to discuss this question today, I still ask Ledebour: does he have the courage now, under capitalism, to give up the colonies?

Perhaps he can also tell us what he would do about the overpopulation of Europe. Where would the people who must migrate go, if not to the colonies? What does Ledebour want to do with the growing production of European industry if he does not want to create new export markets in the colonies? And does he as a Social Democrat want to shirk his duty to work continually for the education and further advancement of the backward peoples?

We are tempted to quote more extensively from this discussion as we have in past documents. However, the point is made perfectly clear here: there is a solid, clearly understood material basis for white opportunism that is not limited to the U.S. or to the "backward," "duped" white working class. It includes its most advanced sector, communists who claim to be organized to struggle for the power to lead the world to a new day of society free of oppression and economic exploitation.

African Internationalism is not simply an empty discussion dealing with purely abstract questions. It is a theory that has profound implications for how we understand the world and our approach to changing it, as we must.

This is why this Political Report has become a tome of sorts to dig deeply into the theoretical issues confounding much of the world. As an organization of propagandists the Party is the tool of the advanced detachment of the African working class used to spread the gospel of African Internationalism among the oppressed African workers and all the toilers of the Earth.

IV. The question
of the nation

Imperialist political oracle and Obama adviser, Zbigniew Brzezinski, is a ruling class observer of the crisis of imperialism. In his book *Second Chance: Three Presidents and the Crisis of a Superpower*, cited in Chapter II, Brzezinski makes this observation about the significance of the question of identity today when imperialism is being challenged to its parasitic foundation by the political intervention of the peoples upon whose oppression this system was founded.

> *Global systemic instability...is likely to be prompted in many parts of the world by challenges to existing state frontiers. In Asia and Africa especially, state borders are often imperial legacies and do not reflect ethnic or linguistic boundaries. These borders are vulnerable to increased pressure as heightened political consciousness leads to more assertive territorial aspirations....*
>
> *The largely anti-Western character of populist activism has less to do with ideological or religious bias and more with historical experience. Western (or European) domination is part of the living memory of hundreds of millions of Asians and Africans, and some Latin Americans (though in this case its sharp edge is pointed at the United States)...In the vast majority of states, national identity and national emancipation are associated with the end of foreign imperial domination...This is true in such large and self-confident states as India or China as it is in Congo or Haiti.*

In addition to Brzezinski's consideration of the question, there is a bevy of other publications attempting to address the same issues of the nation and identity. They include David Cannadine's 2013 book, *The Undivided Past: Humanity Beyond Our Differences*, and the 2004 Samuel Huntington book entitled, *Who Are We? The Challenges to America's National Identity.*

Patrick Buchanan's *Suicide of a Superpower: Will America Survive to 2025?* is another of the intellectual forays into the arena of the nation and its future from the vantage point of various representatives of U.S. and/or European imperialism.

These farseeing thinking representatives of the white ruling class are being forced to contend with the earth-shattering consequences of a European civilization resting on the historical fault line of economic parasitism.

The shifting center of gravity in the world, the omnipresent upsurge of the "wretched of the earth" to realize our dreams of happiness and security come at the expense of imperialist stability. The resistance of the oppressed unhinges the previous definitions of social reality that required imperialist-imposed tranquility for its foundation and raises the question of the nation and identity to center stage.

In his 2007 book, *Day of Reckoning: How Hubris, Ideology, and Greed Are Tearing America Apart*, Patrick Buchanan probes the question of the nation:

> *Yugoslavia and Czechoslovakia, it is said, were artificial nations created by the treaties of Versailles and St. Germain in 1919. And the Soviet Union was but the Russian Empire reconstituted by the Red Army, the KGB, the Communist Party, and Leninist ideology, not a nation at all....*
>
> *The sudden disintegration of these three nations into twenty-six seemed to substantiate Strobe Talbott's*

prediction in his 1992 Time essay, "The Birth of the Global Nation":

"All countries are basically social arrangements, accommodations to changing circumstances. No matter how permanent and even sacred they may seem at any one time, in fact they are all artificial and temporary....

"[W]ithin the next hundred years...nationhood as we know it will be obsolete; all states will recognize a single, global authority. A phrase briefly fashionable in the mid-20ᵗʰ century—'citizen of the world'—will have assumed real meaning by the end of the 21ˢᵗ century."

Is the time of nations over? Is the nation-state passing away? Are the bonds that hold them together so flimsy? Since Talbot's essay, events have not contradicted him.

Buchanan's summation is representative of the anxiety of the international white ruling class, whose concerns about defending their world hegemony are reflected in the drone bombings, assassinations, unrelenting war and threats of war.

The current policies of the imperialists designed to crush the will of the peoples' resistance in Afghanistan and the Middle East, all of Africa, Asia, the Americas and the world, are attempts to maintain the shaky empire and its ideological reflections that define identity and the nation according to its interests and will.

Our entry into this discussion of the nation is mandated by the seriousness of the times. It is mandated by the requirement of Africans and the oppressed to provide a summation of reality that reflects our interests and our aspirations. Our summation is based on science and objective analysis grounded in material reality that predicts the defeat of imperialism and the emancipation of the toiling masses of Africa and the world.

Our discussion of the nation is informed by our inevitable elevation as workers to the role of the ruling class in the transition to a world shorn of classes, borders, nations and states. To win our liberation we must know who we are and who our enemies are.

Let us begin.

Most often the question of African nationality is handled in careless, offhanded and vague ways, making no pretense of ascribing to any particular scientific approach or definition.

The common practice among Pan-Africanists of referring to the international African community as African "peoples" is an example. More commonly, there is the practice of characterizing Africans forcibly dispersed from the Continent as African "descendants" with the intent of differentiating the national identity of such Africans from those who suffered imperial white domination on the Continent itself.

Africans are not unusual in the ambiguous manner in which the question of the nation is handled. In the past few centuries there has been much debate concerning this issue among some of Europe's most erudite intellectuals. Their approach is equivalent to the quote: "I don't know anything about art, but I know what I like."

Similarly, it is difficult to get a uniform definition of the nation from different scholars or intellectuals. Some claim outright that there is not an a priori definition of the nation. "I can't tell you what it is," they might say, "but I know it when I see it."

What is probably the most influential definition of the nation is one offered by Joseph Stalin. This is because as leader of the Soviet Union and the international communist movement from 1924 to 1953 Stalin took the question out of the classrooms and into the fray of political movements throughout the world. Stalin applied his interpretation to the real conditions impacting and tormenting millions of people struggling to define their places in the world.

Written at the end of 1912 or early in 1913, Stalin's position, later published in pamphlet form, defined the nation's key elements, which, according to Stalin, included a "historically constituted, stable community of people, formed on the basis of a common language, territory, economic life, and psychological make-up manifested in a common culture."

Obviously the situation for Africans does not satisfy Stalin's definition of the nation, whether applied to the artificially created African "countries" carved out at the imperialist Berlin Conference in 1884-85 or to African people forcibly dispersed around the world.

While Stalin's definition of the nation is one of many, it contains within it elements being offered by others at the time and even today. In fact, Stalin's definition was a struggle against contending definitions forwarded by European socialists at a time when nationalist sentiments were roiling in Europe. These ideas would soon facilitate the European bourgeois war to redivide the world, the First Imperialist World War or World War I.

In his book *The Undivided Past*, referred to above, author David Cannadine challenges many of the prevalent ideas around which the definition of the nation revolves. Here he deals with the requirement that makes language a prerequisite. While not addressing Stalin specifically, Cannadine had this to say about the self-defined European "nations" involved in the First Imperialist World War:

> *To begin with, the idea that the belligerents of 1914 were unified, homogeneous nations does not survive detailed examination. Consider, for example, the matter of common language, often regarded as essential to any shared sense of*

national identity. It certainly did not exist in the nation created by the Risorgimento. "We have made Italy," Massimo d'Azeglio observed at the time, "now we have to make Italians." With less than five percent of the population using Italian for everyday purposes, they had a long way to go. In France, almost half the school children engaged with French as a foreign language, speaking another tongue at home: dialect and patois were widespread, and in departments bordering other nations, it was often Flemish, Catalan, or German that was spoken. A similar picture could be found in Germany, where in the east many spoke Polish as their first language, whereas in Alsace and Lorraine many spoke French; and in Russia, educated people conversed in French, while workers and peasants used a wide variety of Slavic languages and dialects. In Austria-Hungary the array of different tongues was even more varied, including German, Czech, Italian, Hungarian, Polish, Croatian, and Greek, and many of the Hapsburg emperor's subjects were multilingual, speaking one language at school or at work and another at home. Insofar as a common tongue could be considered an essential criterion, none of the major powers that went to war in 1914 qualified as a "nation."

Cannadine challenges other ideas generally used to determine the nation, some of which also dispute Stalin's influential definition. We know many of the limitations of Stalin's work from our own observations. However, this does not relieve us of the need to enter into this discussion.

It is true that nations exist if only because the nation is a commonly held idea along the lines of Marx's maxim that theory, when grasped by the masses becomes a material force. Indeed, the idea of the nation is something that *has* been grasped by the masses to the extent that people actually kill and die in the name of furthering its perceived interests.

Slavery, colonialism basis of the European nation

One of the least discussed questions concerning the nation is the basis for its advent in history. How is it that the world is perceived as a place where for thousands of years there was no such thing as the nation only to have it suddenly emerge in Europe, dominating the 19th century, often referred to as the era of "nation building"?

One attempt at an explanation for the advent of the European nation is provided by Modibo M. Kadalie, Ph.D. in his book published in 2000, entitled *Internationalism, Pan-Africanism and the Struggle of Social Classes*. This rather lengthy and vacuous quote illustrates the general lack of clarity that surrounds this issue:

> *After thousands of years of change, transformation, setbacks, rapid advances, monstrous defeats, uneven-ness in human conflicts with nature and with other human beings, which was constantly changing in its character; the colossal units of production and exchange that have come to be known as the modern nation-state came into being ruled and fashioned by a class of people who resulted from this long and arduous path of dialectical development. The modern nation-state was the creation of the modern bourgeoisie and serves as the political form or funnel through which this class continues to perpetuate itself in its quest for historical immortality.*

> *The most highly developed political formations of this type took place in Europe and later in North America. It is for those reasons that the brutality that has come to be a part of this class slashing its*

*way across the planet has come to be associated
with Europeans generally. Rightfully so. Capitalism
and the European predatory nation state became to
Europe and the rest of the world what feudalism,
in its most advanced forms, was to Asia, and
communal and intricate pre-feudal modes along
with a variety of early forms of social production
were to the continent of Africa....*

*The European bourgeoisies could become
international precisely because they were national.
After carving out and consolidating their sway
within a certain geographical area which defined
its boundaries, a given national state could
continue its expansion. This occurs because of the
organic and predatory nature of the capitalist mode
of production. With this expansion bourgeois rule
spreads. It, therefore, became a highly developed
system for international conquest with its ruling
class at the helm guiding, in a deliberate and
calculating way, its own realization and affirmation
through continuous conquest.*

What Kadalie has done here is to detail the obvious:
indeed, "The modern nation-state was the creation of the
modern bourgeoisie," and indeed, it is predatory. However,
after all is said and done, we still do not know its origin nor
the historical basis for its emergence in Europe. In addition,
we are misinformed by Kadalie who claims: "The European
bourgeoisies could become international precisely because
they were national." In fact, the bourgeoisie and the bourgeois
nation were products of imperialism, the "international"
activities of slavery and colonialism.

This is the point made by Hosea Jaffe in his book *A History
of Africa*:

The 15th century, then, saw the multiplication of the primary accumulation of European capitalism; and Africa played the most important part in the process as the principal arena of European colonialism, the very genesis and foundation of the capitalist system. From the turn of the 16th century the Americas and Asia were added to this foundation, and out of this totality arose capitalism and modern Europe itself. Before capitalist colonialism there was no Europe, only a collection of feudal, mercantile and tribal towns, farms, villages, discrete states and kingdoms vying and warring with each other, just as in Africa, but on a different property basis—that of private property in the land. Europe then was neither a concept nor a reality, at most a vague idea that Arabs— but not "Europeans"—had long ago of some place northwest of Greece. As long as Europe remained isolated from the world, there was no Europe. When it became connected with, and dependent on, first Africa, then the Americas and finally Asia, it began to become a reality and an idea. Only when Portuguese, Spanish, French, Italian, Dutch, English, German, Danish and Swedish confronted and clashed with Africa, America and Asia did the need arise for them to consider themselves as a set, a whole, different from, hostile to and, eventually, superior to Africans, Americans and Asians. Colonialism gave them a common interest.

This "common interest," the sense of sameness, common history and psychological make-up manifested in a common culture—elements contained in most definitions of the nation—was forged through slavery and colonialism. This was the nation-building process; the sense of sameness and common culture of violence are features of the subjective factors identifying the European nation.

Contrary to white leftists and modern-day Marxists, both the white ruling class *and* the white working class owe their existence to this process. They are historical twins, containing the same DNA and spawned by a history of genocide and enslavement of other peoples that is repugnant in its entirety.

The parasitic capitalist economy is the objective factor, the material basis upon which the subjective relies; it is the bonding element of the nation that holds this collective community together.

The European nation, and we do mean "European," with its multiplicity of languages, classes and internal borders, was born as a bourgeois nation, a white, Christian nation, spawned through the blood and gore of slavery and colonialism and resting on a foundation of capitalism benefiting Europe at the expense of Africans and the rest of the world.

Aspects of the European nation's subjective content, its self-perception, were forged through the assault on Islam during the Christian Crusades in the feudal era for control of much of the same territory in North Africa and the "Middle East" that imperialism is contending for today. However, the most essential component of Europe's subjective identification grew out of its history of genocidal aggression against Africa that included colonial slavery.

Herein lies the process that bonded Europe into a single nation, though differentiated by sometimes competing capitalist centers designated as countries and incorrectly identified as nations. This, like the anti-Islamic national component, is residual from the pre-colonial European feudal era where contending European powers defined themselves primarily in relationship to each other, except for the united looting expeditions through the Middle East that occurred under the religious banner of Christianity.

Thus the European nation was born white and Christian. Moreover, it was born as a bourgeois nation, as the center of capitalist production stemming from parasitic accumulation of "capital" flowing from colonial slavery. Even the European working class was born on the pedestal of colonialism and slavery, therefore ultimately realizing the benefits of an oppressor nation and identifying with its own bourgeoisie.

Marx was wrong!

Feudalism preceded capitalism in Europe. Feudal society was defined primarily by the relationship between the nobility, impoverished peasants and serfs, agricultural workers who were tied to the estates of the feudal lords who expropriated most of what the serfs produced.

While serfs could not be individually bought and sold as was the case with Africans, the serfs had little or no rights that were not granted by the lords. The role of the feudal state was to protect this relationship that required permanent attachment of the serfs to the landed estates.

As we know, in describing the transformation of feudalism to capitalism, Karl Marx authored the term "primitive accumulation," naming the European enslavement, genocide, wars and occupations of oppressed peoples around the world as the source of the vast wealth extraction out of which the entire capitalist system was born.

But Marx erroneously includes in his definition of primitive accumulation the internal process of European peasants and serfs being driven from the land through England's Enclosure Acts beginning in the early 1600s that privatized lands that had been collectively farmed by peasants for centuries.

According to Marx from Part VIII, Volume I of *Capital*:

The economic structure of capitalist society has grown out of the economic structure of feudal society. The dissolution of the latter set free the elements of the former.

The immediate producer, the laborer, could only dispose of his own person after he had ceased to be attached to the soil and ceased to be the slave, serf, or bondsman of another. To become a free seller of labor power, who carries his commodity wherever he finds a market, he must further have escaped from the regime of the guilds, their rules for apprentices and journeymen, and the impediments of their labor regulations. Hence, the historical movement which changes the producers into wage-workers appears, on the one hand, as their emancipation from serfdom and from the fetters of the guilds, and this side alone exists for our bourgeois historians. But, on the other hand, these new freedmen became sellers of themselves only after they had been robbed of all their own means of production, and of all the guarantees of existence afforded by the old feudal arrangements. And the history of this, their expropriation, is written in the annals of mankind in letters of blood and fire.

Marx was wrong. Though this process involves the creation of the social mobility and capitalist labor force previously prohibited by feudalism, it is not primitive accumulation.

European capitalist society may have very well "grown out of the economic structure of feudal society" but it was *conceived* by way of:

The discovery of gold and silver in America, the extirpation, enslavement and entombment in mines of the aboriginal population, the beginning of the conquest and looting of the East Indies, the turning of Africa into a warren for the commercial hunting of black skins...

Notably, in *Capital,* Marx devotes far more pages to the conditions of peasants and serfs in the transformation from feudalism to capitalism than he does to the enslavement and genocide that created immense wealth for Europe but destroyed the lives and means of production for millions and millions of African and oppressed peoples for centuries to come.

Equating the removal of the European peasants from their land with the fact that Europe transformed Africa into a "warren for the commercial hunting of black skins" is a historical lie. It relegates African people to mere footnotes of history.

The expulsion of the peasants from the land is a *result* of the process of primitive accumulation of capital, not a part of it. Ultimately, the former serfs became European workers who now also sit on the pedestal of our oppression and benefit from it enormously.

This Eurocentric error by Marx subordinates the historical basis of the existence of Africans and others to the requirements for European development. It objectifies the history and civilization of African people, rendering us invisible and leading to wrong conclusions that disguise the bloody reality of parasitism, making it seem that African people exist merely for the needs of Europeans.

This Political Report is replete with examples that challenge Marx's confusion on this issue. When it comes to objectively describing the historical process that gave rise to capitalism, and its impact on Europe and the development of capitalism, Hosea Jaffe, quoted earlier in this chapter, and the African People's Socialist Party do a better job.

Marx's lack of clarity obviously stems from his own social location on the pedestal of African slavery, a location that provided the superstructure for the European capitalist society within which Marx's consciousness was forged and that his life's work relentlessly criticized.

In *One People! One Party! One Destiny!,* the Political Report to our Party's Fifth Congress, we commented on the tendency by Marx to muddle this issue. Here is a selection:

> *We have to note here as well that Marx's description of slavery as an "economic category," and his concept of primitive accumulation provide outstanding examples of historic objectification of African people by Europeans.*
>
> *The entire historical process that resulted in the total disruption of the political economy of Africa, the imposition of colonial borders and the capture and dispersal of millions of Africans whose forced labor was responsible for the development of Europe and European society is characterized as an "economic category"!*
>
> *Marx reduced the process of European pillage and plunder of the world and the ensuing genocide and enslavement to "primitive accumulation" of capital, a footnote whose function in history is to explain the "development" of Europe.*
>
> *In other works Marx developed the concept of the "fetish of the commodity" to explain how commodity production, production for the market, obscures and mystifies the relationship between people, allowing it to be confused with a relationship between things.*
>
> *A similar thing happened with the concept of "primitive accumulation." Here the relationship between peoples and countries is also obscured and mystified. Marx attributes European "development" solely to the "genius" and productive forces inside of Europe. He is thereby covering over or liquidating the origin of such "development" in the*

parasitic impairment of the capacity of independent development in Africa and other places victimized by Europe.

European nation is white and Christian

The European nation became the means of securing the loyalty of the emancipated laborers to the emergent capitalist state and, by association, ruling class. Now, it is not the feudal state or sheriff of Nottingham that forces the toilers to fight the wars of the ruling class or put the interests of the state above their own.

It is the flag, the national anthem, the pledge of allegiance along with the collective identification with a common history that transcends individual European countries or territories: this is what facilitates the new relations of production[1] necessary for capitalist production, relations of production resting on a parasitic economic foundation whose genesis is colonial slavery.

In summation, the European nation derives from relations of production contained within capitalism that was spawned by slavery and colonialism. It was born as a parasitic capitalist or bourgeois nation that encompasses all classes within it.

The European sense of sameness, self-perception and subjective expression, necessary for binding the emergent working class to its newly forged bourgeoisie, is white and Christian. The material base of the European nation is the parasitic capitalist system that bore it in Europe. The capitalist system feeds the entire European nation through its cannibalistic, parasitic relationship to Africa and most of the world.

---

1 *Relations of production is a Marxist term for the material and human relationships involved in how a society comes together to produce the necessities of life. Relations of production could be capitalist, socialist, feudal, etc.*

I have belabored this discussion and description of the European nation because its arrival on the world historical scene with the advent of capitalism has determined, through the barrel of a gun, how other national expressions would be defined by other peoples in various parts of the world.

It is no accident that Europe would describe the nation in a manner that would not be applicable to Africans, the Indigenous of the Americas and many others whose enslavement was a condition for the emergence of the European or "white" nation in the first place.

European scholars have demanded a common definition of the nation. It is a declaration of European universalism that requires every nation to contain the same elements apparent in the European nation.

It is an extraordinary example of philosophical metaphysics to suggest that we should determine the quality of any social phenomenon without first examining the specifics and history of the phenomenon being defined. It is an extraordinary example of imperialist national narcissism to define the validity of all social phenomena based on proximity to one's own reality.

The function of the European nation was to serve the development of Europe alone; the rise of the European nation is an attack on the development and survival of much of the world.

Historical basis of the African nation state

Our discussion of the African nation and its definition, resting on a real, material basis, must serve African development. The research and writings of Cheikh Anta Diop demonstrate quite scientifically the cultural unity of Africa going back through millennia. Diop authored the book, *The Cultural Unity of Black Africa: The Domains of Patriarchy & of Matriarchy in Classical Antiquity*, that today remains the standard for investigation of ancient Africa by any serious historian.

Below we examine a quote extracted from Diop's otherwise deeply scientific work. Here he not only explores the spiritual aspect of African identity, but he also compares it to that of Europe. This is because the discussion of characteristics specific to national identity always distinguishes one people or nation from an "other."

The nation cannot be defined by measuring itself against itself. If there is no "other," there is no logic for the "nation." The "white man" needed the existence of the "black man" to achieve his identity. So it is with nations.

Of course, the problem for the European nation is that it resulted from a false, self-serving European definition of the African. Since this false definition was the basis upon which the sense of white sameness, necessary for the definition of the European nation is anchored, the ability of the African to successfully achieve self-definition marks the beginning of the end of a crucial subjective factor necessary for European national coherence.

Diop's works place significance in what he characterized as the Southern or Meridional cradle of human development versus the Northern cradle, and how the differences in material conditions peculiar to each of them contributed to shaping the worldview and character of their respective inhabitants. This is Diop's summation that contributes to defining the national character of African people as compared to Europeans:

> In conclusion, the Meridional cradle, confined to the African continent in particular, is characterized by the matriarchal family, the creation of the territorial state, in contrast to the Aryan city-state, the emancipation of woman in domestic life, xenophilia, cosmopolitanism, a sort of social collectivism having as a corollary a tranquility going as far as unconcern

for tomorrow, a material solidarity of right for each individual, which makes moral or material misery unknown to the present day; there are people living in poverty, but no one feels alone and no one is in distress. In the moral domain, it shows an ideal of peace, of justice, of goodness and an optimism which eliminates all notion of guilt or original sin in religious and metaphysical institutions....

The Northern cradle, confined to Greece and Rome, is characterized by patriarchal family, by the city-state...; it is easily seen that it is on contact with the Southern world that the Northerners broadened their conception of the state, elevating themselves to the idea of a territorial state and of an empire. The particular character of these city-states, outside of which a man was an outlaw, developed an internal patriotism, as well as xenophobia. Individualism, moral and material solitude, a disgust for existence, all the subject matter of modern literature, which even in its philosophic aspects is none other than the expression of the tragedy of a way of life going back to the Aryans' ancestors, are all attributes of this cradle. An ideal of war, violence, crime and conquests inherited from nomadic life, with as a consequence, a feeling of guilt and of original sin, which causes pessimistic religious or metaphysical systems to be built, is the special attribute of this cradle.

However, notwithstanding the usefulness of the works of Diop and similar scholars, all of which had to battle against hundreds of years of European prejudice disguised as scholarship to reach the light of day, our discussion of the African nation will revolve around the same time period to which the birth of the European nation belongs. It is clear from what has already been revealed in this Political Report that there is a direct causal relationship between the existence of the European nation and the aspirations of Africans to consolidate the African nation.

Like the European nation, the emergent African nation is a response to necessity. We are facing the historical requirements for advancing and developing Africa and African people, whose generally oppressive conditions of existence derive from the stuff resulting in the emergence of the European or "white" bourgeois or capitalist nation.

One People! One Party! One Destiny! addressed this necessity. It raises the issue of the consolidation of the African nation as a practical political problem that we must solve to forward the national liberation of our people from imperialist domination worldwide. African Internationalism is a theory of practice, as exemplified by this passage:

> *An African Internationalist investigation...leads us to conclude, among other things, that key to the liberation of African people is the defeat of the parasitic stranglehold that has been imposed on us by imperialism.*
>
> *Moreover, as African Internationalists we recognize that Africa has been under some kind of attack for millennia, but that our struggle today is contextualized by the fact that the world economy that gives life to our oppression is a capitalist economy.*
>
> *Our struggle is not fueled by a subjective need for vengeance against every group that has historically attacked Africa. This means that the struggle must be waged against the capitalist social system that is the basis of our exploitation and wretched conditions of existence today. Our struggle for the unification and emancipation of Our Africa and our people is also a struggle against capitalism.*

Hence, our struggle, if it is to be fought to its successful conclusion, must be led by the African working class. It must result in the establishment of a united, socialist Africa responsive to the needs of African people worldwide.

African Internationalism teaches us that slavery, colonialism and neocolonialism, along with African disunification and dispersal, provided the material basis for the European bourgeois national consolidation, the sense of white sameness resting on the pedestal of the oppression of African and colonized peoples.

Hence, we understand that a key function of the revolutionary struggle for the permanent defeat of imperialism and to liberate Africa and her scattered children is the reunification of African people worldwide into a revolutionary, proletarian nation.

"It is slavery that gave the colonies their value; it is the colonies that created world trade, and it is world trade that is the pre-condition of large scale industry." These words by Marx recognize the role of the plunder of Africa in the establishment of capitalism and carry within them the suggestion of what it will take to destroy the capitalist world economy. The African who gave value to the "colonies" is now the oppressed and exploited inhabitant of the colonies that are sometimes incorrectly referred to as nations.

Our conditions of existence in the "colonies," and elsewhere in this world of imperialist-created borders are centered in and derive from the conditions of existence in Africa that are the consequence of the primitive accumulation of capital, the "original sin."

Our revolutionary struggle for liberation, unification and socialism in Africa, throughout the "colonies" and other areas of the world to which we have been forcibly dispersed in the construction of capitalism, will prove to be as significant in the defeat of the capitalist social system as the slave trade was in its advent.

The socialist liberation and unification of Africa and African people under the leadership of the African working class will be the central factor in the defeat of world capitalism and will provide the material basis for the advent for world socialism.

African Internationalism, which demands the total revolutionary liberation and unification of Africa and African people worldwide under the leadership of the African working class, is informed by this scientifically sound dialectic.

Hence, the African Internationalist struggle for the liberation and unification of Africa and African people is at the same time the key factor in the achievement of socialism as a world economy. It is the way forward for those Marxists and other socialists who are confronted with the false conundrum surrounding the question of "socialism in one country."

As capitalism was born as a world economy with its basis in the enslavement and dispersal of African people, leading to [as Marx wrote] "considerable masses of capital and labor power in the hands of producers," so, too, will socialism be born as a world economy in the process of reversing the verdict of imperialism.

Hence, socialism will not be born in one country, but in many countries that are tied to the defining economy of a liberated and united Africa and people under the revolutionary leadership of the African working class.

This is why a fundamental task of the African revolutionary is the consolidation of the proletarian African nation.

African petty bourgeoisie attacks Garvey, nation

This was not the extent of our discussion of the nation in the Political Report to our Fifth Congress. Then, as now, we were engaging in serious struggle with the ossified notions that have hampered and misdirected our struggle since the political defeat of the Universal Negro Improvement Association (UNIA) led by Marcus Garvey in the 1920s.

At that time the struggle for African national consolidation, though seriously debated, was essentially being advanced by the program of the UNIA with its membership of 11 million Africans around the world and its slogan of "Africa for the Africans, those at home and those abroad."

Since its founding in 1919, the Communist Party USA had joined with an assortment of African liberals and the U.S. government in hounding Garvey because of the UNIA's position on the African nation. In 1928 a resolution of the Sixth Communist International held in Moscow admitted that Africans constituted a separate nation inside the U.S., just as the now deported Marcus Garvey had explicitly stated all along. The Communist Party USA was forced to reluctantly comply with this position.

This came after the CPUSA, NAACP and others had eagerly promoted and united with the U.S. government's attack, imprisonment and deportation of Garvey to Jamaica, the island of his birth. The Comintern's position on the "Negro Question" suggested that Africans were a nation within a contrived national homeland of the "Black Belt South" in the U.S.

This manufactured nation of sorts, as described in the "Negro Question," was designed to take advantage of the obvious national consciousness among the African population of the U.S., influenced by the successful Garvey Movement that the CPUSA helped to destroy. The CPUSA attempted to infiltrate the UNIA with undercover communist organizers.

As I stated in "African Internationalism versus Pan-Africanism," presented at the Conference to Build the African Socialist International held in London in 2005, and printed in my book *One Africa! One Nation!*, the Communist Party "… did not address the fact that our homeland had been taken away from us and we from it, which is what Africans were responding to by joining the Garvey Movement."

The CPUSA "Black Belt South" position, moreover, completely obscures the fact that the land of what is now called North and South America—including the "Black Belt South"—was stolen by Europeans from the Indigenous people in the same genocidal process that brought about the birth of parasitic capitalism and the consolidation of the white nation. The Indigenous people continue to suffer the consequences of this assault even today. This land belongs to the Indigenous people.

The CPUSA's position nevertheless implicitly recognizes the commonality of national interests linking Africans worldwide. This passage is one example of that:

> *The Negro race everywhere is an oppressed race. Whether it is a minority (U.S.A., etc.) majority (South Africa) or inhabits a so-called independent state (Liberia, etc.), the Negroes are oppressed by imperialism. Thus, a common tie of interest is established for the revolutionary struggle of race*

and national liberation from imperialist domination
of the Negroes in various parts of the world.

The 1928 Communist International Resolution on the Negro Question became the template for succeeding positions on the question by various Marxist communists and an assortment of black nationalists, some of whom were not communists and sometimes even anti-communist in their outlook.

One of the most influential advocates of this position before his defection from the Communist International to the ranks of Pan-African anti-communism was George Padmore. Padmore was a well-known Trinidad-born activist who penned an authoritative book entitled *The Life and Struggles of Negro Toilers* that was published by a section of the Communist International in 1931.

Like the entire worldwide Marxist movement that made up the Communist International, Padmore was a rabid, visceral anti-Garveyite.

The introduction to Padmore's 1931 work, written during the Great Depression, could have easily been written today considering the current economic crisis. Whether intentional or not, Padmore's book exposes his own opportunism and that of the Communist International he represented. Padmore uses all the evidence that supports Garvey's efforts to organize the liberation of the African nation as the basis for joining and celebrating the attacks on Garvey. It was attacks such as these that helped to destroy Garvey's extraordinary anti-imperialist movement for the happiness and material well-being of African people.

Padmore's introduction inadvertently supports our Party's position concerning the commonality of African conditions and interests internationally, our common national identity, its class character and the African national territory that helps to define us as the nation, though dispersed.

Here's Padmore:

It has been estimated that there are about 250 million Negroes in the world. The vast majority of these peoples are workers and peasants. They are scattered throughout various geographical territories. The bulk of them, however, still live on the continent of Africa—the original home of the black race. There are, nevertheless, large populations of Negroes in the New World. For instance, there are about 15 millions in the United States, 10 millions in Brazil, 10 millions in the West Indies and 5 to 7 millions in various Latin-American countries, such as Colombia, Honduras, Venezuela, Nicaragua, etc., etc.

The oppression of Negroes assumes two distinct forms: on the one hand they are oppressed as a class, and on the other as a nation. This national (race) oppression has its basis in the social-economic relation of the Negro under capitalism. National (race) oppression assumes its most pronounced forms in the United States of America, especially in the Black Belt of the Southern States, where lynching, peonage, Jim-Crowism, political disfranchisement and social ostracism is widespread; and in the Union of South Africa, where the blacks, who form the majority of the entire population, have been robbed of their lands and are segregated on Reserves, enslaved in Compounds and subjected to the vilest forms of anti-labor and racial laws (Poll, Hut, Pass, taxes) and color bar system in industry.

The general conditions under which Negroes live, either as a national (racial) group or as a class, form one of the most degrading spectacles of bourgeois civilization.

> *Since the present crisis of world capitalism begin, the economic, political and social status of the Negro toilers are becoming ever worse and worse. The reason for this is obvious: the imperialists, whether American, English, French, Belgian, etc., etc., are frantically trying to find a way out of their difficulties. In order to do so, they are not only intensifying the exploitation of the white workers in the various imperialist countries by launching an offensive through means of rationalization, wage cuts, abolition of social insurance, unemployment, etc., but they are turning their attention more and more towards Africa and other black semi-colonies (Haiti, Liberia), which represent the last stronghold of world imperialism. In this way the bourgeoisie hope to unload the major burden of the crisis on the black colonial and semi-colonial masses.*

Padmore's introduction continues to assert:

> *It is also necessary for the workers in the capitalist countries to understand that it is only through the exploiting of the colonial workers, from whose sweat and blood super-profits are extorted, that the imperialists are able to bribe the reformist and social-fascist trade union bureaucrats and thereby enable them to betray the struggles of the workers.*

There are a number of erroneous assumptions found in Padmore's words. It is clear that he does not recognize that capitalism was born as parasitic white power that liberated the European bourgeoisie *and* working class from the fetters of the feudal social system. He does not understand that this occurred at the expense of Africans and the oppressed of the world that are overturning that historical relationship at the very moment of this, our Party's Sixth Congress. Capitalism represented progress only for European development, for the workers, the bourgeoisie and society in general.

Padmore does not explain why the imperialists would try "to find their way out of their difficulties" by "turning their attention more and more towards Africa and other black semi-colonies." Of course, for African Internationalists, 21st century Garveyites, the answer is simple: it is the raw, terror-laden exploitation of Africa upon which the entire imperialist edifice rests.

What Padmore warns the white workers about, the super-profits coming from the colonies, is normal capitalist functioning. There is nothing "super" about these profits. The thing that may make the profits appear to be super is simply the fact that white workers, as part of the white nation, share in the imperialist exploitation of the rest of us.

The concept of "super" profits muddles the fact that the vast majority of Africans and other colonized workers constitute the true base of capitalist exploitation and always have. The fact is that the level of profit extraction from this relationship is normal! White workers achieve a greater return for the value of their labor power because they exist as part of a parasitic nation that originates from parasitic capitalism stemming from slavery and colonialism.

"Super" profits infer an exceptional level of exploitation. However it is the white or European oppressor nation worker that experiences the exceptional relationship with capitalism. Ours is not an exceptional relationship. It is the norm. It is the European oppressor nation worker that experiences a "super" relationship with capitalism that is revealed in the different conditions of existence experienced by European workers and the rest of us.

Padmore's concern about the "reformers" and "social-fascist trade union bureaucrats" is also misdirected. While reformism certainly is a problem, when it comes to the issues within the European/white nation, the real question is opportunism, the tendency to sacrifice the long term interests of the struggle against imperialism rooted in the colonial question for the short term interests of white workers, which can only be served at the expense of the rest of us, something the white working class as a social force has never hesitated to do.

Perhaps the root of Padmore's opposition to Garvey and true African national liberation can be found in his characterization of "social ostracism" as one of the oppressive consequences defining the conditions of existence of Africans colonized within the U.S. The question is: social ostracism from whom? The issue of social ostracism only concerns those whose interest is in integrating, assimilating into the social domain of the white oppressor nation, not those who recognize their interests in liberation of the African nation.

This struggle for black or African national independence is usually called black separatism, a subjective response by whites who never speak of the Declaration of Independence proclaiming the establishment of the U.S. bourgeois state on stolen Indigenous land as a "Declaration of Separation."

However, it is in the section of his book entitled "Revolutionary Perspectives" that Padmore unleashes the full force of his venom on Garvey and the struggle for African national emancipation. According to Padmore:

> The struggle against Garveyism represents one of the major tasks of the Negro toilers in America and the African and West Indian colonies.
>
> Why must we struggle against Garveyism? As the "Programme of the Communist International" correctly states: "Garveyism is a dangerous ideology which bears not a single democratic trait, and which toys with the aristocratic attributes of a non-existent 'Negro kingdom'! It must be strongly resisted, for it is not a help but a hindrance to the

mass Negro struggle for liberation against American imperialism."

Garvey is more than a dishonest demagogue who, taking advantage of the revolutionary wave of protest of the Negro toilers against imperialist oppression and exploitation, was able to crystallize a mass movement in America in the years immediately after the war. His dishonesty and fraudulent business schemes, such as the Black Star Line, through which he extorted millions and millions of dollars out of the sweat of the Negro working class, soon led to his imprisonment. After his release Garvey was deported back to Jamaica, his native country. Isolated from the main body of the organization, Garvey has been unable to maintain his former autocratic control over the movement, as a result of which there has been a complete disintegration of the organization, which is now under the control of a number of warring factional leaders.

Padmore continues:

Despite the bankruptcy of the Garvey movement, the ideology of Garveyism, which is the most reactionary expression in Negro bourgeois nationalism, still continues to exert some influence among certain sections of the Negro masses. The black landlords and capitalists who support Garveyism are merely trying to mobilize the Negro workers and peasants to support them in establishing a Negro Republic in Africa, where they would be able to set themselves up as the rulers in order to continue the exploitation of the toilers of their race, free from white imperialist competition. In its class content Garveyism is alien to the interests of the Negro toilers. Like Zionism and Gandhism, it is merely out to utilize the racial and national consciousness for the purpose of promoting the class interests of the black bourgeoisie and landlords. In order to further their own aims, the leaders of Garveyism have attempted to utilize the same demagogic methods of appeal used by the leaders of Zionism. For example, the promise of "Back to Africa," behind which slogan Garvey attempts to conceal the truly imperialist aims of the Negro bourgeoisie.

We have been generous in the space given Padmore because he is one of the best representatives of this backwards view on the struggle for African national liberation that poses as progressive. It is clear that without intending to do so Padmore validates Garvey's position when he says "the oppression of Negroes assumes two distinct forms: on the one hand they are oppressed as a class, and on the other as a nation."

However, echoing many of the written attacks on Garvey by W.E.B. Du Bois, Padmore goes on to manufacture conclusions about Garvey's intentions that cannot be substantiated by science and rely solely on clearly prejudiced, subjective rantings.

It is instructive that Padmore's great fear is the "imperialist aims" of the Garvey Movement at a time when there were only two nominally independent countries on the Continent of Africa and the entire African world was locked in the stranglehold of white colonial slavery.

It borders on insanity that Padmore's fears would be directed at an alleged intent of Garvey to create a black imperialism in Africa that would, in fact, overturn a real, existing white imperialism! The movement to stop Garvey, of which Padmore was an illustrious participant, was in reality a movement to protect white imperialist domination of Africa from African people ourselves.

It is clear how Padmore's position against Garvey mirrors that of the white ruling class, blaming Garvey for the imperialist attacks that were responsible for Garvey's imprisonment and deportation as well as the destruction of the UNIA, events that Padmore gleefully describes.

His barely concealed joy at the downfall of Garvey and the UNIA reveals a commonality of interests among the imperialist white ruling class, Padmore and the Communist International on one side, and Garvey, along with the millions of Africans who supported him and the UNIA vision of national liberation on the other.

Three years after the publication of his book, Padmore left the Communist International, perhaps after discovering it was the headquarters of "reformers and social-fascists" from whom he wanted to protect the white workers. He would eventually end up a Pan-Africanist in the company of W. E. B. Du Bois, whom he had characterized in this same book as a petty bourgeois reformist. He was now a virulent anti-communist and author of the book, *Pan-Africanism or Communism,* for which he is probably best known and revered by petty bourgeois Pan-Africanists.

As we stated in "African Internationalism versus Pan-Africanism," quoted above:

> People ask, "Can there be revolutionary Pan-Africanists? I think that's an oxymoron, a contradiction in terms. Pan-Africanism does not have the ability to recognize the class question, therefore whoever wants to be a Pan-Africanist can be. [Kwame] Nkrumah was a communist, but I've been in London with people who call themselves Pan-Africanists who are anti-communist. A Pan-

Africanist is whatever somebody who calls himself
a Pan-Africanist wants to be."

Pan-Africanism liquidates the class contradiction that's killing us all over the world. To win the total liberation and unification of Africa and consolidate our nation we have to be absolutely clear. African Internationalism informs us that the African working class aligned with poor peasants must unequivocally lead this struggle for African liberation. Every other class force wavers in its loyalty to imperialist white power that affords them the promise of material or other benefits at the expense of the suffering African working class and the subjugated African nation.

The success of the Garvey Movement and its program is the best concrete evidence of the sense of sameness experienced by Africans worldwide. The UNIA was an organization of several million members and supporters throughout the world, including Australia.

Its influence continues to be experienced by Africans even today, a century after its founding. The Garvey Movement's 1920 Convention of the Negro Peoples of the World, held in Manhattan at Madison Square Garden attracted between 25,000 and 50,000 people from throughout the African world. This was an amazing accomplishment at a time when communications and transportation were considerably more difficult than they are today and our national oppression placed formidable constraints on our mobility, both within the U.S. and in the colonial territories in Africa and elsewhere.

The historic Garvey Movement convention was the only place in the world that afforded Africans a democratic opportunity to vote their political preferences. Marcus Garvey was elected the Provisional President of Africa by convention attendees and the Red, Black and Green flag was adopted as the national colors for African people.

It was also at this convention that the delegates enthusiastically adopted the Declaration of the Rights of the Negro Peoples of the World as their program giving political definition to the collective, national interests of the struggle of Africans worldwide. The 1920 Garvey Movement convention addressed the common issues of oppression and resistance. It cemented a united, world African consciousness and expression of power that sent the Communist Party scurrying to the U.S. government to collaborate in the attack that would imprison and deport Garvey and destroy the Garvey movement.

The crushing of the Garvey Movement took the combined endeavors of the U.S. and other imperialist governments of the time, along with a motley assortment of enemies of various hues and ideological leanings, who were all opposed to the notion of our national liberation as Africans. With the destruction of the Garvey Movement went the dreams of African people who aspired to consolidate our African nation—an aspiration left to our Party to accomplish.

The African nation and commonality of culture

The African nation is real. It is distinguished by a number of elements, both objective and subjective. Clearly there is a sense of sameness, something that European and Negro scholars often pretend does not exist, but which nevertheless exposes itself to public view every time Africans come to harm from or achieve victory over imperialist white power.

Few quibble that black people in Africa itself are some variation of African, although sub-identities of ethnicity or "tribe" and/or religion often challenge the significance of the fact that they are African.

The colonial, dividing borders imposed on Africa by Europeans are part of the parasitic process of achieving European national identity through destroying the African collective identity and facilitating the colonial theft of African resources. One function of the borders has been to prevent the consolidation of a single, continental-wide national economy that would be the primary, material foundation of national unification, including one African language.

The commonality of African culture and language would consolidate, develop and flourish under the influence of African self-serving economic forces unleashed from the distorting, limiting imposition of borders that divert all things of value to the service of external forces. Historically our resources and labor have benefited Europe and Europeans primarily, but today this increasingly involves China, India, Turkey and every imperialist-aspiring predator capable of entering the feeding frenzy on Africa's soil.

In the U.S. it is generally agreed that Africans constitute a distinct community, with a distinct history and culture. No scholarly studies are needed to make this point. There is disagreement, of course, on the question of whether these distinct features contribute to the definition of Africans as a distinct nation.

Some of the problems surrounding this question in North America revolve around two issues. One is the fact that Europeans themselves are new to this continent, having wrenched it from the custody of the Indigenous people through brutish, horrendous, genocidal aggression that contributed to the culture of violence that defines the European nation. To admit that Africans constitute a nation is to thrust to the surface an underlying question that the white nation cannot tolerate. Namely: "If they are Africans, then who are we?"

Secondly, there is the question of the size and viability of the African population inside the U.S. Of course, there are more African people in North America than white people in some European countries that pose as nations. Nevertheless, Africans are held to a different standard on this issue.

This takes us back to Garvey and the UNIA. This takes us back to the African People's Socialist Party and the African Socialist International. This takes us to the recognition that the African nation is *not* confined to the borders imposed on us by Europe, whether in Africa or the various places to which we have been forcibly dispersed.

As African Internationalists we recognize that the basis of our struggle is the European attack on Africa, the forced dispersal and colonization of untold millions of its inhabitants and the creation of artificial borders used to facilitate the alienation of Africans from each other, from our resources and from our national identity.

Our position here does not ignore the fact that false national consciousness has been imposed on Africans worldwide through the violence of the imperialist state and imperialist-imposed ignorance.

In West Africa there is a territory known as Cameroon, named for the Portuguese word for shrimp after the Portuguese colonizers discovered an abundance of shrimp in its waters. The fact that there are thousands of Africans there that refer to themselves as shrimp does not make them shrimp any more than an African in England is a "Black Brit" or an African in the U.S. a "Negro" or "African-American."

Africans throughout the world continue to exist under some form of colonial domination. In this era, that takes the form of indirect or neocolonial rule by the European imperialist state in disguise. The capitalist-imperialist state, unlike its feudal predecessor, was born as an "international" state through imperialist colonial slavery, the foundation of capitalism and the European nation.

The bourgeois state manifests itself in Europe as relatively benign in relation to white people. In Nigeria, Sudan and all of Africa, as well as in Ireland, India, the Middle East, Asia and in all the colonized territories of this planet, including inside the U.S., the North American-European imperialist state has been highly armed and unremittingly violent.

Hence, the British state that was vicious in its colonies, bragged about police not carrying guns in England. That is until their colonial subjects emigrated to England in enough numbers to create *domestic* colonies like the ones found in the U.S. since its bloody advent through genocide and colonial slavery.

The United Nations, the North Atlantic Treaty Organization (NATO), a host of international institutions along with the U.S. Africa Command (AFRICOM) and the various U.S. and European military function as arms of a combined European capitalist state with the purpose of violently barring us from seizing control of our African nation. This is also the case for the neocolonial African governments that for the most part rely on charity handouts from imperialist states or institutions for funding, training and leadership.

Nevertheless, we can say without hesitation that the African nation does exist. We are one nation in need of consolidation, a nation definable by objective and subjective characteristics, with features arising specifically in response to historical necessity—just like the European nation. While the objective, material foundation of the African nation is fundamental, this does not limit or undermine the subjective element, the sense of sameness experienced by Africans everywhere.

The most important defining, material or objective element of the African nation is its derivation from Africa, the national homeland of African people. This is the critical component of African identity from which most of the subjective factors derive. The African nation is also defined in part by physiognomy. We are black people of and from Africa, the equatorial continent.

This common connection to Africa carries with it deep and profound cultural connections going back thousands of years, as previously shown in the quote by Cheikh Anta Diop. In 1962 Joseph Ki-Zerbo made similar assertions about the African nation. Included in a 1975 anthology entitled *Readings in African Political Thought*, Ki-Zerbo discusses in, "African Personality and the New African Society":

> *Contrary to the colonial image, which presents pre-colonial Africa as a collection of tiny groups torn by internal strife and tribal warfare, sociologically frozen at the stage of a protozoan or an amoeba, African society was highly organized. Its principal features, in my opinion, were the following: first, the authority of the old people...[I]n Africa the hierarchy of power, of consideration, and of prestige, was in direct rapport with the hierarchy of age...The council of elders in traditional Africa was the supreme political master of the city or the tribe. It was often this autocracy of the old that evolved into a veritable cult of ancestor worship....*
>
> *Another important characteristic of the traditional society is solidarity, and this point is too obvious to require any lengthy examination. I would, however, like to say that this solidarity is not just a phenomenon of the superstructure, a trembling of the spirit, or a tenderness of heart towards others. This solidarity is imprinted on the very basic structure of African culture, and especially in its economic organization. You know that in the traditional African society the notion of property was defined in terms of the family, community or the village and not in terms of the individual. The concept of personal property in terms of the individual is generally alien to African social concepts. Fields are often common property and work is most often collective. Another social*

manifestation of this solidarity is hospitality, which, it is true, is obviously not an African monopoly but which nevertheless is particularly strong there; and here I am pleased to associate North Africa with the rest of the continent....

Another important feature is the equalitarian character of African society. Naturally, I do not intend in any way to idealize or present traditional Africa as the best of all possible or imaginary worlds. Africa has had its tyrants, as have other nations throughout history. But it must be stressed also that the traditional African society often included classes based solely on functional differentiation. There was, for instance the mason class, the blacksmith class, the warrior class. But the fact that in Africa property was common, the fact that there was no class that accumulated the capital property and reduced others to the state of mere tenancy—mere peasants or farmers whose toil was used to amass profit—well, that fact proves that the exploitation of man by man never achieved the status of a system in the traditional society of Africa. And, moreover, by reason of the unlimited solidarity of which I have just spoken, the true principle of such a society was "To each according to his needs," to the extent of the complete utilization of common revenues.

Who is an African?

We can see our commonality in Africa, but as we pointed out earlier, no nation is defined solely in relationship to itself. To say that the nation is one thing is to say that it is not another. Dark skin is a product of equatorial Africa, the land of "black" people. "Black" people among ourselves would be incapable of defining ourselves as such. It is through our relationship with "white" people and the dialectic of the oppressor nation and the oppressed nation that Africans became "black."

We can say, therefore, that the African nation is one born of its historical ties to its African national homeland, with a core sense of sameness that includes a common culture, history and physiognomy.

Still, to arrive at a full definition of the African nation we must say more than this. The African nation is informed by historical necessity, determined by our conditions of existence at this very moment, hundreds of years subsequent to our defining conflict with the European predator nation. Europe's parasitic attachment to Africa and Africans shapes and determines both its successful existence and our national incoherence.

A critical feature of our conditions of existence as a people is the imperialist near-total control of the economic life of Africa and African people wherever we are located in the world. Neither Africa, the land, nor Africans, the people—both fundamental components of the productive forces—have been accessible to Africa for the production and reproduction of real life for Africa and Africans.

Hence Africa has created staggering wealth for imperialism that has benefited the entire European nation—ruling class, middle class, workers and others at our expense. Everything they have was stolen from our labor, resources and knowledge! We have a historical mandate to take back what is ours and fulfill our destiny as a united, independent, self-governing nation in control of our own Continent and future.

This is an immensely profound reality that must be internalized by Africans and all peoples throughout the globe who have an interest in destroying forever this blood-sucking culture of violence stemming from U.S.-European imperialism.

Therefore, historical necessity—the absolute requirement of any people to produce and reproduce life as a condition of existence, survival and a meaningful future—*requires* the consolidation of the African nation. The consolidation of the African nation is a prerequisite for overturning the abject, genocidal conditions of existence of Africans everywhere.

There is no separate solution for the liberation of African people based on colonially-defined borders or identity any place on Earth. Clearly the African Liberation Movement has run into its limitations when fought within the context of these borders. Civil rights and "flag independence" only serve to obscure our oppressive exploitation, not overturn it.

Millions of Africans have been forcibly dispersed from Africa throughout the world. Europeans and others have come to Africa, some as colonizers, some as subjects of colonial powers who were allowed privilege in Africa as intermediary colonial agents functioning as buffers between Africans and our oppressors, a situation contributing to absolute African dependency and the atrophy of African productive forces. Other occupants of Africa are descendants of the Arab conquest in Africa preceding that of Europe.

How do these various forces fit into our definition of the African nation?

First of all, all black people forcibly transported to diverse parts of the world as part of the process giving rise to capitalism and the European nation are Africans. Period.

Secondly, all black people throughout the world are potentially part of the African nation, whether they were part of the forcible dispersal or whether their presence in other places predates the assault on Africa. This includes black people in Australia, India and other places who generally experience a sense of sameness associated with African blackness and the oppression we share because of our blackness. Under imperialist world domination, blackness is universally perceived as justification for our oppression.

For those Africans forcibly dispersed from Africa, we are directly connected to each other by the parasitic capitalist world economy under whose weight we continue to groan in poverty and oppression as the economic foundation of the European nation. All our cultural expressions, found everywhere we are dispersed—music, dance and other art forms and traditions—have their foundation in Africa.

The African nation and Arabs, whites, others in Africa

On the Continent of Africa, our national homeland, there are many Europeans who came as colonizers. They have chosen to remain in Africa after nominal independence was declared in some territories, including Zimbabwe, Namibia, Kenya and South Africa as prime examples. In South Africa white people called themselves Africans prior to independence.

Are these white people genuinely a part of the African nation by just declaring themselves so? The fact is that all Europeans, including those in Africa, are beneficiaries of the imperialist economy derived from African colonialism and slavery. This means they live at the expense of Africans. This places them concretely and objectively in the category of the European nation, even as they may now be forced to disguise their European national identity for the purpose of maintaining a parasitic attachment to Africa. This attachment of European colonizers to Africa objectively undermines the consolidation of the African nation whose blackness is an identifying badge of exploitation and oppression.

This does *not* mean that whites from the colonizing nation cannot become a part of the African nation. What it does mean is that whites would have to commit "national suicide," abandoning the interests of the European parasitic oppressor nation and uniting with the historical trajectory of the African nation to achieve "black power."

Whites in Africa must unite with the capture of total economic and political power by African workers in a borderless Continent. Power in the hands of African workers is the only way to unleash the productive forces of Africa, allowing Africa and Africans to engage fully in the process of producing life for Africa and Africans the world over. Objectively this would mean white people in Africa would have to voluntarily relinquish to the African nation the vast resources they have accumulated through their past identification with the parasitic European nation.

In the final analysis the struggle against world capitalism, resting as it does on the exploitation of the majority of the peoples of the world, will require the destruction of the "white" or European nation that requires for its existence a parasitic relationship to the majority of humanity.

The national liberation of Africa and African people will be a leading force in that destruction. The role of genuine white or European communists will be to actively engage in the commission of national suicide by becoming one with the national liberation of Africans and others. This is a far cry from the current position of most self-declared white communists who talk instead about the need of the oppressed of the world to unite with their narcissistically-defined European version of history.

A similar situation is that of the Arabs who came into Africa as conquerors, initiating their enslavement of African people that lasted 1,500 years, and paved the way for the European trans-Atlantic slave trade. Similar to Europeans, Arabs must embrace the historically necessary trajectory of Africa toward black power as their own.

We saw the potential for this kind of unity in the 1960s when Gamal Abdel Nasser of Egypt stood as one of the strongest allies of Kwame Nkrumah in his attempt to create a united Africa. Ahmed Ben Bella, revolutionary fighter and first president of liberated Algeria, was another who cast his lot with the African nation. Both men shared with Africa a sense of sameness that showed promise for consolidating all of North Africa into the African nation.

In addition to the practical examples of Nasser and Ben Bella there is the example of black Haiti, which upon achieving independence from France in 1804, created a constitution declaring citizenship and land ownership for blacks only, but which defined whites, including the Poles who fought with Africans in the struggle for independence, as "black" for the purposes of citizenship. This was a historic case of whites committing national suicide and consciously abandoning the pedestal upon which the European nation rests as a parasite on Africa and the world. This is a case of Europeans accepting as their own the struggle for the achievement of revolutionary black power.

We also mentioned the presence in Africa of people from India and other former colonies who were brought to the Continent by the British for the express purpose of acting as a colonial buffer between the imperialists and the often-resisting African masses.

There are literally millions of Indians in Africa today, most of whom live at a much higher standard of living than both the majority of Africans and the majority of people in India. This shows how the pedestal upon which Europeans sit on our backs can be and has been opened up to petty bourgeois sectors of formerly colonized countries who now enjoy the benefits of white power at our expense.

Thus, Arabs, Europeans and residents of Africa from other European colonies *can* become African if they commit national suicide and abandon their parasitic relationship to African people. They must financially, politically and in every other way unite with the leadership of and become one with the African working class and the aims of a united and liberated Africa.

We are Africans because we say we are!

The African nation, then, is a community of people whose core identity is based on historical ties to the equatorial continent of black Africa, contributing to a common culture, history and physiognomy.

The African nation is also comprised of all those African people who have been forcibly dispersed to various places in the world through colonial slavery. Dispersed Africans were part of the process of the development of capitalism and the European nation, a process that requires our subjugation and national incoherence.

Additionally, the African nation is comprised of many who experience a sense of sameness, a subjective connection to Africa, mainly because of skin color that helps to define their imperialist-inspired impoverished and oppressed state of existence. The Dalit in India, the Indigenous of Australia and other areas where the African presence goes back to earliest times, such as in the Asia-Pacific region, are included in this category.

Finally, the African nation can include people of other nationalities living in Africa who commit national suicide, becoming part of the African working class and abandoning all allegiance to a predatory, colonial relationship to African people.

The truth, stated simply, is: we are Africans, whatever else we may be called, because we say we are Africans and we feel like we are Africans.

Africa is the national homeland of all black people worldwide. It is the land to which the identity of the African nation is firmly and irreversibly affixed. Our historical connection to Africa represents the critical element of the material basis for African nationality. For although we have been forcibly dispersed by colonial slavery and related factors subsequent to the initial European attack on Africa, our current conditions of existence, both in Africa and abroad, are essentially defined by the consequences of our forced dispersal.

Here we remind ourselves that it was Europe that divided Africa with the illegitimate borders that now still function to facilitate the theft of Africa's still vast resources by various imperial forces. The colonial division of Africa continues to separate Africans from each other and from our resources that are being expropriated without cessation.

The 54 delineated territories currently characterized as African nations were created in a conference held in Berlin, Germany in 1884-1885, attended by contending European states that parceled Africa out among themselves, resulting in the map that is known as Africa today.

The result of this European invention has been the evolvement of a false national consciousness that fits the interests of the imperialists who created it at the expense of Africans ourselves. There were *no* pre-colonial borders separating Africans from each other. Now borders surround 54 colonially-created entities, many of which cut right down the middle of ancient family or kinship territories, dividing and pitting against each other Africans that lived together for time immemorial. Clearly, this physical and psychological separation has facilitated false national consciousness, not to mention a myriad of other traumas.

The practical significance of this clarification concerning the African nation and its relationship to the European imperialist nation was discussed in our book, *One People! One Party! One Destiny!*:

> *The anti-imperialist struggles of the world's peoples for repossession of our sovereignty and*

resources, both human and material, are the basis of the current, deep crisis of imperialism. They are struggles to remove the pedestal upon which the entire rotten edifice of imperialism rests. They are struggles that enlist the vast majority of humanity, the laboring masses of every nation, in the creation of a new world without exploitation and oppression, without slaves and slave masters and, ultimately, without borders.

We recognize that the struggle for the liberation and unification of Africa and African people, the struggle for the consolidation of the African nation is ultimately a struggle that undermines the solidarity of the European nation-state. We understand that under imperialism those who were enslaved, colonized and oppressed as a people will have to win liberation as a people.

We are also clear that the successful nation-building struggles of Africans and others under the leadership of the working class is at the same time the beginning of the process of the withering away of nations.

The European nation was born as a bourgeois nation at the expense of whole peoples and their territories. As we have seen in this discussion, it is a nation that requires the oppression and exploitation of whole peoples for its successful existence.

Hence, African people have to resist the imperialist bourgeoisie as a people. Our assumption of consolidated nationhood will function to destroy the bourgeois nation. Thus the rise of revolutionary worker nation-states destroys the material basis for the existence of nations and borders that function to distinguish and separate one people from another.

This is easier to understand when we finally realize the significance of the fact that capitalism at birth came wrapped in the skin of the racialized European nation-state. It is this reality that made impotent the Marxian assumption of communism resulting from the withering away of the European bourgeois industrialized state.

However, the fact that the European bourgeois nation-state achieves life and definition from its relationship to Africa and the oppressed peoples of the world means that our victory over imperialism, with the African working class at the helm will result in the withering away of nations. This will leave bare and make possible the withering away of the bourgeois state, which will have become historically redundant.

Consolidating the African nation and building the African People's Socialist Party as the tool to achieve that goal must be at the top of the agenda of every African on Earth. Every struggle must lead to this end; every border must be broken down; the crisis of imperialism must be deepened daily. It is on the shoulders of Africans alive today to complete the struggle that our people have waged for more than 500 years: the liberation of Africa and reunification of African people everywhere—the consolidation of the African nation.

Independence, unification and socialism in our lifetime!

V. The history of the Party

The development of our Party has been dialectical, containing within it the history and struggle of African people from the past, which informs our understandings of the present and our projections for the future. Our Party emerged in 1972 from the actual resistance of Africans fighting colonial domination in the U.S. and in Africa. Our ideological trajectory comes directly from our attempts to solve the real, pressing, practical problems confronting our movement against imperialist white power.

Our history is based in the most radical, activist sector of what is popularly known as the Civil Rights Movement. Unlike the Civil Rights Movement and organizations whose focus was on changing or reforming America, ours was a selfish motivation to win the liberation of African people, led by the African working class, regardless of its consequences for America or any other power.

Our Party was born of the brutal repression that destroyed our movement for happiness and the return of our stolen resources in the 1960s. Our mission was defined in part by that repression. We were the living embodiment of the words of Fred Hampton, Black Panther Party leader murdered by U.S. agents on December 4, 1969: "You can kill a revolutionary but you can't kill the revolution."

The 1960s saw the imperialist murders of Patrice Lumumba and the wounded and captured Che Guevara, along with the overthrow of Kwame Nkrumah. Malcolm X, Dr. Martin Luther King, Jr., Fred Hampton, Bobby Hutton and Carl Hampton are among the victims of the imperialist counterinsurgency that attempted to reverse the course of history. As revolutionaries were jailed and assassinated throughout the U.S. and the world, the birth of our Party constituted an organizational way forward.

It was necessary to move beyond the era of protest and organize to win and wield political power. This required the existence of a political party, the highest expression of the will to acquire power. The founding of our Party was an explicit statement of our recognition that we were not fighting for just any kind of power, but revolutionary power in the hands of a revolutionary class—the African working class.

Prior to the emergence of the African People's Socialist Party, the Black Panther Party was the only revolutionary political party of consequence, bearing the brunt of much of the counterinsurgent repression that left its remnants in a state of retreat. Most other remaining African political groupings preferred to shun designation as a party and avoided the internal dynamics necessary to shape and define the class character of a revolutionary organization. This resulted in ambiguity that most often allowed militant, nationalist petty bourgeois organizations to hide their class content behind radical sounding names.

However, we were clear that we had to have a revolutionary party rooted in the African working class and committed to African liberation, unification and socialism. We were also convinced that the tendency of some groups to move toward coalition building as the central component of their work was wrong. We needed a revolutionary party to lead the revolutionary African working class to power.

Political parties exist in class societies and always serve the interests of particular classes. An examination of their programs usually reveals what class is being served by a particular organization. Our objective was to create a party explicit in its class content and its mission to liberate Africa and African people under the leadership of the African working class.

Our commitment to the elevation of the working class to power does not come from a misguided romantic attachment to our own version of the white man's "Noble Savage." Rather it is due to an understanding that all value in society, all the wealth that constitutes a summation of social production, stems from the labor of the workers, who under capitalism never receive the value of their labor.

This is a fundamental contradiction within the system of capitalism: the *private* ownership and control of the means of production versus the *socialized* production by workers who only own their capacity to do work.

The capitalist class owns all the wealth produced by the labor of the workers. Because of private ownership, the capitalist class monopolizes authority in society, while the workers are just so much jetsam, easily replaced from the ranks of millions of others made desperate by the fact that the product of their labor is perpetually expropriated by a non-producing parasitic ruling class.

The African liberation sought by African Internationalism is a liberation that will empower the working class and resolve the contradiction in society revolving around private ownership and socialized production. African Internationalism means black power to the African working class; it means elevation of the African working class to the position of ruling class.

The Black Liberation Movement of the 1960s was crushed before the various contending political and ideological lines within the movement could develop fully and play themselves out on the political battlefield of revolutionary ideas.

Our Party represents a revolutionary continuum, linking the immediate past of defeat with the present and future. We were never a part of the defeat. We were born as a revolutionary organization that simply moved from one level of struggle to another—higher—level of struggle.

The imperialist U.S. colonialist state never succeeded in driving us completely underground and out of active political life. Although one Party co-founder was assassinated and I was frequently imprisoned, we were always engaged in some form of resistance. The ideological questions littering the bloodied battlefield of counterrevolutionary repression did not go unattended. We rescued, resuscitated and resolved them through the ongoing work of our Party.

Consequently, the development of our theory and political line was continuous and benefited from our uninterrupted practice in solving the real problems of the Revolution.

The origins of the Civil Rights Movement

As the immediate history of the African People's Socialist Party is tied to the period of raging struggle of the 1960s, our Party found it necessary to analyze the social and political forces that gave birth to this period.

History shows us that the Second Imperialist World War resulted in the near-decimation of European and Japanese productive capacity and the elimination of England as the mainstay of colonialism and the imperialist world monetary system. This left the U.S. as the most significant economic and political power, the leader of international capitalism.

With massive resources from world colonialism now flowing into the U.S. after the war, the demand was created for new industrial workers in the system. The liberal bourgeoisie needed African workers from the rural South transported to Northern factories to transform the raw materials coming into the economy from previously European-dominated colonies that were now opened to U.S. corporations for exploitation.

This set the stage for the alliance between the U.S. liberal white ruling class, represented by forces such as John F. Kennedy and Lyndon Baines Johnson, and the African petty bourgeoisie, represented by forces including Dr. Martin Luther King, Jr. and Roy Wilkins.

In order to realize its ambitions to integrate into the capitalist system the liberal Southern-based African middle class or petty bourgeoisie sought access to the electoral process and the removal of all colonially imposed legal restrictions on their social, political and economic mobility.

This revolution-from-above that came to be known as the Civil Rights Movement mobilized millions of African working people whose own interests lay in overturning the naked, daily terror and humiliation inflicted on our people by the colonial state, white mobs and individuals acting as extensions of the colonial state. The people also wanted freedom from the backbreaking, near-slave labor to which we were relegated without any hope of ever experiencing the benefits of our toil or an opportunity for our children to know a better future.

Herein lay the convergence of interests that united the liberal white ruling class, the African petty bourgeoisie and the masses of African working people. This is the context for the political turmoil that was the Civil Rights Movement and the emergence of its key players such as the Southern Christian Leadership Conference, Dr. King and the Student Nonviolent Coordinating Committee (SNCC).

It was in this context of political upheaval, church bombings, popular white-mob anti-African violence, political mass arrests and fierce resistance that the Junta of Militant Organizations (JOMO) and then the African People's Socialist Party were born. Herein lies the stuff that shaped and defined our worldview and political character. Herein lies the basis of our tenacity, of all the lessons learned in a process of continuous development. This is the beginning of the 41-year long process that prepared our Party for the enormous tasks of today.

In this period, revolution was the main trend in the world as countless anti-colonial liberation struggles rose up around the globe. Political and social turbulence was the natural consequence of the struggles of Africans and others everywhere that were fighting for a just social order, a world where the labor of the oppressed would go toward filling the stomachs and aspirations of our own peoples instead of the bank accounts and supermarkets of a parasitic imperialist oppressor nation and ruling class.

The historical links of our Party to the actual struggle of the African working class is also the primary reason that our Party was forced to fight for science in understanding and changing the world.

For this reason our Party has solved, through the unity of theory and practice, the most pressing questions of our time: the relationship of class to race, the class basis of neocolonialism, the relationship of white people to the African Revolution, the African nation and the state.

JOMO and the birth of the African People's Socialist Party

The Uhuru Movement preceded the organization of the Party. In 1966, when I was an organizer for the Student Nonviolent Coordinating Committee based in St. Petersburg, Florida, we launched the demonstration that resulted in the defiant removal of a hideous, eight-by-four-foot, racially demeaning mural that had hung on the wall of the City Hall for more than 30 years.

In 1968, from a prison cell where I was serving time on felony charges stemming from taking down the mural, and during the thick of the Black Revolution of the '60s, I formed the Junta of Militant Organizations.

JOMO was the Florida-based leader of the African workers' movement that bore some resemblance to the Black Panther Party that had arisen on the West Coast of the United States in that period.

The Black Panther Party and JOMO emerged on the scene at an important historical intersection, when the interests of the African working class rose up inside the movement that had up until then been dominated by the interests of the African petty bourgeoisie. SNCC, the militant wing of the struggle for democratic rights led by mostly young, student-based Africans, was the crucible for this class struggle, transforming the movement from one primarily for reform to an anti-colonial movement for black power.

Many of the young students and workers in SNCC came under the ideological influence of Malcolm X, who had been assassinated by the U.S. government in 1965. As the public face of the Nation of Islam before his break with that organization, Malcolm X made incessant forays into revolutionary politics, challenging the philosophical idealism that characterized the Nation of Islam.

In 1965, SNCC organized the Lowndes County Freedom Organization (LCFO) in Alabama. LCFO represented an ideological and political escalation of the struggle for electoral political power that broke with the near total loyalty of Africans to the bourgeois Democratic party and the principles of philosophical nonviolence. The Lowndes County Freedom Organization's symbol was the black panther that soon became iconic when it was taken up by the California-based Black Panther Party (BPP) at its formation in 1966.

Almost simultaneously the SNCC chapter in St. Petersburg, made up of African workers free of the petty bourgeois idealism of philosophical nonviolence, adopted the black panther as our symbol that adorned the outer wall of our office building on 22nd Street South.

The St. Petersburg workers' SNCC organization also adopted and popularized the slogan-demand, "Uhuru," meaning "freedom" in Swahili. The slogan "Uhuru" had been initiated by the Kenyan Land and Freedom Army or Mau Mau that fought the British for independence in Kenya in the 1950s. Malcolm X introduced the slogan in the United States.

JOMO was organized in 1968 after I began to recognize the limitations of the Civil Rights Movement in the wake of the repression that targeted SNCC. The formation of JOMO was an attempt to respond to those limitations through what I conceived as a united formation of SNCC-like militant groups, a "junta" that I naively envisioned would provide leadership for the entire movement throughout the U.S.

A later attempt led by SNCC leader James Forman to merge SNCC and the Black Panther Party was a similar effort to resolve some of the same contradictions.

Shortly after our formation in 1968, JOMO launched *The Burning Spear* newspaper in tabloid form as our political journal, still published today by the African People's Socialist Party.

The pages of *The Spear* over the years remind us that our history of struggle for our liberation was forged in contention with the various and sundry organized representatives of the imperialist white ruling class as well as with opportunist sectors within what has generally been considered the African Liberation Movement.

Four years after its creation, it became clear that JOMO had also reached its limitations. With the decision to form the African People's Socialist Party, we understood that the only way to end our oppression was through the struggle for political power in the hands of the organized African working class. We saw the Party as the highest expression of the will to struggle, to win and to wield political power.

The creation of the African People's Socialist Party was our practical answer to the question: struggle towards what end?

JOMO coordinated an intense effort to build the Party prior to the formal merger of the three organizations that became the Party of today. For months, meetings were held in different home-base cities of a number of militant organizations throughout the state of Florida whom JOMO targeted for consolidation into a single party.

During this process the work of an apparent agent provocateur resulted in scurrilous, inflammatory and dangerous ruling class newspaper allegations in an article claiming the murky existence of "kill whitey."

Regardless of the intent, the suspicious article was the kind of provocation common to U.S. government tactics used to justify the destruction of our movement and the Black Revolution in that period. The party-building efforts were stalled when the various organizations proved too liberal to criticize and eject the article's author from our ranks.

Finally, in May 1972, despite all obstacles, when JOMO joined together with the Black Rights Fighters and the Gainesville Black Study Group to become the African People's Socialist Party, the "Uhuru Movement" was already at least six years old. It had already established a legacy based on our bold campaigns and organizing throughout the region that would continue to develop and define the Party.

The Gainesville Black Study Group was an organization of mostly students who were organized by Party co-founder Katura Carey, a school teacher in the Gainesville, Florida area. The Black Study Group brought us into our first meaningful political contact with Africans from the Continent, primarily political refugees representing the independence struggle in white settler-colonial Rhodesia.

The other Party co-founder, in addition to myself, was Lawrence Mann who was later killed in a mysterious, COINTELPRO-type car accident shortly after our founding. Based in Fort Myers, Florida, Mann was an organizer in the migrant workers community and a leader of the Black Rights Fighters. The work with the Black Rights Fighters brought us into contact with, and consciousness of, the plight of African workers tied to Florida's migrant stream, where workers were often held in near-slave conditions and their labor ruthlessly exploited, sometimes at gunpoint.

The Party solved key political questions

The political and theoretical issues that were roiling our movement at the time of our founding included the questions of the relationship of class to race and the place and role of white people in history and in our struggle. We were also consumed by the need to achieve our true national identity that would challenge the false identity imposed on us by our colonial oppressors. Other questions being debated in this period included: what were legitimate tactics and strategies for liberation and was violence or armed struggle a viable option?

While today there is an academic industry that pretends to speak to these issues, it does so without the benefit of revolutionary social practice. Generally speaking, it is an industry that has separated theory from practice, offering up pristine ideological products emanating from efforts to explain the world without being engaged in, or concerned with, the practice of changing the world.

One of our first important political pamphlets that attempted to contribute ideological coherence to our struggle was "Colonialism: The Major Problem Confronting Africans in the U.S.," published in 1975, giving clarity to the African working class as one of the many attempts by our Party to challenge superstition and idealism in the midst of a struggle for the rights and liberties of our whole people.

From the beginning we recognized that "race" is a colonial invention originating from the enslavement and colonization of Africans and Africa that gave birth to capitalism and, simultaneously, to the European nation. Rather than defining the system of our oppression, "racism" is a concept that denies Africans our national identity and dignity and relegates to us the Sisyphean task of winning acceptance from, and often of becoming one with, our oppressors.

In *Izwe Lethu i Afrika*, the Political Report to our Third Congress, I quote a passage from a presentation I made in 1978 in San Francisco that elaborated on our views on racism and explained the ideological departure that helped to distinguish our Party in the struggle for revolutionary science. This presentation acknowledged unity on the part of a variety of African leaders and intellectuals on the question of defining our struggle as one against colonialism. I cited Malcolm X and Stokely Carmichael (later known as Kwame Ture), but clearly showed how our Party developed the discussion beyond previous understandings:

> [W]hat our Party did discover that made for a qualitative leap in understanding how to move toward liberation is that in the U.S., colonialism represents the relationship of class to race. Prior to this discovery our Party was one with most of the pro-independence movement in describing ours as a struggle against racism at the same time we were also calling it a struggle against colonialism.
>
> That is to say, our movement, still under the ideological influence of the primitive-petty bourgeois Civil Rightists whose colonial mentality often equated freedom with their proximity to white people, incorrectly used the terms racism and colonialism to define the same set of circumstances and oppressive structures responsible for our condition.
>
> However, at the moment we were able to understand that what we had been describing as institutional racism was the same thing we meant

by the term "colonialism," and that these same sets of circumstances and oppressive structures imposed on our people were also defined as colonialism historically throughout the world, our ideological and political development increased a thousandfold. This understanding of colonialism helped to place the responsibility for our oppression squarely on the shoulders of the North American ruling class.

Our Party was able to discover that our main or primary struggle is against colonialism, which is an imperialist form, therefore necessarily having class connotations, and which utilizes the ideology of racism to justify and obscure the fundamental relationship that African people within the U.S. have with the capitalist-colonialist ruling-class state.

This was a major theoretical advance made by our Party, clearly helping to move our struggle forward in a manner that undermined imperialism and initiated practice that would contribute to the crisis of imperialism being experienced today. I continued:

We discovered that colonialism is the condition we suffer from as a people and that racism is the ideology that justifies or obscures that relationship. Colonialism is real and concrete. It is a human-made condition that can be struggled against.

On the other hand, we discovered that racism is the ideas in the heads of North Americans: racism is the attitudes displayed by North Americans which makes you [whites] dupes, allies and collaborators with your ruling class in its attacks on us which reinforce and maintain our colonial relationship to the U.S. North American state....

Our understanding of colonialism as the relationship of class to race within the U.S. has also revealed for us the inherent reformist character of a struggle by black people against racism. For ultimately the struggle against racism, when it is given material form, boils down to a struggle for "equality" with the exploited North American working class, that is to say equality within capitalism.

We cannot overstate the significance of this contribution to the body of African liberation theory. While all of this is now obvious to members of our Party and followers of our movement, many people are still trapped in the ideological quagmire that would have us seek an end to racism rather than struggle to win our national liberation as African people.

Our Party's early years

We were born a Party of theory and practice, recognizing that practice is primary and that all theory must meet the test of practice for its development and validation. We did not sit around contemplating the universe and creating various theories to explain the world. We were engaged in the struggle to change the world and in this way our theoretical work was initiated, informed and tested.

Our Party has always recognized the centrality of practice. We have engaged in campaigns that helped to educate the entire African Liberation Movement on how to advance our struggle and that helped to enhance the capacity of our people to lead. It was the struggles in defense of our Party and its leaders that is partially responsible for our surviving the terrorist counterinsurgent repression that defeated our movement.

The efforts to keep me out of prison, the push to free Connie Tucker and Dessie Woods and to defend Party co-founder Katura Carey, were popular campaigns that involved thousands of people throughout the world. Our reputation for struggle is what propelled the board of the Florida state NAACP to call on our Party to provide leadership in the months-long campaign in Pensacola, a northern Florida backwater, following the 1974 police murder of young Wendell Blackwell.

Our years based in Gainesville in the early seventies were important, formative years for our Party. Under the leadership of Katura Carey our work during this time involved building the first support committee in the U.S. for the Zimbabwe African National Union (ZANU), the ruling party now in power in Zimbabwe. We toured ZANU members throughout the country and played a major role in assisting them by raising funds for the sustenance of the organization and their organizers. We actually put staff in ZANU's United Nations office in New York.

Our Party came under political assault in many ways in Gainesville. An elementary school teacher in the county, Katura Carey was the target of FBI harassment and other counterinsurgent activity resulting in the loss of her job. In addition to the other work we did in defense of Katura Carey, we ran her for school board with a progressive education program.

While we had no expectations to win the election in this politically backward county that was under the economic and political thumb of the University of Florida, we did use the campaign to hold off some of the attacks on Katura, expose a history of sexual extortion of African women teachers and raise up the possibility of better education for the masses of our people.

Shortly after the initiation of our Zimbabwe work, our Party began working with the Pan Africanist Congress of Azania (PAC) that at the time was engaged in political and armed struggle against the Apartheid state in South Africa. For many years PAC members were a ubiquitous presence at Party events throughout the U.S. We regularly organized PAC support actions and spoke on its behalf at the United Nations on more than one occasion.

Our Party printed most of PAC's propaganda in the U.S. and gave the organization material support in the face of the wealthier African National Congress (ANC) that had the backing of the international European Left due to its "Authentic Six" designation by the Soviet Union. Our Party participated in the various debates within the PAC, where we stated our opposition to the negotiated settlement that led to the dismantling of Apartheid as the form of the capitalist state in South Africa.

In our efforts to unite the worldwide African Liberation Movement we met with several PAC leaders when they were in the U.S. to participate in U.N.-related affairs. The Party recruited into the Party a PAC member who appeared to understand and unite with the arguments we were making with the PAC about the need to join the African Socialist International. We were struggling for PAC to become a class-conscious political party under the leadership and serving the interests of the African working class and poor peasantry.

These were struggles we did not win. After Zimbabwe's independence in 1980 and the capitulation of the Apartheid state in South Africa in 1994, most of the militants based in the U.S. from both territories returned to their respective birth lands, ending our relationship for many years to come.

The Pan-Africanism of both organizations lent itself to convenient ideological adaptations to win international African support for their efforts to evict the white minority regimes from power. They both focused primarily on exercising or winning power within the parliamentary system put in place by the colonial powers they formally replaced.

By the late 1980s, while still holding on to "Pan-Africanism," Robert Mugabe and the Zimbabwe African National Union officially abandoned their designation as "Marxist," leaving behind all pretense of being a socialist organization presiding over a socialist state that would empower African workers and poor peasants.

Years later in 2002, African People's Socialist Party members traveled to what is now called Mthatha in the Eastern Cape of Occupied Azania for the Eighth Congress of the PAC. I delivered the keynote presentation and a general program for struggle in South Africa to this congress. The response to the Party's line of African Internationalism was overwhelmingly enthusiastic. The entire hall packed with hundreds of people leapt to their feet in cheers and revolutionary song.

Clearly the struggles for liberation in Southern Africa have not achieved liberation for African people and will only be able to do so under the program of the African Socialist International to unite Africa and African people everywhere under the leadership of the African working class.

Free Dessie Woods campaign resurrected our movement

Throughout our history, all our practice has been wedded to our theory of African Internationalism. There cannot be practice for the sake of practice. We have never been a Party that simply bows to spontaneity, blindly dragged by events from one action or situation to another. This is the stuff from which opportunism—the tendency of sacrificing the long term interests for short term gains—is born and nurtured.

Some of the key campaigns of our formative years had worldwide impact both politically and ideologically. This was a time when the Party was one of the few organizations capable of leading successful struggles in the wake of the counterinsurgent defeat of our movement of the '60s.

The Party-led effort to free Dessie X. Woods became the signature campaign for the U.S. Front of the African Liberation Movement of the 1970s. Not only did the campaign help to resurrect and reunify a nearly dormant movement within the U.S., it also mobilized Africans and democratic forces throughout Europe in a massive display of solidarity with the struggle against U.S. domestic colonialism.

The story of the Dessie Woods campaign is told with some elements of accuracy in a 2010 book edited by Dan Berger entitled, *The Hidden 1970s: Histories of Radicalism.* The title of the book is itself a statement of the times, when revolutionary activism was the exception following the U.S. government's assault on our movement that was the driving force of the 1960s.

Dessie Woods was an African woman associated with the Nation of Islam who killed a white man, Ronnie Horne, with his own gun after Horne attempted to rape her and a friend, Cheryl Todd, at gunpoint. In a struggle for their lives, Woods successfully wrestled the gun away from Horne and shot him.

In the face of a weakened African Liberation Movement, the case was initially jumped on by an assortment of pseudo-communists. These forces were inebriated with their sense of self-importance. In their attempts to build themselves, they were fast demoralizing Africans attracted to Woods's defense with their esoteric Marxist phrase-mongering debates in the campaign meetings.

Our Party was successful in turning the struggle around in the committee meetings, successfully establishing African leadership for this campaign. We defined the fight against colonial terror represented by Woods's case to the extent that one of the self-defined African Marxists exclaimed in exasperation that someone white had to be on the program of a major campaign event, "even if it's Rockefeller!"

The worldwide, African-led campaign to free Dessie Woods became the organizational and political model for how such work should be done. A passage in the Berger book partially described the impact of the Dessie Woods campaign as led by the Party-created and led National Committee to Defend Dessie Woods (NCDDW):

> *Damesha Blackearth, Chairwoman of the NCDDW, traveled through Europe, speaking about Woods's case and the systematic human rights violations of black people in the United States. Blackearth's tour garnered increased international attention: every July 4 until her release, protests demanding Woods's freedom were held throughout the United States and Europe, with thousands of people marching, holding aloft drawings of Dessie.*

The African People's Socialist Party defined the struggle to free Dessie as one directed against colonial violence. This went against the existing political grain. At the time the bourgeois feminist movement, another key white opportunist force that rose up after the defeat of our revolutionary movement of the '60s, fought to define Woods's campaign as one supporting the right of women to self-defense. The bourgeois feminists played a big role in the struggle to free Joan Little just a few months earlier, another African woman who had killed a white rapist—Little's jailer in North Carolina.

However, we were determined that the case of Dessie Woods would be properly defined as part and parcel of the historical struggle of African people against colonialism. We knew that the fight to free Dessie Woods must advance the total movement of our people for self-determination, something most of the white movement fought against.

Our defiant and definitive campaign slogan of "Free Dessie Woods! Smash Colonial Violence!" characterized the most important, clearly anti-colonial movement of the period. It was one of the Party's campaigns that would play a major role in helping to rehabilitate the African Liberation Movement within the U.S. The anti-colonial definition of the Dessie Woods work was especially important during this period when the Party was determined to rebuild the anti-colonial movement after its devastating military defeat by the U.S. government that received ideological support from North American leftist opportunists.

Created and led by our Party, the National Committee to Defend Dessie Woods invited and won the participation of thousands of people around the world, many of them as members of the committee.

The Dessie Woods campaign impacted on the white bourgeois feminist movement, helping honest forces begin a process of class suicide by abandoning the self-serving, white rights interests of bourgeois feminism that sought success at the expense of African people. Many former feminists joined the struggle to free Dessie and defeat the colonial domination of African people. Several of those forces are working with the movement under our Party's leadership today.

It was precisely because of our correct line around the defense of Dessie Woods that remnants of the Black Liberation Movement could become reinvigorated by uniting with the campaign. Through the campaign to free Dessie Woods, the Party organized national mobilizations that contributed to the revitalization of the entire struggle against colonialism.

Through the Dessie Woods campaign, we led the first significant African-led national mobilizations against U.S. domestic colonialism subsequent to the defeat of our movement. These mobilizations gained national and international media attention, taking place not only in San Francisco, but in

Atlanta, Hawkinsville (the site of Dessie's trial) and Plains, Georgia, the hometown of then-U.S. president James Earl Carter.

Virtually all elements of the U.S.-based African anti-colonial movement participated, if initially somewhat reluctantly. For the first time in years the terms had been set for principled participation by various North American Left organizations to demonstrate solidarity with our aspirations for total independence from U.S. domestic colonialism.

Revolutionary Puerto Rican and Mexican nationals, themselves representing struggles against U.S. colonialism, also expressed practical solidarity with these mobilizations and with the struggle for our national liberation.

Dessie Woods was released from prison in 1981. She moved to Oakland, where she was known as Rashida Muhammad and remained a true friend and supporter of our movement until her untimely death in 2006.

Our Party led on the colonial prison question

The apparent unity of the U.S. Front of the African Liberation Movement that was spurred by the Dessie Woods campaign had a direct impact on our decision to build the African National Prison Organization (ANPO) in 1979. We initiated ANPO after discussions with leaders within the pro-independence movement with the intent of building on the unity that was expressed during the Dessie Woods campaign.

Our expressed intent was to take on the prison question as a joint project since our whole movement was concerned about this question, especially the issue of our political prisoners who had fallen during the defeat of our revolution of the 1960s. We also witnessed the criminalization and massive round up of African people into the rapidly expanding colonial prison system, understanding this as part of the U.S. counterinsurgency against our whole community following the government's COINTELPRO attack that dismantled our movement of the '60s.

Our Party's position that the U.S. prison system is a colonial prison system is clear in our 14-Point Platform, adopted in 1979 and revised at our First Party Congress in 1981. Point 6 states: "We want the immediate and unconditional release of all black people who are presently locked down in U.S. prisons."

Point 7 states: "We want complete amnesty for all African political prisoners and prisoners of war from U.S. prisons or their immediate release to any friendly country which will accept them and give them political asylum."

ANPO was a vehicle through which the anti-colonial tendency of our movement could unite around practical work through collective leadership. In this way we felt we could establish working unity so our political line differences could be struggled around and resolved through practice instead of debates around abstract questions.

The founding conference of ANPO was convened in Louisville, Kentucky, in September of 1979. Attendance was high, comprised of mostly-enthusiastic Africans who were relieved to see our movement functioning at such a high level of proficiency and resuming control and leadership of our own struggle for national liberation.

Unfortunately, the leaders of the attending organizations were enmeshed in political line differences with the movement of the African working class led by our Party. Their differences essentially revolved around whether the prison question would be targeted in the context of an anti-colonial struggle or whether it would be taken on as a single issue within the status quo of imperialism.

For example, one argument put forward at the conference was that ANPO should be led by prisoners behind bars, suggesting that the prison question was separate from our total colonial reality and could be resolved independently. We recognized that these were petty bourgeois, often adventuristic forces. Many of these forces were strongly supported by the radical oppressor nation white Left, including Prairie Fire Organizing Committee (PFOC), that rose up after the U.S. defeat of our movement of the '60s. PFOC substituted "white and male supremacy" as the enemy rather than U.S. and European colonialism.

These forces refused to acknowledge that the terrorized masses of African people were under siege by the U.S. counterinsurgency being waged against the entire African working class in an attempt to keep it from rising up again.

This was such a critical issue in this period that our Party waged serious struggle for many years within the pro-independence movement, publishing a book based on articles that had appeared in *The Burning Spear* newspaper. The book, *Black Power Since the Sixties: The Struggle against Opportunism within the U.S. Front of the Black Liberation Movement*, was published in 1991.

In the book's introduction I wrote:

> *For us in the African People's Socialist Party this is not just an abstract discussion to demonstrate our paranoia concerning the North American colonial state or to prove that we are knowledgeable about counterinsurgency. We initiated this discussion, this struggle against opportunism, as part of a process to solve the outstanding problems of the revolution.*

ANPO did succeed in raising the issue of prison as a tool of colonial control of our people and created an organization that, though short-lived, won Africans in and outside the prisons into a dynamic organized resistance.

"You're not in America now!"

In January of 1979 our Party had been thrust into the international limelight when the people of Iran took possession of their sovereignty by overthrowing the Shah that maintained Iran as a U.S. military forward operating base in the Persian Gulf. This happened some 27 years after the U.S. overthrow of the elected government of Mohammad Mosaddegh.

The success of the Iranian Revolution and the capture by the Iranian people of the U.S. embassy that functioned as a "nest of spies" in Iran, inflamed the patriotic passions of the U.S. North American population, raising the possibility of direct U.S. military intervention.

Within the U.S., North Americans began attacking anyone from the Middle East, Arabs as well as Iranians. North American students were holding rallies on university campuses that were punctuated with cries of "Sand niggers, go home!" and "Send the Klan to I-ran!" These jingoist rantings by white mobs appear to have been the first pro-war demonstrations in the U.S. since before the sixties and the U.S. imperialist humiliation by the courageous people of Viet Nam who won their liberation.

Our Party had already developed a working political relationship with Iranian exiles and students, particularly in Gainesville. We participated regularly in the demonstrations they held demanding the ouster of the U.S.-imposed Shah. The North American students on the campus of the elite University of Florida in Gainesville, where we had a significant presence, began holding rabidly anti-Iranian and white nationalist demonstrations.

In the face of this knee-jerk clamor from the government and on the streets and campuses throughout the U.S., our Party organized a mass mobilization in defense of the Iranian people in Gainesville that was attacked and disrupted by hundreds of flag waving white people chanting "America!"

They were all mistaken, however, if they thought frothing at the mouth patriotic white nationalist mobs could silence this Party. On the following week, to the dismay of the police department and the Negro ministers of the local churches who advised the African community not to join us, we marched again, behind the Red, Black and Green.

This time, because our first demonstration and its disruption were picked up by media all over the world, the Gainesville police department came out in full force to escort our march. When we were again greeted by thousands of beer drinking, flag waving, America-chanting whites, some of whom were members of motorcycle gangs, we marched right into the mob and faced them down with our own chants of "Africa! Africa! Africa!"

I took the platform in the middle of the city hall plaza and announced to the crowd, "The Sand Niggers are here!" Then, to their own amazement, the crowd was stilled while I read a statement from the then-prime minister of Iran. After this, we began to march away.

Following us with chants of "America," the rabid white mob attempted to intimidate us only until we reached the African community. At this point Africans rushed out of their homes and local establishments loudly responding to the whites, "You're not in America now!"

This display of unity and support for our movement proved to be dissuasive enough to send the whites scurrying back to the politically rancid America with which they were so enamored except when threatened with consequences for their actions.

The Party made reparations a household word

Our Party gave life and definition to the movement for reparations for African people and colonized peoples worldwide. While we did not initiate the contemporary demand for reparations, we built the reparations movement. With a goal to make reparations a household word, we were the ones that popularized the reparations demand in the U.S.

Prior to the involvement of our Party, the issue of reparations essentially involved efforts to win some kind of legislative or judicial recognition in U.S. courts or by the state or federal government. There was no real mass involvement.

We recognized that reparations had to become the property of the masses if it was to be a significant political question. On November 13 and 14, 1982 we held the historic first session of the World Tribunal on Reparations for African People in the U.S. in Brooklyn, New York.

The Tribunal found that the U.S. owed African people in the U.S. trillions of dollars for stolen labor alone, the first empirical quantification of the value of capitalized African labor. The research arriving at the amount of $4.1 trillion was laid out in our book, *Stolen Black Labor: The Political Economy of Domestic Colonialism.*

The tribunal also gave us another opportunity to advance our strategic goals for liberation. The reparations demand was consistent with Point 11 of the Party's 14-Point Platform that called for reparations to African people from a colonial system built on the genocide of the Native people and the enslavement of Africans.

Most important politically, the tribunal utilized existing international law as the basis for its proceedings, initiating a practical example of incipient state power in the hands of the colonized African masses. Through the tribunal the Party demonstrated to Africans colonized in the U.S. the potential for the exercise of state power by our colonially dispersed African nation.

As I stated in my role as the People's Advocate at the opening of the proceedings:

This tribunal will determine whether, even in the absence of state power, the rights of the oppressed will be recognized as rights which may be respected in the form of applied international law, whether they may be respected in the form of an international trial of an oppressor state power.

Following testimony from African people on nearly every aspect of our brutal conditions of life under colonialism, the panel of international judges ruled that the U.S. government is guilty of genocide against African people and owes at minimum the designated $4.1 trillion in reparations to African people in the U.S. for stolen labor alone.

Immediately after the conclusion of this historical event, we launched the African National Reparations Organization (ANRO), whose sole objective was to win the reparations demand in the consciousness of African people.

Following the 1982 tribunal, I toured Europe with the reparations message, going first to London and Ireland, and then to France and Germany, meeting with hundreds of Africans in different settings. We won explicit support from the Irish Republican Socialist Party, which at the time was locked in a life and death struggle against British colonialism.

Subsequent trips to Europe, most often to England, promoted the reparations campaign. In the U.S., ANRO continued to hold reparations tribunals in various cities over a 12-year period, allowing for the presentation of more and more testimony and evidence supporting the reparations demand and winning greater mass consciousness to the issue.

Following the first tribunal in 1982, we published the book, *Reparations Now! The Abbreviated Report from the International Tribunal on Reparations for Black People in the U.S.* A few years later, African Socialist International Secretary General Luwezi Kinshasa was recruited to the Party after he found and bought the book in a Paris bookstore.

Our Party's work to raise the question of reparations to African people laid the foundation for the popularity of the reparations movement throughout the African world. It was a forerunner and catalyst for the historic UN-sponsored World Conference against Racism, Racial Discrimination, Xenophobia and Related Intolerance that took place in Durban, South Africa in 2001. That conference resulted in slavery and colonialism being declared a crime against humanity and reparations a legitimate response.

The Party's participation in the reparations work also expanded the issue beyond the question of slavery, which was the main issue for which reparations compensation was being demanded by most others prior to our involvement. We exposed the fact that the rate of exploitation of Africans has been greater *since* slavery. Moreover, we determined that reparations are due to Africans for crimes of colonialism and neocolonialism, and for the ever-expanding discrepancies in the conditions of existence between Africans and Europeans.

Our view has always been that the reparations issue is a revolutionary issue, informed by the understanding of parasitism or primitive accumulation as the essence of capitalism that was *born* of our enslavement and colonization. We have always understood that almost all the resources of Europe and North America—the largest economies in the world—owe their existence to the forcible expropriation of value from Africa, Africans and others upon whom Europe depends for sustenance and vitality.

During this process, we were able to win the African People's Solidarity Committee (APSC) to the conclusion that reparations to African people is one of the solidarity organization's most important issues/demands.

ANRO, ANPO exposed class struggle inside movement

For our Party the African National Reparations Organization (ANRO) was an opportunity once again to attempt to unify the pro-independence tendency of our movement that had met a counterinsurgent defeat by the U.S. state and the opportunistic white Left whose political lines have always been in contention with the struggle for African liberation on our own terms.

Our Party was often considered a lunatic fringe by African liberals and white leftists because of our demand for reparations during this time. Like the imperialist bourgeoisie, they were unable to concede the fact that the U.S. had built itself off enslaved African labor and other stolen resources, both human and material. Or, when able to concede this fact, they were incapable of believing in the efficacy of a reparations demand.

We also saw ANRO as a means of winning the masses of our people to the reparations position by raising a question that the imperialists cannot answer and thrusting the colonized African population back into active political life independent of the imperialist Democratic party.

Inevitably, various nationalist groups saw the Party's leadership as an assertion of the leadership of the African working class and a threat to the prevailing, outdated petty bourgeois nationalist outlook around the issue of reparations and revolution. The critical question was that the Party recognized reparations as a demand forwarding the African Revolution, while most of the others saw reparations as a *payday* to be achieved within the context of the existing colonial relationship.

Our difficulties with various elements within the U.S. Front of the African Liberation Movement were primarily based on contradictions left unresolved prior to the defeat of the Black Revolution of the Sixties. The presumed tenuous unity of the movement of the 1960s was being frayed even before the defeat of the revolution, but the defeat of the revolution resulted in an ossification of positions that did not have the benefit of development from practice.

Our Party's attempts to build ANRO and the African National Prison Organization were efforts to unite our movement in practice while creating a forum within which ideological positions could be struggled around and developed. The intent was to move the revolutionary process forward despite ideological differences that we felt could be resolved through the test of practice.

However, that was not to be. In fact, the process of building ANRO and ANPO served to illuminate and better define the contradictions. It was the test of practice in building these organizations that exposed the chasm of class differences separating the Party from most others.

The general unity within the liberation movement was based on the issues of self-determination and independence. Most agreed that Africans should be independent of the U.S. white nationalist state power but the questions of class and social transformation were generally left unaddressed. In fact, the Black Panther Party's fledgling position on socialism is what drew the most criticism against them from many nationalists in the 1960s.

The New Afrikanist tendency of our movement only began to identify itself as socialist after a blistering series of African People's Socialist Party polemics was directed against a leading proponent of the tendency.

Published in *The Burning Spear* and later in the book *Black Power Since the Sixties: The Struggle Against Opportunism within the U.S. Front of the Black Liberation Movement,* this struggle was initiated after a former leader and founder of the Provisional Government of the Republic of New Afrika (PG-RNA) publicly celebrated his unity and complicity with the U.S. counterinsurgent "war against drugs." Our Party has always been clear that what is called the war on drugs is merely a political cover for a war on our community focused primarily on the African working class.

The working class was the source of the militant anti-colonial resistance in the 1960s that had shaken the U.S. imperialist domain to its foundation and the "war against drugs" was simply a part of the counterinsurgent mopping up process.

Once our movement's leaders and organizations were destroyed or neutralized, the U.S. government drenched our impoverished communities with illegal drugs and an illegal drug economy to prevent African workers from regrouping and rebuilding the African Revolution. The drugs, along with military occupation and mass imprisonment of our communities, as well as the assassinations of our leaders, are all a part of counterinsurgency, one front of which is known as COINTELPRO.

Many are still confused about this point today. Like every Party, we are simply the advanced detachment of a particular class. Since we have always been clear that ours is the Party of the African working class, we have always defended its interests even after the working class suffered severe defeat and was pushed into a morass of demoralization, demonization and imposed drug use.

Our Party has never condemned the African working class for the myriad of colonial contradictions it might be embroiled in at any given moment. We have always called on the class to rise up to its full stature in opposition to colonial oppression and through membership in its vanguard Party.

Another tendency within our general anti-colonial movement was Pan-Africanism, primarily in the form of the All-African People's Revolutionary Party (AAPRP). Unlike the New Afrikanists, the AAPRP members shouted their socialist credentials to the skies, proclaiming themselves "scientific socialists."

However, the "science" of the AAPRP never characterized their "socialism" as the ascension of the African working class to the position of ruling class and custodian of the independent, united socialist state.

Instead the AAPRP defined *students* as the critical social force for the socialism they were seeking from secure classrooms in various places in the world. Theirs was a middle class or petty bourgeois socialism.

These were some of the ideological barriers that undermined all our efforts to unite the U.S. Front of the African Liberation Movement during those decades of the 1970s and '80s. Similar barriers would reveal themselves with our work throughout Europe and in Africa.

These differences in class outlook severely frustrated the achievement of our strategic aim to unite our movement after its military defeat and in the face of the ideological assault launched against it by the opportunist North American Left.

In 1989, seven years after ANRO's founding, U.S. president Ronald Wilson Reagan decided to grant a pittance that he called "reparations" to survivors of the U.S. concentration camps imprisoning Japanese during the Second Imperialist World War. Only then did some of the same organizations become firm believers in African reparations, finally deciding to build their own, separate coalition around the issue of reparations.

Nevertheless, ANRO did succeed in putting the reparations demand on the political agenda for Africans within the U.S. and around the world. We took the question of reparations out of the classrooms, sterile conferences and limited discussion groups and built a genuine mass movement around the issue.

We popularized the reparations demand by tying it to common struggles, such as the numerous instances of police violence and murder that our people were familiar with in our occupied communities.

Theoretical direction for Party work

The theoretical basis for our political work is located in the 14-Point Working Platform of the Party, published in every issue of *The Burning Spear* newspaper.

It is also reinforced by our Political Reports and other documents and resolutions at our Congresses. However, one longstanding guide for our political work that has stood the test of time and can be seen in almost every political goal we have set for ourselves as a Party is our pamphlet, "The Political Aspects of Building a Mass Movement—The Tactical and Strategic Objectives For Black Liberation."

The Tactics and Strategy paper was given by me as a presentation to a black organizers' conference at Amherst University in 1977 that included the participation of the venerable Ella Baker, and Robert Williams, who was a notable figure in the African Liberation Movement. The conference was organized by Max Stanford, a founder of the Revolutionary Action Movement (RAM), associate of Malcolm X and at the time a staunch proponent of liberation for African people.

These strategic goals and aims have guided our work consistently over the years, with all of our major campaigns fitting into one or more of these categories.

Stated concisely, the "Tactics and Strategy" pamphlet calls for:

1. Winning African people to the position of political independence. "If the masses of black people are not won over to the position of independence, there will be no independence for black people. It is as simple and clear as that."

2. Establishing the leadership of the pro-independence movement. "In building our mass movement, then, we

see that it must be designed to clearly demonstrate the leadership of our movement."

3. Winning support for the independence position within U.S. borders. "The main targets for this effort to win support for the independence position should be the general anti-imperialist forces within current U.S. borders, other oppressed, subject and colonized nationalities and progressive U.S. North Americans."

4. Creating dual or competing or contending governmental powers. "That is to say to the degree possible our movement must assume the real and actual responsibilities of government for our people."

5. Exposing the oppressive nature of the U.S. government. This would constantly undermine "it within and without the current U.S. borders. The U.S. government must be exposed as an imperialist danger to the entire world which practices colonialism within its own borders and Puerto Rico."

6. Winning international support for the independence position, "contributing to international diplomatic encirclement of the U.S."

7. Building an African People's Liberation Army.

The Tactics and Strategy paper also identified three main targets for struggle:

1. The U.S. North American ruling class. "As this is the enemy most responsible for the barbaric treatment of our people, and upon whose system colonialism depends, we must, without letup, strike our main ideological blows here."

2. Black, primitive petty bourgeois collaborators. "These collaborators (neocolonialists) represent colonialism's first line of defense within the dispersed U.S. North American colony."

3. Ideological imperialists. "These are the U.S. North Americans who call themselves socialists and communists, but who deny the right of African people to be led by our own advanced fighters, by liquidating the nationalist character of our movement; obscuring the colonial contradiction; raising the secondary contradiction between African people and our relation to production to a primary contradiction, and seizing hegemony of our movement."

Anyone familiar with the work of our Party can see that, with the exception of building a liberation army, all the work we have been and are involved in can be located within the strategic objectives laid out here.

We are now and have always been a revolutionary Party with revolutionary objectives. We have always understood that revolution is not about who can best cast verbal aspersions against white people or the U.S. or imperialism in general. Revolution is not about who is willing to blow up buildings or the effort to hold massive mobilizations, though the significance of either of these things is not being debated here. It is about all our actions, especially now, being able to respond to the question: toward what end?

Party defined role of white people in our struggle

The question of the relationship and role of white people in history and in the struggle for socialism and African liberation is one that has long plagued our movement.

African people have a bloody history with the white population. White people have historically functioned as arms of the oppressive colonial state against us, motivated to do so by the reward of colonial booty, elevated social relevance and a putrid ideology arising from a vicious social system based on genocide, slavery and colonialism.

White people have created in the African world conflicting responses that run the gamut of hatred, awe, fear, servile obedience, permanent suspicion and unrelenting resistance.

The bestiality and inhumanity of the colonial treatment of Africans and others have done much to mystify Europeans or white people in the eyes of the oppressed, making it difficult to develop a political response to their presence and location in the structures of our oppression. This has been further complicated by the "whites who love us," as they were called by Comrade Robert Mangaliso Sobukwe, founder of the Pan Africanist Congress of Azania.

The whites who love us are the "communists" and other liberals of different stripes with their generally patronizing stances that reflect their imperialist pedigree. Their existence confirmed the worst fears of those in the African world who were skeptical of the ability of whites to end their self-isolation from the world and join in the fight to overturn imperialism, which for most of its existence has had a white face.

This has not been an easy struggle. On more than one occasion we have engaged in physical battles with white dilettantes who, after discovering oppression or exploitation in the pristine environs of a library, would rush into the African community to reward us with their newly attained wisdom, sometimes disrupting genuine campaigns against imperialist white power.

The African People's Socialist Party has also been part of the general discussion within the liberation movement around the question of how to understand white people and their role, if any, in the struggle for the liberation of Africans and the movement toward a non-oppressive, non-exploiting society.

Some of the conclusions we reached laid to rest outmoded, colonialist-serving concepts of "race" that served to place people in permanent contention based primarily on biology or genetics.

Our own experiences also forced us to examine the behavior of too many Africans who betrayed the interests of our people—Africans such as Mobutu of Congo, Duvalier of Haiti and the preachers, lawyers and other traitors in our immediate communities. Obviously, their actions could not be explained by their "race," so there was clearly some other explanation that had to be explored.

We were informed by how the people of Viet Nam and others involved in anti-colonial movements were able to win support from within the imperialist oppressor nations and how clearly and scientifically identifying that our struggle is one against *colonialism* can assist us in winning allies of any nationality or "race."

We learned too that an examination of the history of Africans in the emergence of the capitalist system within which whites and Africans live and contend, would reveal to us the origin and foundation of white power. This revelation not only guides the struggle for our liberation as Africans, but the liberation of the peoples of the world.

As we have made clear in this report, fighting against racism is a dead end street. We are colonized Africans, in Africa, in the U.S. and throughout the world. Our colonization must be overturned and we *can* build a strategy to end it, one that allows for a role by anyone of any nationality or "race" in the effort—including white people.

When we are clear that we are struggling against colonialism, we are capable of identifying anyone who works to obstruct the struggle, regardless of their "race," even if they are Africans. We are also then capable of identifying any genuine ally. This is why the Party fought so hard against the designation of our struggle as one against racism, especially at a time when most of the world was in an uproar to end colonial domination by Europeans.

In 1976 the Party worked with the Puerto Rican Socialist Party and an assortment of African and North American activists to build a July 4 mobilization in Philadelphia termed, "A Bicentennial Without Colonies." This event was held to challenge the hoopla initiated by the U.S. ruling class to build patriotic fervor among the North American population on the 200th anniversary of the bourgeois American revolution.

We saw this as an excellent opportunity to win support for the U.S.-based African struggle against colonialism and mobilized our members and supporters from the U.S. to participate. We also used this anti-colonial momentum to identify many North Americans who had indicated friendship with our Party over the years and win them to an organizational relationship.

In September of that year, we pulled these North Americans together in St. Petersburg, Florida, to launch the African People's Solidarity Committee, an organization of North Americans or so-called white people who would work directly under the leadership of our Party in the struggle against our colonial oppression as we defined it.

The launching of the African People's Solidarity Committee did not occur without struggle. The fact that the Party had identified certain forces and pulled them together to work under our leadership did not automatically mean that these whites would simply overturn their own history and tradition in the structure of our oppression.

Some North Americans have always been able to offer charity to African people, even within the most oppressive expression of our relationship going back to slavery. Genuine, principled, material solidarity based on opposition to U.S. colonial domination of our people was another question.

In the relationship with Africans, either directly or indirectly, whites have a tradition of being boss and Africans have a tradition of being bossed. All of this had to be overturned.

There was the notion in the minds of many of the whites being organized under our leadership that we were entering into a relationship of equal, parallel struggles. Some of the forces imagined that solidarity work meant North Americans doing their "own thing" to free white women or white homosexuals or white workers while Africans as recipients of their occasional charity would be permitted to handle the Africa question. It was many years until this notion was overturned.

The fact that all the work was subordinate to the liberation of Africa and African people; that all white people exist and benefit from the pedestal of the oppression of African and other colonized peoples; and that the task of the solidarity movement is to win support for the Black Revolution inside the white community as a strategic component of our struggle to overturn white power where the oppression and exploitation of the world is centralized—this took some time to win.

For years the creation of APSC was met with a barrage of criticism, most of which was surreptitious, sometimes in the form of slanderous whisper campaigns from North American leftists and black nationalists. Nevertheless, history has shown us to be correct in building this arm of our Party.

Many of the APSC comrades have proven themselves strong African Internationalists, opening up another, heretofore unavailable front for black power within the North American community, something that is valuable unto itself. This organizational relationship provided another means of challenging the empty race nationalism that inadvertently contributed to the overall weakness of our struggle against U.S. colonialism and imperialism in general.

The creation of APSC helped us to end the counterinsurgent isolation imposed on our movement by the U.S. secret political police. It gave us an avenue through which we could break out of the information quarantine blocking the ability of our movement to engage in political debate and struggle outside our colonized community.

The existence of APSC has also forever changed the limitations North Americans and Europeans have imposed on how genuine solidarity should be defined. Now, it is not they, but we who define solidarity with our struggle for liberation.

It is true that nearly all the value extracted from our colonial communities throughout the world is in some white community or another. APSC has assumed its responsibility to concretely build white support for reparations to African people. The solidarity committee is achieving its own capacity as an organization of white people contributing to our just reparations demand and also winning other North Americans and Europeans to contribute to reparations with material support for our liberation struggle. This is truly the significance of APSC, the *organization*, even in the face of certain *individuals* in APSC who have, from time to time, betrayed its aims.

The work of the Party has resulted in APSC members having to confront police repression in a number of campaigns from New York City, to Oakland, California, to St. Petersburg, Florida. APSC has also been custodian of assorted Party-owned institutions for a number of years and its members have experienced arrest, kidnapping and various forms of repression as arms of our Party.

Today, many of those who attacked us in the past for the relationship with APSC, a relationship that is principled and aboveboard, have been forced to abandon previously held rigid racial views that disallowed the development of non-African allies.

Party theory developed through struggle with white Left

Many of the theoretical breakthroughs made by the Party took place during the 1980s when we were based in Oakland, California. This was a crucial period when the development and consolidation of the African People's Solidarity Committee involved serious struggles with and in APSC and the solidarity movement under the leadership of the Party. In addition, our Party struggled with other political lines within the sector of the white Left that characterized itself as being in solidarity with others oppressed and exploited by imperialist white power.

One such line is the concept of "white skin privilege," the notion that the struggle is against the privileges that white people are afforded by their skin color. The many problems with this white self-centered position are glaring to us within the Uhuru Movement today.

This is a position that maintains the centrality of white people as subjects of history. It is one that obscures the parasitic relationship existing between Africans and white people, who function as the oppressor nation sitting on the socio-economic pedestal regardless of status or income. This relationship stems from the colonial parasitism that gave birth to the system of capitalism and the concept of whiteness itself.

The idea that Africans would be essentially tied to a struggle to end white skin privilege is one that undermines the reality that our concern is not about the "skin privilege" of whites.

African people are fighting against white colonial domination of our entire people. The political advantages that whites have in the world are based on the nature of the system that elevated Europeans to significance through expropriation of our political and economic power over our own "rights" and resources.

Our struggle is against white colonial domination imposed to sustain a parasitic economic relationship that requires political repression, both popular and state-initiated.

White skin privilege is an idea that comes out of Euro-American group arrogance born of this parasitic economic foundation—an arrogance whose basic criticism of the system revolves around their own sense of significance. The white skin privilege position is related to the struggle against racism, protecting the actual system by attempting to end privilege without destroying the colonial relationship that white people have to African people.

The existence of "privilege" is a statement of power. White privilege is white power in relationship to those who do not have power. Our fight is not one against the privilege of whites. Rather it is a fighting for black power over our own black lives. That in and of itself undermines the concept and reality of white privilege.

Another related position that we found equally objectionable was put forward by Prairie Fire Organizing Committee (PFOC)—that the struggle is against "white and male supremacy." This position contends with the definition of our struggle as advanced by Africans ourselves and others who have been battling white imperial domination for centuries.

What we would define as colonialism, they defined as white supremacy, while proclaiming that we both meant the same thing. This was not a semantic difference, however. Support for the struggle against colonialism would strengthen the organizational and political position of the colonized and the organizations of the African Liberation Movement. Support for the struggle against white supremacy renders organizational and political support for the white organization.

We needed this work and struggle with the solidarity movement and the white Left in general for our own development. It was a critical means through which another political and ideological window to the world was opened to the Party for examination. We had to find explanations for some of the essential questions confronting the most critical contradictory relationship that Africans have had with the world since the advent of colonial slavery and the rise of parasitic capitalism.

This relationship forced us to expand our theory of African Internationalism through deepening our understanding of the question of parasitism, the foundation of the capitalist system at our expense. As a result of these struggles, we were compelled to find the scientific basis for how the success of white people and white power requires the permanent pedestal of the forced expropriation of value from African and the oppressed of the world.

This gave us the clarity to fully comprehend how the political and economic structures of colonialism exist for all white people regardless of status or income, and providing us the scientific basis for building APSC under our direct leadership.

Although we organized the African People's Solidarity Committee in 1976, it was not until the mid-1980s that the organization was truly consolidated into the formation that was the genesis of what has become the APSC of today.

Part of the work that defined APSC began with the campaign to free Dessie Woods and other Party-led campaigns. Many of the current leaders of APSC came into the work during that time. During this period, we deployed APSC forces in security work for the Vietnamese comrades who were active in Northern California after the success of the revolution that defeated U.S. imperialism in Viet Nam. APSC forces were also key elements in the medical drives for Zimbabwe under the leadership of ZANU supporters in Northern California.

Even as our Party was engaged in serious ideological and political struggles with a host of white leftists on the West Coast during this time, I personally began a regime of ideological and organizational training for APSC cadres, initiating the process for APSC's political consolidation.

After the defeat of the Black Revolution of the Sixties, white opportunist forces were able to take over most of the political space in the Bay Area of California that had only a little more than a decade earlier been the revolutionary center of the Black Panther Party. The struggle to win APSC to African Internationalism took place in this context.

These white Left forces rose to prominence in unity with the success of the brutal neocolonial politicians and the U.S. government's counterinsurgent criminalization of African and colonized communities after our revolutionary leaders had been murdered or imprisoned and our organizations neutralized.

This opportunistic Left had actually begun to speak for the African Liberation Movement, objectively aiding and abetting the assault on our anti-colonial struggle for self-determination.

Some of these North American groups were, in the name of solidarity, providing material and political support for anti-colonial movements around the world, including in Africa. They would offer no support for the African Revolution inside the U.S., however, where both the requirement for accountability and the potential for defeating U.S. imperialism were much greater.

Other white leftists claimed to offer support to African resistance within the U.S. but the conditions were such that they would actually control and dole out the resources as they saw fit, supporting the issues they thought significant. They refused to work directly under the Party's leadership, working instead with African forces in prison or that were otherwise dependent on the white leftists.

It was these struggles that were the basis for the understandings in our book, *A New Beginning*, the Political Report to the First Party Congress in 1981, quoted earlier:

> *Living in a country built and sustained off slavery, colonialism and neocolonialism, the impact of victorious revolutionary struggles reach down into the gas tanks, shopping centers and tax brackets of the North American population.*
>
> *There is an objective relationship between world slavery and U.S. affluence, and up until now the North American population, opportunistically and demagogically led by their stomachs, pocketbooks and corrupt leadership, has chosen the continued enslavement of the world.*

Early on in its existence, APSC provided intermittent material support to the Party. From time to time, in support of one campaign or another or to secure some specific resource, APSC would be called on for assistance. However, the objective character of this relationship was not very different from charity work and it did not necessarily require genuine unity with the objectives of our revolution.

The ideological and organizational training that I initiated with APSC and the struggles waged with a host of North American Left organizations that, because of their deep opportunism were sometimes characterized as Ku Klux Kommunists and ideological imperialists, helped us to redefine APSC work and give it a different, coherent organizational and ideological identity.

There were years of serious struggle with APSC and at one point the Party actually temporarily dissolved APSC, working only with the mass Uhuru Solidarity Organization.

Finally, in 1985 deep political differences erupted inside of APSC, resulting in a split. This arose from issues raised by the Party around the very question of whether APSC would make a commitment to seriously go into the white community to win reparations from the general white population as a key part of the anti-imperialist struggle. This required unity with the understanding of parasitic capitalism and the pedestal upon which all white people sit at the expense of African and other colonized peoples.

This was a call for a real stand of solidarity that was based on their interest in overthrowing colonialism as opposed to something being done *for* us. This gave an entirely different character to APSC's fundraising. Instead of APSC being required to simply raise resources for specific campaigns and/or needs of the Party, APSC's economic or reparations work had to be institutionalized and ongoing based on political principle.

Ultimately, APSC members began to embrace African Internationalism as their own politic. APSC united with the determination to come to the same conclusions as the Party that the main work of APSC is *material* solidarity, reparations to African people, turning back over the stolen resources amassed in the white community to the African Revolution. This 1985 struggle was a key turning point for APSC. Following this the APSC forces began to rapidly build ongoing economic enterprises capable of raising consistent resources for work of the Party.

These Party-owned institutions, which now operate under the African People's Education and Defense Fund (APEDF) include the Uhuru Furniture stores in Oakland and Philadelphia, which have been in existence for 25 and 19 years respectively. Also Uhuru Foods and Uhuru Pies, now part of Black Star Industries, were consolidated during this period, having been initiated by the solidarity work as far back as 1979, when they were carried out sporadically. It was not until 1985 that they were transformed into businesses that function day to day.

The Uhuru Holiday Pies, now 33 years old, is a long-time Bay Area progressive tradition that engages the participation of literally hundreds of volunteers every year at the holiday season. Uhuru Foods' street fairs and Saturday markets in Oakland and St. Petersburg are growing Party fronts immersed in the culture of those two cities.

APSC's current slogan: "Solidarity, not charity!" was born of this period. Now with all of APSC's resource generation functioning as reparations work, APSC's political work is designed to take the struggle for black power into the North American community itself.

Over the years, APSC developed into one of the Party's most invaluable organizations—and it must always be understood that APSC is a Party organization. APSC was created, organized, trained and led by the Party. It has become the custodian of much of the history and expertise of the Party.

The Party's years of struggle in Oakland

The period of Party development and struggle during the "Oakland Years" of the 1980s is an outstanding chapter of our Party's history. The 1980s was one of the most reactionary periods in recent U.S. history when we took it upon our shoulders to complete the Black Revolution of the Sixties and force the interests of the African working class back onto the political agenda again.

Ronald Wilson Reagan had won the U.S. presidency on a platform of political and social reaction with enormous support from the North American white population. His politics and support were based on the revanchist assumptions of recovering the losses to U.S. imperialism in Viet Nam, Nicaragua, Panama and Iran and the growing movement at the time in El Salvador.

In addition, Reagan, who won much of his reactionary reputation as governor of California during the era of the

Black Panther Party, was determined to take back the concessions won by Africans and other subject and colonized peoples inside the U.S. during the 1960s. Much of Reagan's enduring popularity revolves around his role in attempting to push back history and retake all the political and social territory lost by imperialism during that era.

The governor of California at the time of Reagan's presidency was George Deukmejian, who had campaigned as a "tough on crime," law and order candidate. During his reign Deukmejian nearly tripled the California prison population from about 34,000 captives when he took office in 1983 to more than 94,000 by the time of his departure eight years later.

The various cutbacks of social welfare programs in California were glaring in Oakland with its large African population and reputation as the former headquarters of the Black Panther Party. The Black Panther Party had been the center for much of the revolutionary activity in the U.S. and other locations in the world, especially where inhabited by Africans.

The number of people cast out onto the streets by shuttered state-supported housing programs and the economy, which then as now, suffered what was characterized as recession, left a severely battered population in its wake in the Northern California city.

Oakland's African population that had only a few years before been the proud proponents of the Black Panther Party, was now devastated by the U.S. government's counterinsurgent assault on our people. We would often say that we could "still smell the cordite in the air."

The strong beret- and leather jacket-wearing women and men once seen demonstrating or training in front of the Alameda County Courthouse looking out on Lake Merritt were now reeling from the destruction of our organizations, the murder and arrest of our leaders and the deadly influx of drugs in the government's mop-up operation.

It was in this context that our Party came to Oakland in 1981. We held our Party's First Congress there in September of that year at the historic St. Augustine's Episcopal Church where the Panther's Free Breakfast for Children Program had been based and where George Jackson's funeral had been held.

The theme of the Main Resolution of our First Party Congress was aptly named "The New Beginning." This theme was justified by the contents of the Congress's Main Resolution that revealed the deep crisis which U.S. and world imperialism was attempting to resolve through the bombs and war threats of the administration of U.S. president Ronald Wilson Reagan.

This New Beginning was perceived by our Party to be the simultaneous onset of the decline of U.S. imperialism and the growth and vitality of our Party. It designated the potential for the resistance of the world's victims of imperialist plunder. Another, less recognized basis for the Main Resolution's declaration of a New Beginning was the significance of our Party's First Congress for legitimating the Party, its leaders and its defining documents and policies.

We have already discussed the Party's daring and critical work since our 1972 founding, conveying the legacy of revolutionary struggle from the 1960s to the present, within our Party and beyond. We have explored the significance of the Party's founding at the moment the U.S. was convinced of having effectively destroyed the Black Revolution of the Sixties through a wave of terror that included mass imprisonment and murder of select leaders of our movement within the U.S. and around the world.

The period between our Party's 1972 founding and our First Congress in 1981 can be considered the years of "wartime"

Party-building. It was a time when various organizations of police terror were exemplified by the FBI's Counterintelligence Program (COINTELPRO). Open, sometimes bloody police attacks on organizational headquarters of movement forces were common. Phone tapping, other forms of government eavesdropping and intervention were epidemic.

This is the reality that conditioned how the Party would function, including the nine-year delay after our founding before our First Congress. Holding an open congress is not something we could conceive of during the period of government frame-ups and assassinations. While we did regularly hold annual conferences that were used to sum up and establish policies for coming periods of work, and while in many ways our organization was much tighter than now, we did not have the benefit of the level of organizational democracy implicit in the existence and institutionalization of our Congress.

There were regular political reports to annual conferences but they were not mandated. There was no required period of time for their distribution to and study by Party members in preparation for conferences similar to the pre-Congress work required by our Congress. There was no constitutionally required process that held our entire membership, including our leaders accountable to each other and to the Party. In fact, there had been no real democratically-based authority, existing as the highest body of the Party, that vetted our constitution and our leadership.

Our First Party Congress changed all of this. This is why the designation of a New Beginning had a greater organizational significance for the history of our Party: it was truly a new beginning for our Party. It represented a change from the wartime conditions of counterinsurgency where centralism was the outstanding feature of our Party's structure to a process that brought our membership fully into the practice of democratic centralism as the main principle of Party organization.

Our First Party Congress represented a new birth of our Party that has guided our work and defined our character with more or less effectiveness since that time. It was the Congress that marked a turning point in our Party's development, giving democratic authority to our leaders and our Party that has endured since its convocation.

The Oakland Summer Project and Measure O

While headquartered in Oakland, our Party initiated an unrelenting revolutionary campaign to deepen the obviously occurring crisis of imperialism and win the African workers and our allies back into independent political life. Our work in Oakland during this period is outstanding for many reasons, not the least of which is the capacity for a small, disciplined revolutionary Party with the correct line to have a political impact many times greater than its physical size.

With an African majority city council, Oakland provided us one of our most important testing grounds for developing our analysis of, and skills in, defining and struggling against the African neocolonial petty bourgeoisie. It taught us firsthand the neocolonial role in creating class peace by smothering the separate, independent interests of the African working class.

Our struggles were furious and intense, taking place on many fronts. We led popularly supported seizures of city-owned abandoned houses, and organized the Uhuru Tent City for the Homeless in response to the fact that thousands of Africans were forced to sleep in the underbrush in city-owned parks. We exposed a host of crimes by the city government and the Oakland hills-ensconced ruling elite.

In 1984, on the 20th anniversary of the Mississippi Summer Project, our Party organized the Oakland Summer Project that recruited Africans and others from throughout the U.S. along with one person from England. This project did more than provide recruits for our campaigns in Oakland. It gave us an opportunity to provide political education to all the Summer Project participants and spread our influence far beyond our Oakland base area.

During the Summer Project our work intensified with the initiation of a land reform measure, the Community Control of Housing Initiative that was placed on the Oakland ballot. It was a housing measure that aimed to overturn most of the bourgeois assumptions of land use and ownership in the U.S.

The measure challenged the brutal conditions facing the African working class, including the 10,000 homeless people admitted to by the authorities and the 1,400 city-owned abandoned houses that could be used for housing the homeless.

Billions of dollars were being sucked out of the African community by absentee landlords who owned more than 50 percent of the residential rental property and 80 percent of the commercial rental property in East Oakland.

During this period, following the assault on the African Liberation Movement of the Sixties, the neocolonial city officials attempted to remove every vestige of the history of the Black Panther Party and their base of empowered African workers. The goal was to gentrify Oakland for white people and make the city "safe for investment."

To put the housing measure on the ballot, we took advantage of California's initiative provision, apparently designed to allow well-funded and organized white reactionaries to create their own self-serving laws by going around the legislative bodies with slick campaigns to win direct intervention by special interest groups.

The Community Control of Housing Initiative divided the city of Oakland into twelve housing districts according to income and, coincidentally, housing patterns and nationality or "race." These twelve sections would each elect Community Control of Housing Boards from local residents who could own no more than four housing units.

The housing measure prohibited rent from being greater than 25 percent of the average income of the neighborhood. It gave the boards power of eminent domain, permitting compulsory purchase of any property left abandoned for more than six months to be used to house homeless people.

For weeks we conducted well-organized, intensive petitioning, successfully acquiring 33,000 signatures, many more than the 18,000 signatures of registered voters required to get the measure on the ballot. We mobilized all our forces, including the African People's Solidarity Committee, Party-organized community groups and members of the Party in a blistering electoral campaign to win the measure into law that clearly drove the landlords, city government and other opponents including the white Left into a frenzy.

Lawsuits were filed against the measure and on one occasion one white nationalist man physically attacked one of the solidarity workers, breaking her jaw. Something in the range of an identifiable half million dollars was spent in opposition to the Community Control of Housing initiative, and a battery of white Left and Negro opponents were dragged out of the lethargy they displayed in the face of the brutal exploitation of the masses to attack the measure we were forwarding.

The movement won the legal battles and the initiative was put on the November 1984 ballot as Measure O, a state designation intended to dismiss the significance of the initiative in the public mind.

Once on the ballot, the Uhuru Movement enlisted volunteers who walked the streets of the Flatlands of Oakland putting "Yes on O" fliers on 150,000 doorsteps, a number at least equal to the distribution of the bourgeois *Oakland*

Tribune—repeating this process one and a half more times during the six-week period leading to election day.

Our fierce struggles in the interests of the dire needs of African workers broke the class peace and gave our neocolonial and white Left opponents hell! The battle for houses for the homeless was met by a suggestion by one African county commissioner to place the homeless in an abandoned army base located in Alameda County. That base was abandoned because of radioactivity on its grounds.

The landlord and owning class of Oakland were able to mobilize associations of black preachers, black law enforcement officers and a host of other obedient lackeys. All the "progressive" Negro politicians opposed Measure O, one stating that the measure was "too punitive to landlords."

While it was expected that the Democratic and Republican parties would oppose the measure, we were surprised when the Communist Party USA actually *publicly* exposed its opposition to the interests of the African workers and others who were being crushed under the weight of the ruthless landlord class.

But then, the Communist Party USA was an organization of middle class, mostly North Americans, many of whom abandoned Oakland with the rise of the Black Panther Party and Black Power Movement of the 1960s, participating like other whites in mining the resources from our community through ownership of its property.

This is why Angela Davis, at the time an Oakland hills resident and member of the often-discredited Communist Party USA, attempted to come to the rescue of the city and landlords. Pioneering the now prevailing approach to the homeless, Davis proffered a scheme associated with a Negro preacher to deflect the struggle for housing by creating the disease-ridden and dehumanizing homeless shelters.

The San Francisco Chronicle decried Measure O in an editorial with the declaration that ours was not a law about rent control, it, according to the editorial was "rent revolution." On the eve of the election, another newspaper, addressing the significance of the measure, declared that if the measure passes on Monday, governor Deukmejian would order an "airstrike" on Oakland on Tuesday!

Be that as it may, after the dust cleared and hundreds of thousands of dollars were spent to fight the measure—we were never able to determine exactly how much was raised to fight us as monies were hidden and much of it came from other cities and states—Measure O won approximately 25,000 votes, nearly a quarter of the total.

It was a brilliant campaign by a small Party of the African working class that gave the ruling class a powerful fight on its own electoral political terrain.

Revolutionary discipline along with the correct political line that reflects the needs and aspirations of the people is the basis for the Party's influence that is far greater than its size. Our work in Oakland proved that it is better to maintain fidelity to our line and principles than to sacrifice either or both in an attempt to win favor from the ruling class and its lackeys.

Only the Party defined the counterinsurgency

For the 41 years of our Party's existence, we have been the bulwark of the African Liberation Movement. That must be understood by Party members if we are to have the necessary insight, enthusiasm and confidence to complete our mission to lead the struggle for the liberation and socialist unification of Africa and African people worldwide.

Based in the heart of the oppressed and impoverished East Oakland during the Oakland years, our Party clarified our understandings of the U.S. government's counterinsurgency that defeated our movement and continued to destabilize and create hell for us in our communities.

After the military defeat of the Black Revolution of the Sixties, our Party played the pivotal role in the organizational, political and ideological battles to defend and rebuild the struggle for liberation and independence.

The assassinations, imprisonments, organizational destruction and political coups were all implemented with the concomitant mission to undermine our struggle for independence and liberation. They all forwarded the politics of neocolonialism, assimilation and various forms of accommodation in opposition to revolutionary national liberation. They were designed to reinstitute passivity on the part of the oppressed, a situation recognized by bourgeois thinkers as necessary for successful empire.

Killing Patrice Lumumba in Congo was not sufficient. It was also necessary to replace the ideology of Lumumbaism with Mobutuism. Similarly, while the political objective of the U.S. was the removal of Kwame Nkrumah from power in Ghana, the ideological objective was to replace Nkrumahism with neocolonialism, not just as a political reality but also as a clear, acceptable ideological alternative.

In the U.S., Malcolm X was assassinated to remove him as a political presence in the world, but he was also murdered because of the power of his ideological effectiveness in raising and organizing around revolutionary independence in opposition to religious obscurantism and pacifist assimilationism.

Dr. Martin Luther King, Jr., an assimilationist of sorts, was murdered because of his growing ideological advocacy of anti-imperialist resistance. He was moving away from the opportunism of his own organization, the Southern Christian Leadership Conference (SCLC), and tepid anti-racist legalism of groups like the NAACP and others whose analysis limited them to a struggle for acceptance within an imperialist U.S.

In the mid-'60s when the U.S. domestic counterinsurgency program to crush our movement was formalized within the Federal Bureau of Investigation as COINTELPRO, it clearly identified those who rejected pacifism and demanded liberation and independence as "black nationalist hate groups" to be discredited and neutralized.

Attacking the pro-independence sector of our movement was not only designed to remove us as political agents within the U.S., it was also designed to elevate the stature of pacifists, assimilationists and liberals of every stripe and nationality, including many who characterized themselves as communists.

Our Party understood and identified the war being waged against our people and movement as counterinsurgency, an imperialist, military-based counterrevolutionary response to a national liberation struggle utilizing every conceivable method of suppression—economic, psychological and political.

We studied, understood and explained the science of counterinsurgency—its motives, its goals and objectives and its main strategy of resource and population control. We saw it employed in every aspect of our lives as colonized African subjects. We showed how the protected villages and strategic hamlets used by the British in Africa and Asia and by the U.S. in Viet Nam were brought to the housing projects of the U.S.

Drugs—first heroin from Southeast Asia where the U.S. was fighting to keep the people of Viet Nam, Cambodia and the so-called "Golden Triangle" under imperialist domination, and then cocaine from South America, where the U.S. was waging a brutal and bloody counterinsurgency against the Sandinistas of Nicaragua and other revolutionary projects— were used by the U.S. as a counterinsurgency tool against the African Revolution in the U.S.

At a time when other African "liberation" organizations had succumbed and joined the imperialist counterinsurgent attack on the African working class, our Party exposed the fact that Africans are not fighting a drug problem, but a drug *economy*. This is used to keep a faltering U.S. economy afloat, push African people out of revolutionary political life and validate a counterinsurgent war-without-terms on an oppressed and colonized community, now successfully demonized as pathological, drug-crazed and criminal.

Our Party showed that the U.S. government was the real drug pusher that denied Africans the right to employment in the legal capitalist economy. Drugs have been a method of maneuvering us to economic dependency on the illegal capitalist drug economy, thus justifying the violent police presence and mass imprisonment in our communities.

"The White House is the Rock House and Uncle Sam is the Pusher Man," became the Party mantra chanted at countless demonstrations and pickets during the Oakland years. This understanding was immediately embraced by the African masses throughout the U.S. One Party-influenced militant rap group that at various times was a part of our movement launched a successful album that revolved around the U.S. drug-imposed counterinsurgency and which sampled from my presentations on two tracks.

The drug-war front of the counterinsurgency resulted in displaced and destabilized families and communities, thousands of violent deaths and millions of mostly-young Africans shuttled into a burgeoning colonial prison system that also brought revitalized economic life to dying, rural white communities.

The fact that we continued struggling against U.S. domestic colonialism after our movement had been crushed by the counterinsurgency meant that we were obliged to solve many of the problems of the revolution as they revealed themselves in the real world.

This is how we came to recognize that colonialism pure and simple—the ubiquitous presence and authority of the "white man"—shifted its essential form to white power in black face in the U.S., just as it has done in Africa and other areas of the world.

InPDUM founded to defeat counterinsurgency

The impact of the counterinsurgency against our movement and our people led us to build the People's Democratic Uhuru Movement in 1989 in Oakland.

By 1991 we transformed PDUM into the National People's Democratic Uhuru Movement and, ultimately, it became the International People's Democratic Uhuru Movement, our primary mass organization today. The founding convention of InPDUM was held in Chicago on April 6, the 23rd anniversary of the U.S. government's assassination of 17-year-old Black Panther Party member Bobby Hutton in Oakland in 1968. Chicago was the city where 21-year-old Black Panther Party leader Fred Hampton was murdered in his bed on December 4, 1969.

InPDUM was built to win the African masses back into political life and to expose and defeat the counterinsurgency. From its inception InPDUM has led critical struggles pushing back the various attacks on our community on the political, economic, social and cultural fronts.

At the Fifth Annual InPDUM Convention held in St. Petersburg on December 6-8, 1996, I stated in my keynote presentation:

> *The significance of the National People's Democratic Uhuru Movement has already proved itself in the world. It is significant because it is a mass organization built subsequent to the defeat of the Black Revolution of the Sixties when the U.S. government had determined that African working*

and poor people would never ever have another organization or another chance to win our total freedom from U.S. imperialism....

Throughout the country the National People's Democratic Uhuru Movement has been responsible for raising the question of the counterinsurgency against African people and the struggle for our democratic rights. This is the fundamental question of our times: the question of a counterinsurgency, a war initiated against our community....

That is what the National People's Democratic Uhuru Movement is about: turning things around, defeating the counterinsurgency, drawing the masses of poor and oppressed African people into political life.

NPDUM became InPDUM—the International People's Democratic Uhuru Movement—at the annual convention in 2000 after African people in England and other parts of the world joined the organization.

In cities as distant and diverse from one another as Freetown, Sierra Leone, West Africa; Stockholm, Sweden; London, England; Washington, DC, and Oakland in the U.S., InPDUM has taken on such issues as police terror, political prisoners, educational reform, inadequate housing, mass imprisonment and the prison economy.

Today InPDUM has shed its defensive character and developed a Revolutionary National Democratic Program. The changing conditions in the world, the rising motion of the masses demanding return of resources and liberty from a disabled imperialism along with the consistent work of our Party, have all contributed to a strategic difference in how InPDUM must move.

Today InPDUM is leading mass work and campaigns with the intent to raise up revolutionary national democratic forces within our colonized community to power. It has assumed an offensive, as opposed to a defensive, posture.

Party wins dual power in St. Petersburg

The Party's leadership of the masses and the heroic role of InPDUM reached a critical stage when on October 24, 1996, the St. Petersburg, Florida police department shot down an 18-year-old African, TyRon Lewis, in broad daylight in front of scores of witnesses in the African community.

The police murder, which took place three blocks from the Uhuru House, the National Office of our Party, resulted in a fierce response from the African community. Rebelling masses torched police cars and corporate news vehicles. Liquor stores and other white-owned businesses notorious for their unfair extraction of capital from an impoverished community were also targeted.

The police and media used the ubiquitous presence of our Party as a public rationale for blaming us for the uprising. This was especially because Party members were correctly carrying out our responsibility to provide on-the-spot political education to the masses that explained the role of the police as the occupying army of a colonial state. This gave the people's uprising a political character that unnerved the police and the bourgeoisie, both locally and within the federal government.

Occasional spontaneous mass uprisings, although annoying, are generally something the bourgeois colonial state can handle. Sometimes these uprisings are actually helpful to the bourgeoisie as justification for greater repression against revolutionary movements.

Uprisings with political consciousness are different, however. It is political consciousness that generally distinguishes spontaneous uprisings from rebellions that are precursors to revolution. This was clearly a mass uprising with political consciousness.

The bourgeoisie began an intense media campaign that targeted our Party for repression. Police harassment directed at our movement became endemic. Organizers were arrested for selling our newspaper and for distributing political leaflets and pamphlets to the people.

In a futile attempt to prevent our communication with the masses of our people, archaic laws were resurrected and new laws created to abrogate constitutionally guaranteed freedoms of assembly and expression.

On November 13, 1996, three weeks after the police murder of Lewis, hundreds of various military forces associated with the state and city along with an assortment of neighboring police organizations assaulted an InPDUM community meeting at our headquarters.

In an attempt to silence our movement from exposing the grand jury report exonerating the police for the murder of TyRon Lewis, the city attacked the Uhuru House during a pre-planned meeting, unleashing all the tear gas in the city's arsenal on a roomful of about 100 women, men and children. Armed police surrounded the building with murderous intent.

Several people, including some of our leading Party members, were trapped in the tear gas-filled building. Tear gas canisters were purposely shot in the trees in the back of our center, setting several trees afire. The police also attempted to burn the building by shooting the incendiary tear gas canisters onto the roof.

Hundreds of Africans from throughout the community leapt into battle with the militarized police in defense of our building and entrapped leaders. When the police deployed a helicopter over the building, the people, conscious of the same police tactic used against the MOVE organization in Philadelphia in 1985, resorted to an armed response, bringing the helicopter down by gunfire.

The intensity of the politically-informed resistance alarmed the federal government. As a result U.S. president William Jefferson Clinton sent a cabinet member to the city in an attempt to resolve the situation before it became a generalized model for mass uprising throughout the colonized communities of the U.S.

As this resistance unfolded, the Party joined the broad-based African American Leadership Coalition made up of sectors of the African petty bourgeoisie who saw our Party as the clear leadership of the masses of African workers in this struggle.

This was an important development. Even though their motivation was influenced by their prospects for acquiring federal funds to appease the resistance, the coalition acted as a wall of petty bourgeois, national democratic, black "respectability" surrounding our Party and movement that made it difficult for the state to effectively employ a military solution against us with impunity.

The coalition also became a part of the method through which the Party locked the colonial state in political struggle. Through the coalition we defined this struggle as a contest between a pessimistic public policy of police containment of our people versus an optimistic public policy of economic development for a population suffering economic quarantine by the government and capitalist financial institutions.

The Party also organized constant mass mobilizations to push the colonial state back and to bring greater organization and political consciousness to our people, enhancing the relative position of power occupied by our Party and the revolutionary democratic movement we had organized.

The Party exposed the limitations of the state and ruling class and galvanized the African working class and democratic sectors of the African community. Through its media and political mouthpieces the bourgeoisie had claimed the African working class was an inarticulate, uneducated mass without consciousness of its interests and aims. These same forces also claimed that our Party and movement did not represent the masses of African people.

However, with our movement's political demands that the Party forced everyone to recognize as the voice of the working class, it became clear that the masses were very articulate and quite capable of spelling out our interests and aims.

Through the mass mobilizations and the people's armed defense of our movement and its leaders, the world came to recognize that not only did we represent the people, but that the masses were willing to defend us from attacks by the most powerful military force available to the colonial state.

In the following weeks and months and, indeed, for several subsequent years, the Uhuru Movement created a situation of dual power in the city, where there was an actual balance of power between the bourgeois colonial state and the Party and Uhuru Movement.

It was in the wake of the enhanced political consciousness, mass organization and influence of our Party and movement that the city of St. Petersburg hired its first African police chief in an attempt to employ a neocolonial solution of white power in black face.

Our movement's influence and enhanced political position was clear as the chief of police immediately united with our demands for replacement of the public policy of police containment with a public policy of economic development for our occupied and exploited community.

To the consternation of the colonial police department and much of the white population and city council, the African police chief also initiated radical reform in the police department, firing many of the notorious initiators of violence against our community and disciplining all police who were disrespectful to our people.

The *St. Petersburg Times* wrote during this period that the police chief called for the Party's Uhuru House to be treated as an embassy with no arrests being permitted for anyone taking harbor inside the building.

Situations of dual power are never permanent. They are fleeting and temporary. We were not able to win all power to the people and consequently the state has been able to reassert its general authority over our colonized community with a vengeance.

However, because of the leadership of our Party the power of the colonial state has been forever compromised and its limitations permanently etched into the consciousness of the people. We were so effective that it was eight years after the 1996 murder of TyRon Lewis before the police killed another African in the city.

The example of the Party-led St. Petersburg resistance is extremely important. The resultant impact of our Party's character and identity, forged in this period, is profound. We were able to affect every form of struggle, from mass mobilization to armed struggle. We even used the electoral process, running me for mayor in 2001 and Chimurenga Waller for city council and the school board during this period.

This is who we are or, in the vernacular of the young people of the community, "this is how we roll."

These are just some of the work and campaigns that exemplify the organizational, political and ideological work that helped to forge the DNA of our Party over the 41 years since our founding.

The struggle against neocolonialism

Throughout our years of organizing on the ground, our Party has been able to advance the understanding of neocolonialism, giving it a class character and identifying the African petty bourgeoisie as the social base from which it springs.

Throughout the world when the movements for liberation grew to an extent that masses rose up with the blood-curdling cry of "kill the white man" it became no longer tenable for white power to exercise its rule directly.

Indirect rule, neocolonialism, white power in black face became necessary. The mass struggles for liberation necessitated an obvious transfer of political power from the white colonizer to the black colonized. This serves to obscure the fact that the white colonizer continues to dominate the colonized through control of the economy and hence control of the politics of the colonized.

Neocolonialism is the concept developed by Kwame Nkrumah to define the new face of colonialism. Nkrumah taught how the continued control of African economies allowed for indirect rule by the same powers. However, it was our Party that defined African *neocolonialists* according to their *class* character. It was we who recognized the role of class in the implementation of neocolonial rule. This had not been previously understood.

We saw how the Kenya model used by the British against the anti-colonial struggle in East Africa was being carried out in the U.S. In Kenya the legitimate revolutionaries were wiped out by the British through horrendous and bloody mass torture, mass imprisonment and unspeakable, near-genocidal mass murder. The British colonizers then promoted the idea that a pliant, neocolonial surrogate was the "legitimate revolutionary" to whom they transferred the appearance of political power.

In the U.S. this is done mostly through elections. Real black power had been advocated by Malcolm X, the Student Nonviolent Coordinating Committee, JOMO, the Black Panther Party and a host of others, including militant assimilationists like Dr. Martin Luther King, Jr. After many Africans embraced the idea that political power could be won through the ballot box, however, many opponents of black power were raised up by the white ruling class as representatives of black power. They were helped into political office after the revolutionaries were murdered and revolutionary organizations crushed by counterinsurgency.

On the rare occasions that representatives of the legitimate aspirations of our people were elected to office, the counterinsurgency worked with skilled, brutal efficiency to undermine them, often initiating electoral "regime change" to replace them with adherents of capitalism, colonialism and patriots of the white nationalist state.

Various loyalty tests were devised to determine the trustworthiness of African candidates for office. If they refused to denounce certain designated African leaders, they invited the wrath of the white ruling class, media demonization and diversion of campaign monies to more amenable candidates.

The electoral process became the primary method of priming and vetting neocolonial leaders though other methods were used as well. Various leaders of mass organizations functioned as neocolonial surrogates, including the obvious example of Jesse Jackson who became U.S. president William Jefferson Clinton's Africa representative. A similar role is played currently by Al Sharpton as water carrier for Barack Hussein Obama, in his latest display of neocolonial fealty to imperial white power.

Building the African Socialist International

The African Liberation Movement, in Africa and abroad, has run into its limitations when fought within the imperialist-defined borders. Civil rights were given and taken back with little afterthought in the U.S. and "flag independence" in one neocolonial enclave after the other has only served to obscure the imperialist origin of our continued misery.

Africans around the world experienced the brutal defeat of our movement on different continents by a united imperialism that had no regards for borders. We understood that the inherent strength of a revolutionary anti-colonial movement based in several continents could only be realized if it were a movement conscious of its connection and its historical mission.

Our Party from its inception rejected the notion of Africa and African people as permanent charity cases, locked in poverty and despair by a fate reserved for black people.

In the 1960s, the Soviet Union, presumed by many to be the leader of the international struggle against imperialism, declared that the six organizational recipients of its anti-colonial support on the Continent were the only legitimate revolutionary forces in all of Africa. As we discussed earlier in this book, they were referred to by the Soviets as the "Authentic Six."

These six organizations received resources and organizational, military, political and ideological training from the Soviet Union in our struggle to overthrow white colonial rule. A condition for becoming one of the authentic designees was having the "correct" political line and meeting the needs of Soviet foreign policy objectives.

We recognized that Africa must be able to define its own interests without concern for meeting the objectives of some non-African force, whether Soviet socialists or U.S.-supported European capitalist-colonialists. Hence in 1981 at our First Congress, we passed a resolution calling for the creation of the African Socialist International (ASI).

The ASI put the struggle of our people and our homeland squarely in the hands of Africans ourselves and, more explicitly, in the hands of the most revolutionary sector of the African nation, the African working class aligned with the poor peasantry. Only the ASI can transform our individual poverty and powerlessness into our collective wealth and strength.

Our First Congress resolution to found the African Socialist International called for:

• Liberating and uniting all of Africa under a single, all-African socialist state;

• Uniting, coordinating, and giving general assistance and direction for the revolutionary struggles of all African people wherever they occur and whenever the aims of such struggles are consistent with the aims of the international socialist association;

• Achieving the objective consolidation of African nationality for all African people wherever we are oppressed and exploited throughout the world due to the machinations of imperialism.

Point 14 of the Party's Working Platform that quotes Kwame Nkrumah offers an explanation of the Party's approach to building the African Socialist International:

> *We want the total liberation and unification of Africa under an all-African socialist government.*
>
> *We believe that "the total liberation and unification of Africa under an all-African socialist government must be the primary objective of all black revolutionaries throughout the world. It is an objective, which when achieved, will bring about the fulfillment of the aspirations of Africans and people of African descent everywhere. It will at the same time advance the triumph of the international socialist revolution, and the onward progress toward communism, under which every society is ordered on the principle of—from each according to his (her) ability, to each according to his (her) needs."*

The Political Report to the Party's Fifth Congress published as *One People! One Party! One Destiny!* further states,

> *The African Socialist International, the practical expression of African Internationalism, uniting African workers on every continent, provides Africans and the world with the first step in the creation of a real Communist International that for the first time encompasses the enlightened participation of the vast majority of the toiling masses of the world.*
>
> *Workers of the world, unite under the banner of African Internationalism!*

From our First Congress in 1981 the strategic direction of our Party revolved around building the ASI. A considerable portion of all our resources went to this project. Much of this work within the U.S. revolved around attempts to win the Zimbabwe African National Union (ZANU) and the Pan Africanist Congress of Azania (PAC) through engaging their expatriate militant organizers and, in the case of the PAC, through occasional meetings with its primary leaders.

We also worked to establish a relationship with Grenada under the leadership of the New Jewel Movement and sent an organizer to meet with Thomas Sankara, leader of Burkina Faso before his assassination. It was our hope to win unity with the ASI project and launch a founding ASI Congress in either Grenada or Burkina Faso. The fate of both these revolutionary projects was further proof of the urgency of our task to build the ASI.

The first meeting to build the ASI occurred in Brooklyn, New York, the day after the first World Tribunal on Reparations for African People and the founding of ANRO in 1982. From that time onward much of the energy of the Party was directed at building the ASI.

It became our strategic mission to win the recognition that regardless of what we did in the U.S. against our oppression, we would never win our liberation until we created the African Socialist International that organically connects the struggle of Africans in the U.S. with those of Africans worldwide and especially in Africa, our national homeland.

Our ASI work quickly extended to regular organizing trips to Europe, especially London, where many Africans from throughout European colonies were living or were in transit for any number of reasons.

A general resistance from many organized Africans to *revolutionary* organization and ideology complicated our initial work in London. This was especially true of Africans who were not born on the continent of Africa and preferred to identify themselves as "black" with a strategic mission to create what they characterized as "black and Asian" unity. Although some of them considered themselves "Pan-Africanists," they saw their function as expressing "solidarity" with the people and struggle on the African continent, not as an integral part of the same struggle or the same nation.

Nevertheless, after many years of work, we were able to organize a base in London through Comrade Luwezi Kinshasa, a member of an organization we had been attempting to unite with the ASI for years prior to Kinshasa's arrival in London.

Comrade Luwezi's entry into the Party allowed us to change the general strategy for building the ASI. Instead of an effort to locate and win existing groups to the ASI, our strategy now shifted to building the Party in England and wherever else possible as the primary method of organizing ASI component organizations.

With the consistent work that has been done over the years in England and Europe and with major ASI conferences being regularly conducted in London, the ASI was also able to extend its reach to various regions of Africa. The London ASI conferences attracted forces from West Africa, allowing us to establish a base in that region, and from South Africa where we re-established contact with the Pan Africanist Congress of Azania that eventually proved unfruitful.

We have also reached into South America and The Bahamas and are now a growing factor in defining and leading the struggle of our liberation throughout the world. To use a phrase of the 1970s, popularized by ZANU, "We are our own liberators!"

Black is Back Coalition challenges Obama

On September 12, 2009, the Party played a major role in pulling together the Black is Back Coalition for Social Justice, Peace and Reparations (BIBC). This is a diverse group of anti-imperialist Africans that opposes U.S. imperialism throughout the world and within the U.S. itself.

The founding of the Coalition is important for a number of reasons, but none more so than the successful mobilization of this broad group of Africans who, in most cases, had no prior history of working together and who were unlikely to ever do so without the intervention of the Party in initiating the Coalition's founding.

The Coalition involves the participation of different groups and personalities without threatening their independence, while allowing them to magnify their individual significance many times over through their participation.

The Party also benefits from the existence of the Coalition. We are unlike most of the Coalition partners who are motivated by single issues or general outrage against imperialism of the Obama regime, but have no general revolutionary worldview tied to an organizational strategy to defeat imperialism.

Participation in the Coalition gives the Party the ability to advance an anti-imperialist agenda to forge a Revolutionary National Democratic Program in pursuit of black power.

Through participation in the Coalition, the Party is also able to extend our general reach beyond the limits of the Party's membership and direct organizational capacity.

The existence of the Coalition and our Party's participation in it provides us with a greater capacity to pursue the Party's positions around questions of war and peace. While many in the Coalition are offended by and mobilized around some specific imperialist offense, the Party's participation affords us an opportunity to deepen the understanding of the Coalition participants through providing African Internationalist analyses. This is necessary work for building *revolutionary* consciousness within the Coalition and, through the Coalition, among the masses.

Mostly comprised of advocates of African self-determination, BIBC includes individuals who are motivated by different ideological and political beliefs, but who were disturbed by and opposed to the ongoing wars in the Middle East and other wars not being addressed by the traditional white, antiwar or peace movement.

This contradiction was spoken to in the proposal I presented to the Coalition to organize the successful, groundbreaking National Conference on the Other Wars that occurred on March 26, 2011, in Washington, DC.

> *The Coalition's interest in this political intervention in the peace movement is based, in part, on our unwillingness to allow the white Left to monopolize the definition of what the struggle for peace is about. Our Coalition is opposed to an imperialist peace, one that does not disturb the relations of power between the oppressed and the war-mongering imperialist oppressor.*
>
> *It is this historical defect of the U.S. Left that prevents it from giving genuine practical and material solidarity to the national liberation*

struggles of Africans and other peoples within the U.S. Indeed, the U.S. white Left has been generally incapable of supporting any struggles anywhere that did not benefit the leftists organizationally and/or politically or that did not revolve around issues that appear to present an immediate or future challenge to their material interests as U.S. North Americans.

Thus, millions of Africans have been dying in the Congo, most recently since 1998, with little or no alarm by the white Left. Similarly, the bloody U.S.-induced deadly mayhem in Somalia, Sudan, Ivory Coast and other places in Africa receives no attention by the white Left in the U.S., and Haiti is dealt with essentially because of the current crisis related to the earthquake and characterized primarily as responsive to "natural disasters."

Nor are Africans the only ones who are marginalized by the U.S. white Left agenda. The same is true of Mexicans suffering U.S. settler colonialism within the U.S. Immigration raids and special police concentrated in border areas that separate the Mexican people from each other and their occupied lands, along with imposed poverty, a host of social contradictions and massive incarceration are the norm for this oppressed people.

The Native people...like the Mexicans, another Indigenous people...suffer the consequences of settler colonialism. Even now, these survivors of a U.S. policy of genocide as despicable as that of Hitler, the imperialist bogeyman used to deflect genuine criticism of imperialism, are living in horrible conditions in concentration camps euphemistically referred to as "reservations."

Additionally many of the founding members of the Coalition were motivated by the fact that Barack Hussein Obama's presidency was for the first time ever giving a black face to U.S. imperialism. Because of this some felt a special responsibility to show African opposition to this African imperialist stooge, especially in the face of the overwhelming public support shown to Obama by the masses of Africans in the U.S. and throughout the world.

Some felt we had to demonstrate permission to the world's peoples, oppressed and threatened by U.S. imperialism but sympathetic to the struggle of Africans within the U.S., to fight back against the U.S. imperialism of Obama just as vigorously as against the imperialism of Bush and others.

Since its founding, the BIBC has helped to change the face and character of the antiwar movement within the U.S. and has, with help from our Party, extended its organizational reach and influence to the Caribbean and Europe.

On November 7, 2009, the Coalition held the first national demonstration at the White House against the war-mongering regime of Barack Hussein Obama. It was the only African-led demonstration against the U.S. government since Obama's installation as the public face of U.S. imperialism.

In January of 2010 the Coalition held a consolidation conference that laid out its general direction and in February launched a national mobilization in Miami in support of our people in Haiti following the devastating earthquake there. The mobilization, with much participation from the expatriate Haitian community, demanded reparations from the U.S. and France to Haiti for the centuries of ruthless exploitation and the return of Jean-Bertrand Aristide who, with French participation, had been forcibly deposed as president and exiled by the U.S.

The National Conference on the Other Wars, held March 26, 2011, in Washington, DC, was well-attended and posed a fundamental challenge to the traditional white-led antiwar or peace movement. It was an attack on the tendency of the U.S. Left's tradition of allowing the ruling class to define which were valid wars that demanded attention.

Because the U.S. and other imperialist powers were publicly identifying Iraq and Afghanistan as the theaters of war and there was some chance, even if remote, that white young people might have to fight those wars, the white Left was able to oppose those wars. However, the more distant the likelihood of the wars affecting the security of the general white population or the less attention given to the issues by the imperialists themselves, the less significant were the wars to the Left.

This means that the "Other" wars, those being made daily against the internal colonies of the U.S., against the Africans, Mexicans and the Indigenous people, got no attention. There was no civil disobedience at the barrio or "ghetto" police precincts to prevent the daily military mobilizations against our colonized communities. There were no white Left peace protests against the immigration police created for the purpose of colonial containment of the Mexican population on both sides of the illegitimate Mexican border.

The Romani victims of political repression and state murder throughout Europe, the ongoing attacks, including murder of Africans and Arabs from the Netherlands, Germany and Sweden to France, Portugal and Greece, do not make the agenda of the white antiwar or peace movement. These are among the "Other" wars that the Coalition is determined to put on the political agenda as issues that would test the credentials of any movement claiming opposition to war.

One of the resolutions stemming from the National Conference on the Other Wars called for an August International Day of Action Against the Wars on Africa and African people. This resulted in demonstrations of varying sizes and significance throughout Europe, the U.S. and in The Bahamas.

Another highlight of the Coalition's work was the Black is Back August 18-19, 2012 Annual Conference that was held in Newark, New Jersey. Anticipating the upcoming U.S. presidential election and focusing on electoral politics and its possibilities and limitations under imperialism, the title of the conference was, "Obama, the Election and the Struggle for Black Power."

The conference occurred with a full house that included legendary notables from the Black Revolution of the Sixties and a representative from Unión del Barrio, a Mexican national liberation organization, long-time ally of the Party, based primarily in Southern California, whose strong campaign for city council was backed by the Coalition. The Coalition also endorsed the successful candidacy of Chokwe Lumumba for mayor of Jackson, Mississippi.

In January 2013 the Coalition joined with InPDUM in waging a serious successful struggle to free a newborn African child from a Pennsylvania hospital. The child was born to a mother who, because of sickle cell anemia, was prescribed morphine for pain. Upon birth, without any testing and despite the fact that the mother saw no physical need for the treatment, the hospital, against the will of the child's parents and relatives, forced a regime of morphine injection upon the baby.

The Coalition, under the leadership of its Health Working Group, mounted a spirited defense of the child and family, including demonstrations at the hospital and other means of publicizing the kidnapping of and chemical warfare against the child, resulting in a speedy retreat by the hospital and freedom for the baby.

In 2013 the National BIB Conference took place in Harlem, New York. It was preceded by a small rally and enthusiastic march through the streets of Harlem, down the iconic 125th Street. Characterized as a Weekend of African Resistance the conference occurred under the long and informative slogan of "From Trayvon Martin to Stop and Frisk—From COINTELPRO to Black Misleadership, Resist the U.S. War on African People."

The conference featured profound analysis concerning the nature of the imperialist state and revealing testimony from African victims of the colonial police terror with which Africans are confronted daily. Also significant was the decision to give the Coalition a more dynamic and sustainable life by concentrating on building its capacity through the Coalition Working Groups.

This will mean more authority and leadership will automatically be transferred to the various committees that are responsible for its political activities. One of the outstanding committees of the Coalition is the Health Working Group, a team that always attempts to take the initiative around issues involving its mandate. This helps to keep the Coalition in motion between conferences and specially called meetings to deal with urgent questions. All the existing Working Groups are now the basis of building the Coalition.

In many ways the Coalition is one of the most important developments by our U.S.-based struggle for self-determination since the 1960s. It is a coalition that has won many people to political life, providing their first real involvement in the movement. Some of these people have even come into our Party.

The Black is Back Coalition has also challenged the sectarianism that has impacted our movement for decades, since the defeat of the Black Revolution of the Sixties. It has provided the ability of individuals and groups with ideological and political differences to overcome an inability to work together against U.S. imperialism in a common formation.

Many of the people who participate in the Coalition were genuine anti-imperialists before the creation of the Coalition. However, generally speaking they were working in isolation from each other and denied the advantage of collective genius and action.

It was the Party that was capable of pulling us all together, something that is further testimony of the significance of being in place with organization, experience and enough political maturity to advance a genuine revolutionary national democratic program that speaks to the diverse revolutionary national democratic interests within our colonized community.

The Burning Spear chronicles our movement

Throughout the years, *The Burning Spear* newspaper has played a key role in expressing the unity of the Party's theory and practice.

After the influential newspapers of the Black Panther Party and Nation of Islam had been effectively neutralized, *The Burning Spear* continued to project the ever-developing aims of our movement, not as eulogizer of the fallen or the past, but as the primary advocate of the basic ideals that the U.S. counterinsurgency was designed to silence.

The Burning Spear pre-dated the African People's Socialist Party by several years, having been founded as the political organ of JOMO. *The Spear* served to keep the masses connected to the ideals and surviving organizations of the pro-independence movement.

Through *The Spear* we have been able to fortify the morale of our people who were suffering the vicious counterinsurgency defeat with its political assassinations, mass police roundups of militants and imprisonment of some of our leaders, including this writer.

The tireless on-the-ground campaigns of the Party: freeing political prisoners, exposing police violence, denouncing the countless attacks on the African working class around the U.S. and the world are chronicled in the pages of *The Spear*. Our Party's journal has always been a lively forum for discussion and struggle on political and practical questions facing the African working class from all walks of life.

The Burning Spear reports on the victories of the people of Viet Nam and the ongoing struggles throughout the Americas. We exposed our people here to the struggle in Zimbabwe and its connection to the movement within the U.S.

The New Jewel Movement of Grenada, the resistance of the people to the U.S.-imposed dictatorship of the Shah of Iran, and other issues impacting oppressed peoples around the world were all kept before Africans in the U.S. and other areas of the world where our newspaper was distributed. We covered the continuing battles of the besieged leaders of the Black Panther Party and the Provisional Government of the Republic of New Afrika as well as those we were involved in ourselves.

The Burning Spear was the primary organ used to convey to the world the ideological developments of our Party that pushed our struggle forward, moving it beyond the stagnation imposed on it by the repression that resulted in many who survived the assassinations and imprisonment, being forced into exile or into often inactive underground existence.

Today, *The Burning Spear* newspaper and its online version, Uhuru News, continue as a unique, vital international forum engaging and informing African workers and our allies everywhere.

Expression of people's will to struggle

As a revolutionary Party we have the responsibility to lead around every question. In the pamphlet, "Build and Consolidate the African People's Socialist Party," published in 1984, we were very clear about what it means to be a revolutionary African Internationalist Party:

Today the Party has come to terms with the fact that not only must we not be apologetic for leading, it is our absolute responsibility to lead.

The Party must help the mass organizations, the community organizations, prison collectives and campus groups to work out the correct political line and to properly direct their activities toward political independence, African liberation and socialism.

This is the Party's task because all the Party's work prepares it best for this responsibility, and because the Party is the most perfected and highest form of black working class organization and the highest expression of the people's will to struggle.

Within the ranks of the Party are the most advanced, most conscious representatives of the colonized African population, the black working class and the toiling masses, the representatives upon whose shoulders rest the ultimate responsibility for raising up the revolutionary scientifically-guided consciousness of the black working class.

It is clear that the liberation of our people and the emancipation of our class cannot be won by just any kind of organization. It is even clearer that many existing organizations have absolutely no interests in making revolution and that even some of the radical nationalist organizations are only willing to go just so far.

However, the role of political leader can only be fulfilled by the Party as the highest form of organization for national liberation and the emancipation of the black working class....

Political leadership is a science and an art. It is not something that one does automatically. It requires skill and the capacity to quickly choose and change forms of struggle.

V.I. Lenin, the successful Russian revolutionary, correctly, declared:

"We are the Party of a class, and therefore almost the entire class should act under the leadership of our Party..."

However, with the victory of the struggle for democratic rights, which came as a concession to the black petty bourgeoisie and at the expense of the Black Revolution of the Sixties, the black petty bourgeoisie realized its fundamental political aim and lost any historically derived progressive character it once had.

Thus the mantle of leadership—both for the struggle for national liberation and socialism—has fallen upon the shoulders of the most despised and feared black working class.

Therefore, as the advanced detachment of the black working class, the African People's Socialist Party assumes the leadership not only for "almost the entire class," but also for "almost the entire people."

Therefore, we resist any efforts to reduce the activity of the Party to that of a passive recorder of spontaneously developing events in the manner of some so-called "revolutionary" organizations whose theory or program does not require intervention in the practical struggles of life.

Our entire mission and the basis of our existence are to become actively involved in life. Our task is to mold the consciousness of the working class and

*all the toiling masses and to permanently lead the
revolutionary struggle of the masses for political
independence, African liberation and socialism.*

Self-determination institutions distinguish the Party

Leading the struggle of the entire people places the
responsibility for the liberation of the dispersed African nation
on the shoulders of the African working class through its
fighting, revolutionary class organization, the African People's
Socialist Party. Concretely this means that the Party leads the
struggle for national self-determination.

Over the years the Party has created numerous institutions
and organizations that function to create reserve forces for the
Party and the revolution. Some forces may have revolutionary
inclinations but are not yet ready for admission to the Party.
Many of these people will come under the leadership of our
Party through InPDUM, the mass organization created for
that purpose.

In addition to InPDUM, the Party has created a number
of other organizations that act as avenues into the general
ranks of our movement. These include civic-like organizations
with specific missions that appeal to revolutionary national
democratic interests such as education, health, and
general community improvement and self-reliance. These
organizations operate within the U.S. and, like InPDUM, in
various places around the world.

It is important here to mention the role of the All African
People's Development and Empowerment Project (AAPDEP).
This formation was organized by the Party to build important
development work within our impoverished communities in
the African world. A critical significance of AAPDEP is its
capacity for Africans throughout the world to cooperate in our
own development. This is what we mean when we say that

African Internationalism is a theory of action, a theory with a plan.

This work is currently led by Comrade Aisha Fields who has steered the organization into campaigns that are mobilizing African people into development work that contributes to self-determination. This is especially true in Sierra Leone where AAPDEP has acquired hundreds of members and initiated institutions and programs that affect the lives of thousands of Africans.

In an initial period of eight months and under incredibly difficult conditions AAPDEP established clinics, schools, subsistence farming and a boat-making project, among other things. All this has been enthusiastically accomplished through the unity and initiative of ordinary African workers that literally have to struggle for bare necessities of survival.

We are all familiar with the conditions in Sierra Leone, a neocolonial state with one of the highest infant and maternal death rates in the world, and where diamond mines are daily looted by international corporations, some of which are also rapidly purchasing beach land to create luxury retreats for rich tourists that consume more in a day than the average African will in his or her lifetime.

Africans from various parts of the world have participated in collective work in Sierra Leone under the leadership of AAPDEP. This has included work to create a rainwater harvesting program in one community where clean water was inaccessible, as well as training in health care services and resources to improve facilities at our infant and maternal wellness clinic there.

This work to unite Africa and Africans is clearly more important than all the combined empty Pan-Africanist conference resolutions giving abstract recognition to African unity.

We have always had a dynamic Party, which when at its best, fights for and maintains close connections with the masses of our people. Mass organizations are our most important tools for maintaining this relationship with our people. In our pamphlet, "Build and Consolidate the African People's Socialist Party," cited earlier, this point is clearly made:

The mass organizations are the transmission belts from the Party to the people. Work in these organizations and winning them over to the side of the Party is one of the first duties of an African Internationalist.

The Party is the leader and teacher of mass organizations of the oppressed and colonized working people. The Party elaborates the correct political line, defines the tasks and direction of the political work and strengthens the mass organizations with leading personnel.

The African People's Socialist Party has also had to assume the responsibility of building mass organizations for the people subsequent to the defeat of the Black Revolution of the Sixties, a defeat that was also experienced as the destruction of many of the genuine mass organizations founded to address the material contradictions of U.S. domestic colonialism....

Hence, it has been the responsibility of the Party to build mass organizations which can address the needs of the people....

The basic methods of Party leadership in the mass organizations are persuasion, education, ideological influence and the development of the initiative of the organizations in every way.

The line of the Party in the mass organizations comes as a result of the African Internationalists who work in them.

Each African Internationalist is also expected to conduct work among the masses.

The fact is that everyone can win others to African Internationalism if the agitator or propagandist can approach her/him in such a way to transmit African Internationalist ideas.

If an organizer, a Party cadre, an agitator, speaks in a language he or she can understand and makes use of facts of ordinary life which are known to the colonized African being addressed, that African can be won to African Internationalism.

There is so much more that we can and must say about our Party and its history. We shudder to imagine the state of the beleaguered and oppressed African working class if it were not for our Party summing up the war waged against it and always advancing struggle that points the way forward to the future of a united and liberated Africa and African people. There is a book that must be written, a chronicle that must be recorded of the magnificent journey of the African People's Socialist Party that started out as a handful of comrades and that now influences the world.

VI. The One People! One Party! One Destiny! Campaign

We did not come to our Sixth Congress to rest on our laurels. As powerful as our history is, our Party's significance will be determined in the long run by what we do now at this historically critical moment. Our four decades of history is only important if it functions as the springboard to the future.

The purpose of our Fifth Party Congress, held in 2010 in Washington, DC, was to position us on this springboard. It was a Congress that would challenge many of the old ways of doing things in order to prepare us to seize the time during the crisis of imperialism.

In the three plus years between our Fifth Congress and this one, the Party has been dedicated to carrying out the mandates of that Congress even as we have continued to intervene in the most critical issues confronting our people and struggle as they have emerged.

In February of 2012, the Party conducted our National Plenary in St. Petersburg under the title: "On the 40th Anniversary of the Founding of Our Glorious Party, Raise High the Banner of African Internationalism and Build the Revolutionary Party of the African Working Class."

The Political Report to that Plenary is instructive for its determination to win our Party to a greater capacity to carry out our revolutionary responsibilities to our people and to the oppressed peoples of the world.

Reflected in the document is recognition of the need to concentrate on the organizational nuts and bolts necessary to construct in our Party a real capacity to lead our people to victory over imperialism at this time when history is summoning imperialism's gravediggers to the forefront.

The National Plenary Political Report challenged our ways of doing things in the recent past and placed organizational development and everything needed for its achievement at the vanguard of our efforts.

In that Political Report we put our current organizational situation in perspective:

> *On November 1, 2010, barely four months after the Fifth Congress, I was waging struggle with the leadership of our Party to carry out our Congress mandate. In a paper entitled, "Abandon organizational disarray and unite to build organizational efficiency and accountability," the following struggle was initiated within the Party's National Central Committee:*
>
> *"The internal resistance to organizational cultural transformation can be seen in part by the difficulties to institutionalize our offices and provide Plans of Action for the leading, strategic, components of our work....*
>
> *"The struggle being led by the Office of the Chairman is to prevent the abortion of this new organizational culture....*
>
> *"We have a number of campaigns, resolutions and projects to which our Congress committed us, but for the entire year our work must prioritize organization and be dedicated to organizational consolidation.*
>
> *"Centering our work on organization will prevent us from allowing this critical question, the one that has plagued us from before the Congress, to be sidelined or to slip between the cracks as it has too often in the past. It is only organization that*

will make it possible and necessary to implement decisions of the Congress and advance our revolutionary capacity.

"The Congress presented us with a host of projects and resolutions. None of them can be done effectively unless we give priority to how the work is to be done. The critical issue is organization and this will be our focus for the year....

"The revised Party Constitution, the Political Report to the Congress, the resolutions and the post-Congress Organizational Manual are all contributing to a higher, better-politicized unity upon which to build.

"The Office of the Chairman has grown its administrative capacity in many different ways, but most importantly, it has achieved an unprecedented ability to oversee, direct and hold accountable all the work in every department. We have achieved the ability to relentlessly pursue all the directives of the Fifth Congress and the organizational efficiency and accountability necessary for our progress and our revolutionary success.

"And, we have been, and will continue to be, relentless. This is a profound change that must not be overlooked. My office has withstood every effort to hold onto the old organizational culture, to undermine, stall or otherwise prevent the emergence of an organizational culture of efficiency and accountability.

"In the past we have conducted Party congresses, plenaries and assorted conferences only to remain incapable of carrying out the changes and determinations called for and sometimes voted on. We have complained of this Party shortcoming

over the years and now we are actively in the process of overcoming this limitation.

"Although they must be standardized, the required Plans of Action (POA) and Monthly Summary Reports are beginning to stagger in. Some of them will require more work after they have been submitted and the fact that they have not been delivered on time is unacceptable.

"But this process is changing the character of our organization. The POAs and Summary Reports do not only establish the plans and activities of our leading committees and structures. They also serve to inform the entire leadership and organization of what we should expect of each other and of our leaders.

"Our National Headquarters is the busiest it has ever been since our location in this renovated center. Party leaders are increasingly moving toward regular office operational hours. This does not mean that we have become 9-to-5 revolutionaries. Instead, it means that we are busy at work struggling with Plans of Action and achieving stated goals and objectives for concentrated periods of time. In the past our offices were too often unattended while we were too busy doing anything but achieving goals and objectives tied to concrete Plans of Action.

"This is a most important struggle against organizational anarchy. Our leaders are forced to work from a predetermined agenda. We don't simply 'DO' things. The things that we do are informed by a PLAN and we are consistently kept up to date on progress toward accomplishment of the plan by the required Summary Reports.

"With the institutionalization of this new, improved, efficient and accountable organizational culture; with the ongoing push to grow the capacity of our respective offices, other changes are also emerging. Now we are achieving the permanent organizational capacity to bring more people into a relationship with the Party and our movement. We are creating the structural and organizational foundation for leading others when they come into the embrace of the Party or our movement.

"This has been slow, mind-numbing work when compared to the exciting adrenalin-inducing character of anarchy. However, it is going to pay off in the long run by institutionalizing our practices, making our work less dependent on the personalities, enthusiasm and relationships of the individuals involved; but, instead, reliant on the organizational, political and Constitutional principles enshrined in our structures.

"Our work for this...period, subsequent to the Fifth Congress...must be characterized by the struggle for organizational renewal consistent with the Directives from the Office of the Chairman, mandated by the Fifth Party Congress as expressed through the revised Party Constitution, Congress Political Report, Resolutions, Organizational Manual and basic organizational principles found in other important documents such as 'Build and Consolidate the Party' and 'Standards of Party Life.'

"In all of our efforts, campaigns, struggles, etc., the critical guiding principle that anchors our efforts must be organization building."

We are still engaged in this struggle. Our Fifth Congress Political Report demanded that we solve the problem of recruitment, recognizing that the "current crisis of imperialism has resulted in ever growing numbers of Africans seeking membership in the Party and a relationship with the movement under our leadership."

To take this on we changed the Standard Party Agenda to place recruitment on the top. This was a change to make sure that its last place on the agenda would not continue to have recruitment treated as an afterthought that sometimes didn't get discussed if the meeting lasted too long. We even changed the Constitution to create an Office of Recruitment and Membership.

While today we can boast having someone on the National Central Committee responsible for this office, the fact is that an office holder does not necessarily represent organization, especially as spelled out in the "Abandon Disarray" document, which states further:

"Organization must mean upholding the fundamental principles of democratic centralism, recognizing that for every organizing effort there must be designated leaders and followers and that all our committees have recognized goals, objectives and timelines and appropriate divisions of labor to carry out their functions."

This is not the situation with our Recruitment and Membership Office. There has not been a general membership and recruitment policy guiding the work of our Party and movement. There has not been a meaningful organizational development of the National Office of Recruitment and Membership (NORM) through which policies can be developed and pursued.

This must change. We are not a motley group of individuals who happen to agree on certain philosophical principles; we are the African People's Socialist Party, African Internationalists, which by definition means that we are an organization of theory and practice bound by strict organizational principles, the chief one being democratic centralism.

The Political Report to our Fifth Congress stated clearly what is being called for:

"Consistent with the need for greater accountability, I have directed members of the Party's Central Committee, including the Political Bureau to write Plans of Action to define their work and offices and to establish measurable guidelines and timelines for judging accomplishment. These are important developments, especially necessary for these times of crisis of imperialism and growth in responsibility and membership of our Party and movement."

This National Plenary must be a stepping stone in our work to build the future as history propels the subject and oppressed peoples of the world into irreversible motion to destroy imperialism that is experiencing death throes.

Following the 2012 Party Plenary and months of internal Party struggle and experimentation, the Party's National Central Committee devised a plan to build our organizational capacity and follow through with the mandates found in the Political Report, general resolutions and other initiatives from the Fifth Congress.

This plan was one that would build an intense campaign under the direct leadership of the Office of the Chairman which created an ad hoc structure that would complement and sometimes supercede the National Central Committee.

This structure was designated the One People! One Party! One Destiny! (OPOPOD) Committee, a process that ended with the Party's Sixth Congress in December 2013.

The OPOPOD Executive Committee contained within it members of our National Central Committee and the Chairwoman of the African People's Solidarity Committee functioning under the direct leadership of my office.

The OPOPOD Committee gave the leadership of the Party immediate access to the most critical components of our entire Party and movement, pulling together all the movement's expertise, skills and experience, sometimes located in isolated pockets, and made them available for the purpose of forwarding our top goals and priorities.

No one falls through the cracks!

The One People! One Party! One Destiny! Committee launched a campaign that infused the entire Party with fierce determination to realize the mandates and carry out the resolutions of the Fifth Congress.

Fixating on recruitment, the One People! One Party! One Destiny! Campaign demanded a new level of organizational inter-coordination under the Party's Office of the Chairman with greater centralization which has strengthened not only the leading bodies of the Party but all organizations and departments.

This has provided greater leadership and accountability and at the same time maximized the effectiveness of all skills, resources and understandings in the Party, minimizing duplication of work, inefficiency and uneven development throughout our ranks.

Formed in June 2012, the OPOPOD Committee declared its commitment to never allow any possible recruit to "fall through the cracks." The campaign went beyond the simple task of signing up new members; it determined to turn followers into members, "members into cadreş and cadres into leaders."

One of the most important results of this campaign is that it brought science, protocols and a great deal of attention to the process of outreach and recruitment both on the level of the Party and the mass organizations.

During its 18 months of existence, the OPOPOD Committee began by meeting five days a week and then weekly until its culmination after the Sixth Party Congress. This process went way beyond the question of recruitment, giving intense scrutiny to nearly every aspect of Party-led work. The campaign raised the bar for everyone's work and enforced Party standards for what it means to be a cadre.

This process forced every possible contradiction to the surface to be confronted and resolved by the committee. The OPOPOD Campaign approximated a cultural revolution within our Party and movement.

Some Party and movement forces, including veterans, found themselves unable to stand up to the new terms of our Party fighting a besieged imperialism in a state of irreversible crisis. They have been moved aside, many voluntarily. At the same time this led to new, dynamic forces stepping forward to assume leadership and responsibility.

In some cases, Party recruits put into important areas of the work proved to be self-serving opportunists, something to be expected during the crisis of imperialism when the neocolonial aspiring petty bourgeoisie will attempt to hitch a ride on the rising tide of the people's struggles.

This has not, however, been the defining character of our work during this period. The overwhelming response to the Party's presence and call, and to the OPOPOD Campaign, has been passionate affirmation. Most of the Party's cadres, as well as the new contacts and recruits, have welcomed this intensive campaign of the Party as a reflection of the seriousness of the new situation presented to the Party and the world during this Final Offensive.

A concise summation of the significance and success of the OPOPOD Campaign includes:

- Close oversight and intervention by the OPOPOD Executive Committee into all Party departments, organizations and areas of work.
- Strong emphasis on recruitment that includes holding it accountable through monthly reports and mandates for recruitment protocols to be carried out with the slogan, "Every African on board; no one falls through the cracks!"
- Manuals and protocols created for work in nearly every area.
- Strong emphasis on cadre stance, leadership and taking responsibility.
- Cadre development and training on how to successfully lead and build Party work.
- Building of Party economic and other infrastructures.
- The process of APSC turning back over to the Party knowledge gained through training under the Party's leadership over the years: This means that some APSC veterans now work in Party departments.
- Increased exposure of the Chairman and other Party leaders in Europe, Africa and throughout the U.S. at events coordinated by Party members and supporters in those localities.
- An OPOPOD process that is uniting the Uhuru Movement across the planet by holding worldwide movement meetings and political education.
- A strong push within the Party for self-government and self-determined leadership led by the African working class Party.

- A strong move by the Office of Economic Development and Finance to lead, direct, develop and hold accountable the various economic institutions, several of which have been historically managed by APSC, building the Party's economic infrastructure and creating Black Star Industries.
- A deepening of the Party's political line of African Internationalism, especially regarding the African nation, the white nation and the question of white opportunism, as clearly shown by this Political Report to the Sixth Congress.
- A deepening process of struggles against liberalism with individual members, from the leadership of the Party to the rank and file, along with an overall intensification of struggles inside of the organization for members to rise up to lead.
- A strong commitment and priority to build cadres and popularize the cadre stand throughout the Party.
- A commitment to developing a political education and cadre-building process that will standardize the stance of cadre and generalize the understandings of African Internationalism throughout the Party.
- Struggles exposing neocolonialist individuals and organizations in the world that claim to represent the African working class.
- The struggle for greater general influence over the political arena through the Black is Back front.
- The struggle to publish and sell The Burning Spear monthly throughout the movement, as mandated by the Party's Constitution.
- Faster pace in accomplishing work and goals.
- Centralization of work and skills—especially agit-prop and graphic skills.

Party's Agit-Prop Department moves forward

Many of the contradictions in the Party that I discussed in my Political Report to the 2012 National Plenary have been diminished or overturned through the OPOPOD Campaign. We are now seeing most of the Party's departments and organizations moving forward well.

For example, September of 2013 marked a full year of consistent monthly publication of *The Burning Spear,* our flagship political journal published since the earliest days of our movement.

Of course, this is not without contradictions. We must still reinstate the culture of active distribution of *The Spear* by Party members, something that is complicated by this era of electronic media, in which children cut their teeth with smart phones and social media.

Nevertheless, the "digital divide" is real. As many as half the people living in poverty in the U.S., a category that would be heavily African, do not have computers in the home. Selling the print version of *The Spear* is critical for reaching and organizing the most oppressed sector of the African working class.

Also, more than a million African workers are in the colonial prison system within the U.S. on any given day. Most of them do not have access to computers and *The Burning Spear* is the primary method we have of reaching them, notwithstanding our running battles with prison camp authorities to get *The Spear* in to the captives.

Some Party leaders still may not recognize the significance of the regular publication of *The Burning Spear.* There is really no substitute for the political organizer who puts *The Spear* in the hands of Africans and others, engaging them in political discussions and struggles that magnify our presence many times over.

The distribution of *The Spear* is the most important day-to-day work that a Party member can do. It is one of the most important morale boosters for the entire colonized African population to regularly experience its freedom fighters on post, distributing the people's media and promoting their interests.

Despite the accomplishment of monthly publication, *The Spear* needs to realize greater financial solvency. If nothing else, this, our Sixth Congress must help our Party members and supporters to understand the critical contribution of Agit-Prop to our work and revolution.

In its development since our Fifth Congress and the criticism raised about the department at our 2012 National Plenary, Agit-Prop has been developing its capacity in other ways. It has conducted its work according to the protocols of the OPOPOD Campaign. Manuals have been developed to institutionalize much of its work and members of the department are becoming ever more competent in running the department.

Uhuru News, the online version of *The Burning Spear* is growing as an outstanding anti-imperialist Party news site. There is no comparable news site anywhere in the African world. It is not simply a site that records important events, Uhuru News is a site that is involved in making events.

Additionally, the OPOPOD Campaign has contributed to Agit-Prop's development of Uhuru Radio. Despite the need for resources to upgrade our equipment, Uhuru Radio has been consistently raising its level of professionalism and promises to grow even more with newly recruited talent and expertise in the coming period.

The enthusiasm with which Comrade Dedan Sankara has demonstrated assuming interim leadership of Agit-Prop has been infectious. He has established long-term plans for Agit-Prop's development that inspire the belief that it is a department that is coming into its own as a self-mobilizing, capable entity of the Party that has fully accepted the critical role of Agit-Prop as something that must be achieved expeditiously.

Likewise, many contradictions raised with the International People's Democratic Uhuru Movement in 2011 have been mostly relegated to our rearview mirror.

The organizational protocols have resulted in the growth of InPDUM as an international institution with committed members building branches in Europe, North America and West Africa.

We still have problems in the National Office of Recruitment and Membership. The efforts to build the office with cadres filling out the NORM structure have not yet achieved success. I am, however, impressed by the consistency of work within the office and have reason to believe that the OPOPOD Campaign will result in consolidation of the office.

Already there is a greater, more efficient capacity for dealing with new Party recruits. The OPOPOD protocols are being adhered to and a struggle is being led by NORM calling on all Party organizations to base their relationship to new Party recruits on the principles and protocols set forth by NORM.

Cadre-building must be our focus

One of our most important tasks now is developing cadres— building the capacity of forces who are prepared to lead the masses of the people through a deep internationalization and understanding of African Internationalism, especially as it is expressed in this Political Report.

We plan to popularize the cadre stand to a generation of Africans who were born subsequent to the defeat of the African Revolution and the world revolutionary movement that was the main trend in the world in the 1950s and '60s.

Today, we again experience a world in which oppressed peoples are rising up in what imperialist pundit Zbigniew Brzezinski, quoted earlier in this Report, called the "global political awakening," and what our Party calls the mass resistance of the Final Offensive against Imperialism.

The resistance of oppressed peoples has grown so powerful that it has shifted the balance of power by deepening the economic and political crises of imperialism, complicating Obama's war agenda and threatening the already uneasy equilibrium.

It is on the Party's shoulders to politically educate and train the world revolutionary forces. This Political Report will play the crucial role in winning the whole world to understanding the missing theoretical link of parasitic capitalism and primitive accumulation of capital. Once the theory of African Internationalism grips the masses of Africans and oppressed colonized workers of the world it will become a material force in overturning imperialism once and for all.

In the next year, our Party will develop standardized political education curriculums and will build cadre schools and programs. Today our Party is working to implement the same cadre-building process that Chairman Mao's Communist Party in China laid out in 1937, more than 75 years ago when he wrote in "Win the Masses in Their Millions for the Anti-Japanese United Front":

> *Our Party organizations must be extended all over the country and we must purposefully train tens of thousands of cadres and hundreds of first-rate mass leaders. They must be cadres and leaders versed in Marxism-Leninism, politically far-sighted, competent in work, full of the spirit of self-sacrifice, capable of tackling problems on their own, steadfast in the midst of difficulties and loyal and devoted in serving the nation, the class and the Party. It is on*

these cadres and leaders that the Party relies for its links with the membership and the masses, and it is by relying on their firm leadership of the masses that the Party can succeed in defeating the enemy. Such cadres and leaders must be free from selfishness, from individualistic heroism, ostentation, sloth, passivity and arrogant sectarianism, and they must be selfless national and class heroes; such are the qualities demanded of the members, cadres and leaders of our Party.

The Political Report to our Fifth Congress addressed at length the significance of cadre development for our Party.

More than anything we must give the greatest significance possible to the task of development of Party cadres. By this we do not mean simply filling the ranks of the Party with new forces or having sterile political education classes that will simply allow them to memorize text that can be regurgitated on command. We mean that members of our Party must be prepared to lead.

In practical terms this certainly means that they should be able to lead the particular areas of work for which they may be responsible. Their leaders must give them complete understanding of this work. But they must also be able to lead the masses in general—in their communities and on the campuses, in prisons and at their workplaces. They must be won to a love for the revolution and an undying love for the Party that is the instrument through which the revolution will be pursued and won.

This deep and profound respect and love for the Party is an absolute necessity for our cadres in this period. The Party cadres must be capable of recognizing the programs, commitments, strategy and struggles of the Party as their own. They must see the contradictions as well as victories of the Party as their own.

This means that subjectivism and opportunism, tendencies that place the interests of individuals at the forefront, have no place in Party cadres. The same is true of adventurism and other forms of individualism that substitute personal significance over the significance of the Party and our collective mission.

Individuals displaying subjective tendencies may be able to work in mass organizations under the leadership of the Party, and may be even in the ranks of the Party itself, but they cannot be considered cadres, regardless of the shortage of forces we may be contending with at any given time.

No matter how great or genuine the problems or significance of individuals, they cannot be allowed to undermine the responsibility to place the interests of the revolution and the Party first, above all else. This means that within the Party all our members must aspire to becoming cadres.

Cadres must be taught to understand that the Party is everything, without which our people will be left with another 500 years of misery, should we survive the desperate aggressions of this imperialism in crisis at all. If there is to be independence, unification and socialism in our lifetime it will be because our Party, deeply united in our mission, is successful. This cannot happen with an organization of whining self-serving, individualistic members incapable of seeing beyond their own real or perceived pain or genius.

Our cadres recognize the value of democratic centralism as the main organizational principle of the Party. They recognize why this is so and how this reflects the fact that we are an organization of unity of will and action, something that is absolutely necessary for making the revolution that will end the misery of our people.

Our cadres understand that to come into the ranks of our glorious Party is to submit to its will, to make the will of our Party our own will as opposed to the tendency of attempting to make our own will the will of the Party, as has been occasionally demonstrated by some Party members, past and present.

Cadres must be schooled in the history of our Party that fought decades of struggles and held true to revolutionary principles while others all around us abandoned the field of battle in the face of our imperialist enemy. They must not only know the history in terms of dates and places of struggles, but cadres must also be made familiar with the tactics and strategies employed by the Party during various periods and in different struggles. This will arm them with a bank of experience that they can call on when faced with similar circumstances.

Our cadres must also know the history of our Party as it is represented by the exemplary stances of various comrades who have undergone sacrifices, including alienation from friends and family as well as jailings, beatings, bombings and other attempts on their lives. The history should include the examples of those comrades who have traveled throughout the U.S. and the world to organize the African resistance under the most difficult circumstances. It must be a history that helps to steel cadres for the hardships and victories to come.

Our cadres must be taught African Internationalism. They must study the critical theoretical documents of our Party, especially those developed to explain the world as we were involved in struggle to change it.

This would obviously include texts such as the Constitution of the African People's Socialist Party and Political Reports to the First, Second, Third, Fourth and this Congress.

We must also study "The Dialectics of Black Revolution" and "Political and Economic Critique of Imperialism and Imperialist Opportunism." The reports to InPDUM conventions as well as the main ASI documents must also be studied.

Obviously these are not the only materials that should be used for study. Others include works on political economy and dialectical and historical materialism. They also include materials that teach cadres how to be in an organization of this type, based on principles of revolutionary discipline. However, we must remember that the best school for the development of cadres is actual, practical struggle. Otherwise we create forces that are incapable of utilizing anything that they learn. We continue to be guided by the understanding that practice is primary and that it provides the only meaningful test of theory.

Our leaders must organize their work to accommodate the struggle for the development of our cadres. *Every leading committee and department must play its role. Indeed, I am calling on all our Local and Regional Party leaders to present Plans of Action for the development of cadres in their areas of responsibility. This is also necessary for our mass organizations, for InPDUM and AAPDEP as well.*

Obviously the primary organization for carrying out the task of cadre development at this time is Agit-Prop. This is something that Agit-Prop is working on now, but it must be taken on with demonstrably greater urgency. I believe that recent developments in Agit-Prop give it the ability to quickly devise a Plan of Action for cadre development and I am requiring this to happen expeditiously.

Also, the important role of the Party organizations themselves in this issue of cadre development must not be overlooked. For it is in the Party organizations that we have the greatest opportunity to combine theory and practice.

The Party is organized into committees that give it a division of labor that provides the ability for greater efficiency. But this is only if the various committees and departments assume full responsibility for their areas of work. The structural division of labor allows the Party to predict the success of the whole Party by the role of its component leading parts. Hence, if plans are made for the Party—its division of labor—and one or more components of the Party does not enthusiastically and successfully carry out its responsibility the entire plan can be undermined.

Now more than ever the Party must have leaders who are farsighted problem solvers. It should not be necessary to spell out every possible eventuality for leaders of specific areas of the Party structure. They should be the experts in these areas and know them better than anyone. They should be anticipating problems and planning for successes even when no one else in the Party is concentrating on their area of work.

If we move correctly in this period, if we do our work to build cadres and organize the Party rank and file, putting The Burning Spear *in the hands of the masses, it will help to recruit new members into our ranks to assist with the tasks with which many of our committees are faced.*

However, we cannot continue to use the excuse of too few forces in our leading committees. This is simply one of the tasks that has to be solved by the leaders who head up the committees. Otherwise we will always be explaining away our failures because of not having the people to do the work, when in reality the absence of these forces should be informing us of another critical aspect of the work that has to be taken on.

This paper has explained some of the requirements of cadre development. However, I want to add to the context of this discussion by reminding us that our cadres are the primary force through which we seek to capture and exercise power. They are the forces through which we intend to organize the revolutionary national democratic government and to lead and contend for power on every front.

Our cadres will be the foundation of all our mass work, especially in InPDUM but also AAPDEP and the mass organizations that have not yet been built through which the leadership of the Party will be expressed. Our cadres must be capable of finding the line of march and when necessary, to create organization that will increase the influence of the Party beyond our ranks.

Agit-Prop must contribute to a thirst for knowledge among our ranks. It must help us to create our own working class intellectuals. It must re-establish a culture of constant political study. Agit-Prop must also equip Party cadres with the political education and technical skills to make them capable and valuable, not only to our general Party work, but also to the masses we want to organize or who may already be in organization.

The One People! One Party! One Destiny! Campaign and this Political Report to the Sixth Congress are statements, as we said in our Political Report to the Fifth Congress in 2010, "...of our unflinching commitment to the liberation and unification of Africa and the dispersed African nation and to carrying out our responsibility in the worldwide movement of peoples and countries for liberation, peace and socialism."

VII. African economic self-reliance and dual power

Deputy Chair Ona Zené Yeshitela leads the Office of Economic Development and Finance that has the responsibility for the economic work of the Party while developing and promoting economic development for the entire colonially dispersed African nation.

We recognize this is a bold proposition, but no bolder than a program for the total liberation and unification of Africa and Africans the world over. This is the role enthusiastically embraced by our Party. We have always prided ourselves in our ideological commitment to economic self-reliance, reflected in the history of our practice.

We have also recognized that our practical work for national economic self-reliance—work done since the inception of our movement and Party—is a concrete manifestation of our ideology. It represents a measurable example of our political struggle against foreign and alien colonial domination. It is one of the things that shows that the Party's commitment to national liberation is not simply an abstract concept. It is demonstrably real in every way.

In the book *One People! One Party! One Destiny!*, the Political Report to the Fifth Party Congress, we spelled out the responsibility of the Office of Economic Development and Finance based on the current state of the development of our Party and struggle, stating:

> *Not only must this department create real economic development programs for the whole Party, it must anticipate new expenses and plan for meeting the budget requirements of the Party and its various programs. This office must*

also participate in helping to develop contending economic development programs that benefit the masses and help to bring them closer to the embrace of our Party....

The Office of Economic Development and Finance must be bold in its vision and competent in its ever-expanding capacity.

This is the office that must acquire the expertise to anticipate the emergence of an independent African economy growing out of processes and programs of our Party that are developing now as instruments of contending and dual international economic power.

The African petty bourgeoisie, where most of the expertise we need for such development is located, is not readily accessible to us at this time. It is also true that without ideological transformation, the expertise gained through imperialist institutions is not immediately useful to us. However, this will change.

The conscientious work by the Office of Economic Development and Finance will result in the development of the needed expertise within our ranks; the growth of our Party and the movement under its influence will result in class suicide by elements of the African petty bourgeoisie with such expertise. They will abandon the interests of the petty bourgeoisie, which is a dying social force and adopt the interests of the African working class as their own.

The Office of Economic Development and Finance must re-establish the culture of self-reliance within the ranks of our Party and teach the Party how to constantly be in the process of resource generation as a matter of practice on a regular and consistent basis. Party organizations must be taught the principles of financial accountability and resource security.

However, one of the most important tasks of this office is to develop a program to also teach these things to Party cadres. This is not because all cadres will be involved in finance and economic development, but because we want each cadre to have a rudimentary knowledge that will make her capable of functioning in various mass organizations of the people in this struggle for influence and the acquisition of power.

Self-reliance key to national liberation

Leading the struggle of the entire people places the responsibility for the liberation of the dispersed African nation on the shoulders of the African working class through its fighting, revolutionary class organization, the African People's Socialist Party. Concretely, this means that the Party leads the struggle for national self-determination.

One of the things that has distinguished our Party from assimilationist organizations and put us firmly in the camp of Marcus Garvey is our history of building self-determination institutions. Mostly this has happened within the framework of our strategy of building dual and contending power as part of the contest with the existing colonial power.

Assimilationist organizations such as the National Association for the Advancement of Colored People (NAACP) do not have any such obligations because for them the ultimate aim is to integrate into the existing capitalist-colonialist system.

Our quest for dual power is also different from the self-reliance, do-for-self institutions initiated by the original Nation of Islam because our intent is not to build a movement of petty merchants.

For our Party, the work for self-determination and self-reliance is an integral part of the struggle for national liberation under the leadership of the revolutionary African working class.

We are an organization of professional revolutionaries, which means among other things, that we have always sought an ability to sustain certain key organizers. From our earliest days this has meant everything from going into the orange groves for collective orange picking, to holding traditional car washes and dinner sales, to building large, highly successful institutions. We have lived in collectives where one or more persons would take turns working regular jobs in order to pay the way for the group and the work.

We purchased and operated bookstores and record shops in Louisville, Kentucky and Gainesville, Florida, launching the first commercial African-owned newspaper in Gainesville.

For eight years subsequent to our founding, I traveled the U.S., living out of a red Samsonite suitcase, organizing the Party wherever possible. In Atlanta, Georgia, one of our collectives was so dilapidated that the front door had no hinges. At another collective we were engaged in a permanent battle with the water company that would turn off the water due to non-payment of the bill, only to have us turn the water back on once the company's service personnel would leave.

The contradiction of poverty has been monumental for our Party of the African working class. Economic self-reliance is something that we have taken on since our founding.

The peoples of the world are engaged in a cataclysmic struggle for self-determination. Our Party is a part of that struggle, one that must be waged in the world and within our Party as well. We are now moving more vigorously toward economic self-reliance within our Party.

We are redeveloping our economic work as a new *political* front. Unlike the recent past where our economic work was essentially designed to fund political activity, our economic work, more firmly in the hands of the Party directly, is now strategically geared toward the conquest of political power. It will be more clearly defined as part of the struggle for dual and contending power with a dying imperialism.

This time, in the era of the Final Offensive, we intend to win the struggle for power and raise the African working class up to its proper place as the ruling class of a socialist, liberated and united Africa and African people.

Under the leadership of our Party, the African working class is not only engaged in struggle with the imperialists at the point of production. We make this very clear in the Political Report to the Fifth Congress where we declare the necessity of the African working class to lead the struggle for construction of a new world:

> Hence, the African workers must be brought to consciousness of their task to lead the struggle against our national oppression as a strategic necessity for the emancipation of African labor and the elevation of the African working class to the position of the ruling class of a liberated, united Africa and African people worldwide.

The struggle of the African working class to become the ruling class is also being pursued by its own class conscious African People's Socialist Party. All our economic work, our institutions and enterprises constitute a part of this struggle.

Party forces must lead our economic institutions

Since our Fifth Congress, my office has been working at breakneck speed to give better organization and definition to this work. It is our intent to win the participation of our Party, our movement, our people and the peoples of the world in the Party's self-reliance work.

For us, political power in our hands means the Party must take on all the responsibility for self-rule even while we are engaging imperialist colonialism for all power to the people and black power to the African community.

Party leaders must win greater awareness among Party members of the significance of all our economic-related institutions. They must understand that these institutions, currently in the custody of the Party, belong to our people. African people have a shareholder's stake in ensuring the integrity of the Party to carry out our expressed aims without being beholden financially to any other group than the African working class and our allies and supporters.

Clearly, the people have to be actively engaged in making the Party's institutions successful.

Some of our institutions were conceived or built more than 30 years ago during the Oakland Years that we discussed earlier. The Uhuru Furniture store on Grand Avenue in Oakland celebrated its 25th anniversary in 2013 with a community banquet attended by nearly a hundred enthusiastic shoppers and political supporters. The Uhuru Furniture store on Spruce Street in Philadelphia, open for 19 years, is now moving into a much larger space on Broad Street to accommodate its growth.

These stores, which are much-loved political institutions by their local communities, grew out of a fundraising booth selling used clothes and other items at the Ashby Flea Market in Berkeley in the early 1980s.

Uhuru Foods and Pies began in the Bay Area of California during the late 1970s as a fundraiser for the campaign to free Dessie Woods and other Party mass organizations. Uhuru Foods and Pies continues to be based in Oakland, California, as well as in St. Petersburg, Florida, where its breakfast booths are an established and thriving institution at local farmers' markets. Uhuru Foods now functions as a subsidiary of the Party's Black Star Industries (BSI).

The Uhuru Holiday Pie Campaign currently sells close to 2,500 pies per season to hundreds of repeat customers for whom the pies are a way of "bringing the struggle for African liberation home to the family dinner," according to one long-time supporter.

Our leaders and Party members must become aware of the responsibility of Africans in our Party to lead these institutions just as they lead other areas of the work that we readily recognize as political work.

These institutions were initiated and have been in the custody of comrades of the African People's Solidarity Committee (APSC), who have done a remarkable job up to now. However, we have other tasks, some of which are economic related, to which we must assign APSC. Moreover, our understanding of self-reliance demands that Africans begin to play the major role in these institutions.

We have been working to accomplish this for a few years now, especially under the leadership of Deputy Chair Ona Zené Yeshitela. We must be clear that our Party's economic institutions require the highest level of political unity for their success.

Work in these institutions is not simply a 9-to-5 job. It can't be approached in the manner in which we often take on jobs under capitalist ownership. Under those circumstances there is a contest between the bosses and workers in which the boss is attempting to get a maximum out of the workers for little pay and the workers are attempting to get as much as possible from the boss with little or no work.

The truth is that the work in our institutions is hard but highly rewarding and based in the people. The pay *is* low, but the difference is that these institutions are *our* institutions that do not enrich any individual. They provide some jobs, fund our work and the projects of our nonprofit, the African People's Education and Defense Fund, and lay the foundation for the economy necessary for African self-determination.

They also represent concrete evidence, to the masses of our people, of what we can accomplish.

Our work for self-determination and self-reliance functions to undermine the success of imperialism in the same way that struggles by the peoples of Venezuela, Afghanistan, Iran and Iraq challenge U.S. power. We can't state often enough that it is the transfer of the peoples' resources away from the imperialist centers and back to the possession of the struggling peoples that is responsible for the crisis of imperialism.

The struggles of the peoples of Iran, Iraq, Palestine and Venezuela are recognized by the world community as political struggles being waged for self-determination. We must also begin to see that our economic work is political work, tied to the struggle for African liberation and independence under the leadership of the African working class.

Black Star Industries: independent African economy

All of the Party's economic work being led by the Office of the Deputy Chair has been consolidated under the leadership of my office. Our objective is to increase our capacity for resource generation to support the work of our Party and to create institutions and programs to stimulate economic development within our colonized communities.

APSC's resource generation will continue to be important, but its role will be more clearly defined in relationship to the Party's economic work. The economic work of the African People's Solidarity Committee is becoming increasingly supplemental to this strategic approach to our economic work. Their task will be to help facilitate the process of resource transference from the oppressor nation back to the oppressed for use in our march to self-determination.

The assets and enterprises of Black Star Industries (BSI) are presently minuscule and limited in scope. However, our vision is that BSI will be able to initiate major projects and industries throughout the African world.

The whole Party and our movement must unite with this work. BSI is an anti-colonialist project that is designed to shift ownership of production and distribution away from the colonial economy and into the collective ownership of the African masses under the leadership of the African working class in the form of the Party.

Black Star Industries is the economic development umbrella organization, a limited liability company (LLC) registered in Europe and the U.S., through which we are forging the ability to win the international African population to a process of developing a free, independent, liberated and united African economy. Black Star Industries is named for the steamship line created by Marcus Garvey and the Universal Negro Improvement Association and African Communities League (UNIA) in the first quarter of the 20th century.

Through BSI, the dispersed African nation can be consolidated and realize its economic aims and requirements under the leadership of the African working class for the production and reproduction of life for Africans ourselves as opposed to for our oppressors.

Our economic work is only one of the political vehicles through which we are working to achieve power. We are also doing this through development of community food gardens, health clinics and our TyRon Lewis Community Gym in St. Petersburg, Florida, in addition to an assortment of schools and education projects and other fronts. All of our Party leaders and members must accept collective and individual responsibility for the success of these Party-led endeavors. The leaders of this work must become more efficient in winning support and participation of the Party's members.

Besides building our Black Star Industries and other Party institutions of economic development, we must institutionalize the culture of economic work throughout all our organizations. Each member of our Party and movement must take responsibility for the financial security and growth of the Party and our institutions.

This is really part of our Party tradition. We understand the issue of national independence as inextricably tied to the question of economic self-reliance. National independence without economic self-reliance is better defined as neocolonialism. It is not real independence. This is evident in the current crisis of imperialism, which can also be defined as a crisis of neocolonialism, as more and more peoples and countries are busily rejecting neocolonial solutions by struggling to determine their own independent economic destiny, free from European and U.S. domination.

The higher development of Party division of labor has contributed to the notion that all our economic work would be in the custody of the Office of the Deputy Chair under the leadership of the Office of the Chairman.

While it is true that our economic work is developed and led from that office, economic work continues to be a part of the political front in which each Party member and all Party organizations must participate, whether it is work initiated by one of the Party's institutions or by local organizations of the Party.

This Congress will hear a report from the Office of Economic Development and Finance that details its accomplishments and goals. We have seen the development of this office since our last Congress, a development that has had implications for the work of the entire Party.

The Office of Economic Development has brought a level of professionalism and structural coherence that has reverberated throughout the Party and the Uhuru Movement. All of the economic institutions of the Party have become increasingly accessible to the Party for active participation by every Party committee and organization. This means that for the first time in many years all the Party's economic institutions are accessible for participation by all members of the Party and the general colonized African community as well.

But again, we are still faced with the enormous task of winning the leaders of the Party to recognize that the economic front of our work is a major component of the *political* work of the Party. Nothing says more clearly to our people and the world that we are about the assumption of actual self-determination than our economic program through which we achieve self-reliance that is fundamental to the question of self-determination.

We reiterate: there is no such thing as self-determination independent of self-reliance. They go hand in hand. The African Revolution must and will transform the physical economic conditions of African workers around the world. The struggle for dual and contending power is a fight by African workers in our own interest, for our own benefit to win our liberation.

Recognition of this fact by the Party's leadership means that we will begin to incorporate the programs and possibilities afforded us by the Office of Economic Development and Finance into our work. It means that we will see this work to be as important as any other political work with which we are tasked. Indeed, we will see it as more important than most. For the truth is that all our political work is directed towards the ends of self-determination for our people.

Historically, this is something that has always been understood and appreciated by our Party. Throughout the years Party economic work was integrated into the work of all our organizations and committees. Every week, each organization and committee would hold at least one session of political education in addition to the brief study that accompanied each Party meeting.

In addition, every organization would conduct at least one weekly fundraising event, whether it was group car washes, dinner sales or any number of things that the various church groups, fraternal and civic organizations would do to raise necessary resources.

This has been an important part of the culture of the Party. It is unacceptable that this aspect of Party life is not currently generally understood. The rank and file self-sufficiency of the mass organizations must be reinstituted if we are to continue our tradition of struggle for self-determination.

More than anyone else, our leaders should understand the significance of our division of labor as a means of achieving greater efficiency and creating greater accountability for each area of the work. This does not change the reality that every member of the Party is responsible for the success of every program and campaign of the Party, both politically and economically.

The Party must not relinquish our principled stand of absolute and total self-determination of our people. We must give special attention to our joint responsibility for the Party's economic development program as well as the economic and financial health of the Party itself.

Moving forward, in addition to the question, "How many people did you recruit?" we must also ask, "What have you done to promote and support our economic institutions? How much money did you raise to advance the program of the Party and the progress of the revolution?"

The way these questions are answered will be determining factors of the success of every Party committee and organization and, increasingly, it will be the determining factor of the success of each Party member and of the Party itself.

VIII. The state of the Party

The rapid growth of the Party is a reflection of the reality that the primary task for the advancement of the struggle to liberate and unite Africa and Africans of the world; the primary task for driving imperialism out of the lives of the oppressed majority of the peoples of the world is the concerted commitment to build the African People's Socialist Party and the African Socialist International.

All African and freedom-loving people want peace and security. All the people want an end to the conflict, instability and personal insecurity stemming from a world divided between oppressors and the oppressed.

The system ruled by a minority handful that owns and controls the means of production while the majority of the world has been relegated to the position of impoverished and bloodied spectators of our own rape by imperialism and all its various sordid accomplices and contenders must go.

Our entire existence is a response to this reality. As we survey our presence and significance as a Party, we are able to concretely measure our role in deepening the crisis of imperialism by engaging the imperialist order from so many different fronts.

Our growth and participation in the fight against imperialism contributes one of the most important ingredients in the struggle for a new, liberated world without class exploitation and national oppression; one that will ultimately be free of classes and borders. This ingredient is *revolutionary* consciousness and organization.

Clearly, a defining aspect of the crisis of imperialism is the unbridled motion of the world's oppressed, the pedestal upon which the fortunes of imperialism rely for continued success and existence.

We are experiencing the wake of a changed world. Nothing will ever be the same again in terms of the relations of power existing between the historically white imperialist Europe and the vast majority of the rest of us.

The historical insecurity of the majority has begun to be experienced by the minority European populations of the world. The formerly freewheeling parasitic social welfare states of Europe are now facilitating the cannibalization of their white populations, offering them choices of death characterized as "austerity" or "stimulus."

The former is the ruthless elimination of the unearned "social spending" that Europeans have come to take for granted over the years—from nearly free healthcare to six weeks of paid vacation time annually.

Economic stimulus involves printing phony and illusionary unearned money to "stimulate" the growth of a non-producing European-based economy.

Notwithstanding the fact that it has recently lost much of its economic luster and absolute international political influence, the U.S. has been pushing its own version of economic "stimulus"—pumping billions of dollars into the economy—onto their European counterparts as a universal solution to their economic woes.

In reality, the bourgeois economists are being exposed as modern day political alchemists bent on peddling fool's gold to the world. Each new promise of a glowing future for the world's (meaning "European") economy finds itself incapable of surmounting the wall of reality that confronts it.

Nevertheless, it has only been our Party that has clearly initiated a revolutionary political process that is not content to simply protest the conditions with which the peoples of the world are confronted. The Euro-American struggle to regain their social welfare losses can not be successfully realized except through reactionary efforts to turn back the forward motion of the world's majority upon whose backs they have existed as freeloaders for the last five or six centuries.

Euro-America includes the masses of Greece, Portugal, Spain and increasingly France, whose worsening economic plight has thrust them into political motion sometimes bordering on hysteria in protest to the policies of their government, the European Union, European Central Bank and the International Monetary Fund. Some Greeks are claiming that they are being reduced to "third world" status and conditions.

The world's majority—the oppressed peoples, including those of us located inside of the European centers—whose motion constitutes the unrest that destabilizes the existing U.S.-dominated imperialist system, cannot be victorious by simply overturning our relationship with white power, as strategically significant as that is for the emergence of world socialism.

We must implement social transformation that results in an end to the suffering of the masses and forwards the ability of the world's toilers to rise up to their full stature at the helm of their own destiny.

Dual and contending African power

African Internationalism has initiated a concerted effort on different continents to build a revolutionary movement, informed by advanced revolutionary science and dedicated to the overthrow of imperialism and the establishment of an African workers' socialist state. These are not just empty words.

We have developed an economic plan that is at work and constitutes an active capacity. We have created a process of international dual power that might also be spelled "d-u-e-l" power. It is a contending power that, while still unfolding, now owns several institutions operating on many fronts as we have discussed earlier, including Burning Spear Media, an incipient media power that is expanding with the growth of our Party.

Under the umbrella of the network are *The Burning Spear* newspaper, Uhuru News and Uhuru Radio Internet magazine and radio station and Burning Spear Publications that prints and distributes our books.

We are seriously at work improving our political organ, *The Burning Spear* print and Internet journal. We continue to grow Uhuru Radio and expect to add an FM station in the near future.

Burning Spear Media is formally owned by our Black Star Industries (BSI). Uhuru Foods and Pies, a major economic enterprise, is also owned by Black Star Industries while several other enterprises in Europe, the U.S., the Caribbean and Africa are in the pipeline for implementation and development. Our small apparel company, which has a capacity for international commerce, also falls under BSI.

We created the self-reliant non-profit, the African People's Education and Defense Fund (APEDF), under which our community gym in Florida operates, as well as the furniture stores in California and Pennsylvania.

Through the All African People's Development and Empowerment Project (AAPDEP) we were initiators and participants in community development plans and projects in West Africa and in the U.S., including an infant and maternal health clinic, and a community farm in Sierra Leone, along with community gardens in the U.S., among other programs.

The Party has actual organizations and organizers throughout Europe—in Cologne, Wuppertal and Berlin in Germany as well as in Paris and other departments of France, Belgium, the United Kingdom and Sweden.

Dedicated Party organizers are ploughing the ground for our growth in The Bahamas, throughout the Caribbean region and in Colombia in South America. We are also growing in Canada and within the U.S.

This is just a synopsis of our motion. It does not capture the full picture or the influence of our Party's theory.

InPDUM's increasing capacity to lead

The International People's Democratic Uhuru Movement (InPDUM) has enthusiastically undertaken the task of rectifying the errors pointed out during our Fifth Congress. InPDUM delegates traveled to its International Convention, held in St. Petersburg on March 23 and 24, 2013, from various places in the U.S. while other members participated electronically. Representatives were also present from Sweden and the UK, with live presentations transmitted from Germany, New York and elsewhere.

InPDUM is building its organizational capacity to lead the mass struggle for revolutionary national democratic power throughout the world.

In 2010 the Party criticized InPDUM for its promotion of a single leader at the expense of creating its organizational capacity. InPDUM's 2013 Convention was notable for the obvious development of leaders throughout its structures and its progress in organizational development, recruitment and branch building.

The InPDUM Convention exemplified the bold tradition of leadership for which our Party and movement have always been known. With its declaration to "Build Revolutionary Organization to Protect and Defend our Own," the Convention conducted relevant workshops, including its groundbreaking panel on the issues of homosexuality and democracy in the African community.

The workshop attacked the hegemony of the European or white Left on gender issues, defying its attempt to give a European universalist definition to this question, a definition that serves to perfect imperialism for white oppressor nation citizens, enabling white homosexuals to equally enjoy all the benefits of sitting on the pedestal of African oppression.

The white Left's promotion of homosexual rights include gays in the military forces—from the police precincts occupying African communities in the U.S., to the marines occupying communities in Afghanistan and threatening the people of Syria.

InPDUM's Convention panelists, however, identified colonialism, imperialism and parasitic capitalism as the basis of the oppression of the entire African nation, including homosexuals. The panelists rejected white-imposed terms such as gay, lesbian and bi-sexual, in favor of an African designation as "same gender-loving" or SGL.

As expected, this stand resulted in controversy among African activists, most sharply in France. This opposition was primarily based on claims that homosexuality was a foreign import to Africa and that support for equality for SGLs was bowing to European or U.S. pressure that is using the issue against African governments by threatening to cut off aid if they did not comply with U.S.-defined demands for "gay rights."

Controversy may remain around the material, historical basis for the advent of homosexuality in human society, and the U.S. government *does* use the issue as another "imperialist threat" to African governments.

There is no controversy, however, around the fact that all Africa has existed and continues to exist under some form of imperialist domination. Likewise, there should be no controversy around the need to enlist the participation of the entire nation, especially the African working class and poor peasantry in the struggle to defeat our relationship to imperialism, regardless of gender or sexuality.

InPDUM's stance around this question also ridicules the attempts of some African governments to divert attention from their subservience to imperialism by dividing the people with attacks on differences around nonessential issues like sexual identity and ethnicity.

These same traitorous forces allow the imperialists and their citizenry full access to Africa and all its resources, including protection by the neocolonial state that is really nothing but a white power military outpost in our African communities. This is the real foreign import to African communities our detractors should be concerned with.

This stance is just one of the examples of InPDUM's growing political maturation. It represents InPDUM's determination to defeat any idea or tendency that attempts to divide the African nation and working class.

APSC increasing presence throughout white world

The African People's Solidarity Committee (APSC) is also evidence of the Party's significant growth and leadership around every question during this era of imperialist decline and general mass confusion. One area of confusion for the masses as well as organized militants has always revolved around the issue of white people.

The African People's Solidarity Committee has always been a significant weapon in the arsenal of our Party. Its role in the post-Congress One People! One Party! One Destiny! Campaign and the drive to increase its presence throughout the white world, including attempts to organize a base in Europe, accentuate its significance.

APSC is one material, institutionalized manifestation of the Party's theory of African Internationalism. It is a living example that the participation and role of white people in the struggle to change the world does not have to revolve around assimilationist politics, either of the white leftist "Black-and-

White-Unite-and-Fight" or black nationalist "White-Man-is-the-Devil" variety.

The existence of APSC discloses the universality of African Internationalism. It provides practical evidence that it is possible to conduct a dispassionate criticism of capitalism that reveals its foundation, and therefore the well-being and fate of whites in general as built on the imperialist attack on Africa and the world.

It helps us to understand that African Internationalism is not a theory of Africa and Africans separate from our relationship to the world, but a theory of Africa, Africans and peoples of the entire world in relationship to the emergence, existence and future of capitalist-imperialism.

At its January 2013 National Plenary, APSC demonstrated a growing sophistication in showing Euro-Americans how to escape their historical gilded cage of human isolation by becoming one with the world's people in overturning the unnatural parasitic relationship whites have with the world as beneficiaries of patriotism or solidarity with the imperialist white nation state.

Rapid development of ASI is our priority

Developing the African Socialist International (ASI) is the strategic heart of our work and one of our greatest challenges. The African Socialist International is our organization of African People's Socialist Party formations on the ground every place in the world where African people are located.

The Garvey Movement, the closest thing to a precedent for the work we are doing to build the ASI, is nearly a hundred years behind us. There are no well-trodden paths here. It is we who are hacking our way into this generally unexplored territory. It is we who must blaze the trail to consolidation of the single worldwide African organization of the working class aligned with the poor peasantry that will function under the leadership of the general staff of the international African Revolution.

Since the 2010 Fifth Congress, ASI Secretary General Luwezi Kinshasa has done an excellent job winning forces into the Party's process from throughout Europe. Secretary General Luwezi's work on the European Front has implications for building in Africa as well, since many of the comrades in our work in Europe are also tied to Africa through family, citizenship and recurrent struggles on the Continent.

We have conducted two powerful African Liberation Day conferences in Paris as part of our ASI-building efforts, events that have helped to transform the political culture and ideological direction within the African community throughout Europe.

Contributing to this transformation were my European speaking tours in 2012 and 2013, during which we visited Frankfurt, Berlin and Cologne in Germany; Brussels, Belgium; High Wycombe and London in the UK and Stockholm, Sweden. Actor Ron Bobb-Semple accompanied the 2012 tour with his powerful presentation of Marcus Garvey.

Most of these places are locations where we have actual organization or organizers. In others we sought to win organizers, build the Party and the Uhuru Movement and extend our influence.

Our presence within the Congolese community is strong throughout Europe. Organizing there among the masses who have been mobilized by the conditions and struggles in Congo, we have built the We Are Patrice Lumumba Coalition that allows us to connect the struggles of Africans in Congo and Europe to the Black is Back Coalition in the U.S. This coalition enables us to initiate African Internationalist ideological intervention in the mass struggles of Africans based inside of Congo as well.

Even as we see the tremendous potential for the rapid development of the African Socialist International, we acknowledge contradictions in this work. Our focus in the upcoming period following the Sixth Congress includes urgently revitalizing the ASI structure and committees and constructing a strategic Plan of Action that unites and gives direction to all ASI forces around the world.

The work in Europe, North and South America, the Caribbean and Africa will all be part of one coherent structure that will overturn the uneven ideological and political development in many of our target areas.

Our immediate plans include a meeting of ASI leaders to be held during our Congress to fill all the leadership positions of the Executive Committee and to set the agenda for the committee's work for this period. As the Chairman of the African Socialist International, leading and building the ASI is slated to be one of my main priorities in 2014.

The executive component will include the ASI Chair, Secretary General, Economic Development Director and Secretary. Ultimately, we will also have a Director of Organization.

The struggle to build the ASI is related to the pressing struggle for Party cadre development and recruitment. The lack of political education and training necessary to facilitate recruitment and lead the work in some areas is glaring.

Despite our contradictions, the Party's One People! One Party! One Destiny! Campaign has strengthened the ASI-building process. In the areas where there is adherence to the established movement protocols we can clearly see results. In some places Party forces are engaging in actions, holding events, participating in the struggles of the people and bringing in recruits. In Europe, for example, most of the dynamic preparation for my recent tours was carried out by our comrades with enthusiasm and skill.

The general tasks of the ASI will include ideological, organizational and economic fronts. Plans of Action and instruments of work will be developed to maximize the spread of African Internationalism throughout the African world.

Creating and implementing programs of political education in Africa and elsewhere will result in introducing the people to their own relative strength in the battle with imperialism as it manifests itself in the world and in their lives. This will expose to the masses their absolute strength as the foundation upon which imperialism depends.

This will help the people to struggle in their own interests, free from the influence of imperialism and the imperialist poseurs and wannabes. This will transform the urgent spontaneous struggles of the people into revolutionary motion, driven by the selfish and independent interests of oppressed Africans to win power at the expense of the existing imperialism and the incipient imperialists occupying our political spaces and our organizations.

This will direct the general motion of the people in a revolutionary way, moving from demonstrations of disgust, to actions to wrest power from our class enemies and national oppressors.

Spreading Party literature, organizing forums and debates, intervening in the existing and spontaneous struggles of the people with African Internationalist based analyses, is our key, fundamental work.

This is the method we will use to struggle against superstition and awe of the imperialist state with its neocolonial infrastructure. This enables our forces to defeat the dregs of Pan-Africanist influence that feebly exists off the ideological inertia pilfered from the Garvey Movement.

We are working on a strategy upon which to build springboards throughout the African world. We must deepen our influence and extend our work in critical areas, such as Kenya in Eastern Africa, South Africa and Namibia in Southern Africa and Ghana in West Africa. Building the ASI in these strategic places will enable us to strengthen our foothold in Africa.

In this upcoming period the international ASI leadership body will develop our ASI regional leaders and hand over to them the responsibility for advancing the ideological and Party-building work in their areas.

ASI regional committees will then draw up their Plans of Action defining the method of building the Party throughout their territories. Obviously, this must include an analysis of the region and the conditions of existence of our people there, the level of existing organization, its class component and national character, along with the level of political development of the masses and other leading organized forces.

These Plans of Action will include the methods of producing, acquiring and distributing the Party theoretical materials based on the conditions of the people and the skill level available to us. Regional leaders must also sum up the state of the existing infrastructure—roads, Internet accessibility, water and housing within their area—which in some places can be problematic.

Yet, though transportation and communications are a problem in Africa, the people and the local neocolonialists make do with the situation. Our organizers on the ground are well-acquainted with the conditions and must use them as a basis for winning African people to the struggle for the unification of Africa and control of our stolen resources.

In the process of planting our theoretical footprint within each region we must also identify and recruit likely candidates for the ASI. Throughout the region, these recruits must be consolidated into national Party organizations with the primary responsibility of recruiting people just like themselves.

Party members must become professional African Internationalist evangelists and skilled organizers who go out into the world building local Party organizations from city to city wherever they are assigned.

All our cadres must be competent at spreading the gospel of liberating and unifying Africa and African people under the leadership of the international African working class and its independent revolutionary organization, the African People's Socialist Party.

Central to the training within the ASI will be the principles found in the main ASI resolution, its existing Constitution and other documents, including the ASI Manifesto. Basic organizational principles must be studied and embraced, especially democratic centralism as well as opposition to liberalism and the host of termites that can eat away at the organizational and political essence of the Party.

Our trained cadres must internalize African Internationalism, learning how to keep their bearings in every situation, how to be in organization, conduct meetings, build local Party units and events, carrying out all that our Organizational Manual conveys.

These are crucial times. Imperialism as we know it is on the ropes of despair. All its actions throughout the world reek of desperation and irrationality.

The U.S. and the entire European world are beginning to experience hunger and economic insecurity for the first time since being rescued from a diseased and impoverished feudalism by enslaving Africans and colonizing the rest of the world. Europeans inhabit North and South America, Australia and Africa as conquering marauders who suffer convenient amnesia when it comes to their history.

A dying European imperialism is attempting to cut and shoot its way back into historical relevance. At the same time its hungrier competitors, raised from the ranks of the formerly colonized, especially in Asia and especially China, are aggressively digging into the finite human and material resources previously ensconced behind an exclusive door protected by "whites only" barricades.

Today both the imperialists and their contenders are looking to Africa, the critical primary or "primitive" source of capital accumulation, to either rescue or build themselves in their contention with other imperialists.

The interests of Africa and African people ourselves are only considered when they impact on the plans and interests of the desperate predators, some of whom have lived off the flesh of Africa and her children for centuries.

Africa is the battleground and the stakes are high. The European Union, Canada, the perennially prostrate, would-be-white Turkey—all have Africa plans. Some of them are engaged in proxy wars of chaos to cover their looting that has resulted in the deaths of millions of African people within the last few years.

It is they who back the neocolonial stooges who preen on European stages, pretending to be leaders while the birthrights of our people are being carted away on trains, lorries and ships, on structures and infrastructure created only for the purpose of theft.

The U.S. and European powers literally own the governments of Africa as extensions of their own imperialist power. They provide the money for the functioning of government and the salaries of the puppets whose only real function is that of oppressing our people for the sake of the status quo. Backed by imperialism, the neocolonial puppets are funded to reproduce themselves as a totally repugnant, totally worthless social class that survives by eating the flesh of its own people.

It is the U.S. imperialists, the old and decrepit white power, armed to the teeth, and blasting away at its own shadow, that created AFRICOM, the U.S. Africa Command. AFRICOM formally introduced itself to the world with its ruthless and brutal overthrow of the Libyan government and the public lynching of its president in a manner reminiscent of exemplary U.S. Southern justice traditionally directed against our people: "That'll larn ya."

U.S.-funded proxy wars are being directed at the people of Somalia with Kenyan and Ethiopian armies utilized to guarantee that Somalia and Africa will never be able to freely control their own oil and other material and human resources.

This is also true of the proxy wars in which the U.S. is funding and training the forces of Yoweri Museveni in Uganda and Paul Kagame in Rwanda—forces responsible for abetting the imperialist slaughter of more than 7 million people in the Congo in the interest of U.S. imperialist control of the country's minerals essential to Western technology.

From one stretch of Africa to another, for the totality of its 12 million square miles of cornucopian booty that created the white world and its opinion of itself, Africa is being devoured by a remorseless and shameless predator. Until recently this predator monopolized the power to define itself as beneficent civilizer and peacemaker to an uncivilized and violent Africa.

In the meantime, grinning supplicants posing as leaders and heads of states are celebrating the fact that a "generous" China purchased for their use a new headquarters of the African Union in Addis Ababa, Ethiopia.

Clever stooges, these, who consider themselves empowered by being able to play Chinese predators against European predators to win greater favors for themselves. Unless, that is, they go too far and end up like Mu'ummar Qaddafi or on the dockets of the white people's International Criminal Court that was obviously created just to keep them in line.

We have said over and over again that the African Revolution, when fought within the borders established for us by imperialism, has clearly run into its limitations, but when fought as One Africa! One Nation! will bury all the imperialists on the battleground of our homeland.

There will be no successful Ghana, Liberia, Sudan or other African-based revolution. We have seen repeatedly that the "independence" achieved within those borders has only served to consolidate white power in neocolonial black skin. Flag independence has merely empowered a sector of the African petty bourgeoisie to administer the white power imperialist state on African territory, as we have shown.

ASI only meaningful response to African oppression

The ASI is the only solution for Our Africa that is experiencing an escalation of the exploitation of our people and our homeland by an imperialism whose desperation increases daily during this deepening crisis caused by the resistance of the world's peoples.

This greater influx of imperialist financial intervention into Africa, and its designation as an "emerging market" is being extolled by bourgeois economists as evidence of the growing economic vitality of Africa. Of course, in reality this is nothing more than intensified foreign imperialist capital extraction impacting on bourgeois economic indicators. The masses of the people are suffering more than ever.

This economic "vitality" or growth in Africa is a reflection of the increasing numbers of foreign "investors" claiming and speculating on African mines and minerals.

It is the increased number of boxcar loads of diamonds and iron ore leaving the mines of Sierra Leone day after day on ships bound for the U.S., Europe and China. It is the renewed skyrocketing of European and now ever-growing Chinese settlers buying our nation's land for their vacations and retirement or to seek their fortunes in the feeding-frenzy on African soil.

The economic growth and vitality they celebrate is nothing but the same old parasitic growth and vitality used to neutralize the economic growth and vitality of Africa and African people.

With the exception of the incipient presence of the ASI, there is no meaningful political response in Africa to the plight of our people or Our Africa.

Locked ideologically in the past era of direct colonial domination where it was clear that the "white" man was the enemy against whom all of Africa must unite, the African working class and poor peasantry have been defenseless against our class enemies *within* the African nation. These traitors work indirectly for the mostly white power imperialism even as they serve their own class interests.

The African Socialist International, the African People's Socialist Party throughout the world, is the only organization that provides direction for the liberation and unification of Africa and the dispersed African nation under the leadership of the African working class in alliance with the poor peasantry.

In Angola, Mozambique, Guinea-Bissau, Guinea-Conakry, Ethiopia, Eritrea, Zimbabwe and other places that were seen as examples of socialist-influenced and led struggles and governments in the past, there is little pretense of a socialist, collectivized society any longer.

Even in South Africa where the party in power includes partnership with a "communist" organization and where more than one of its contenders from the period of the liberation movement claim socialist credentials, there is absolutely no evidence of class-based struggle. There is no organization that advances the interests of the suffering African workers and peasants and the general African population.

Our African people continue to be pushed into shanties, subjected to subsistence on a dollar a day, repressed as criminals and defined as social contradictions that have to be solved for the benefit of the white dominated status quo.

The former colonial state of South Africa has only been modified enough to allow participation of the African petty bourgeoisie associated with the African National Congress in administering the state instruments of repression of our people and as minor beneficiaries of the parasitic economy.

In Europe our Party work has to contend with the general reluctance among Africans—many of them first generation from Africa—to recognize the issue of class within the African population.

We must help the people understand how power in the hands of the African petty bourgeoisie results in one approach to our oppression and exploitation, and power in the hands of the independent, organized African working class in the form of the Party results in another approach.

African workers and militant intellectuals in Africa and Europe do not have a tradition of organizing to advance the capacity of the African working class to seize political power in its own selfish interests as a class.

These are some of the difficulties that must be overcome.

We must win recognition of the need to build a revolutionary Party that is characterized in part by its approach to national liberation revolving around the capture of political power by the African working class and poor peasantry. These are the critical social forces that have always been used to propel the African petty bourgeoisie to power, only to suffer greater exploitation and oppression in the aftermath.

In Europe, where domestic African colonies are a recent phenomenon, African organizations have been mostly concerned with the politics of self-defense. Sometimes this has resulted in forms of cultural nationalism intending to promote and defend the dignity of African culture against the inherent slander by the European nation.

This is shortsightedness or opportunism incapable of really considering a return to a liberated Africa under the rule of a revolutionary class. This is a politic of despair by a group of Africans prepared to be in Europe forever. They are attempting to carve out enclaves of cultural security and tolerance in exchange for the presumed economic security of Europe—security attained at the expense of the well-being and security for Africans in Africa, even as Europe's security is more and more in jeopardy.

Another expression of African politics in Europe revolves around the effort to be accepted by Europeans into the European nation. Like the cultural nationalists, who seem to pop up wherever we are, this struggle for European acceptance is not peculiar to Europe.

It is something that has also characterized the struggle of African people within the U.S., with the exception being that cultural nationalism and assimilationism have only become the dominant politic among Africans since the defeat of the U.S. Front of our movement fighting for national liberation, if not worker's rule.

Throughout South America and the Caribbean the task of the ASI is to raise up the national and class consciousness of African people who suffer severe economic exploitation, political insecurity and national repression.

In Honduras, Colombia and other areas of South America, lands inhabited by African people, sometimes previously conceded to African communities by those governments, are constantly being seized or are under threat of seizure by governments or government-supported corporations.

South America, like its counterpart to the North, is a territory that achieved its identity by genocidal European appropriation of the land of the Indigenous people.

As we have discussed throughout this book, the fate of the Indigenous people is part of what Karl Marx called the primitive accumulation of capital that gave birth to capitalism, white power and the European nation. For the Indigenous people this was a parasitic infection that has led to disastrous consequences being suffered and fought against up to this day.

The European colonizers of South America, mostly Spaniards, fought their "mother country" for right of sole ownership of the stolen land. These were known as fights for independence, though it was no independence for the Indigenous people and the enslaved captured Africans brought to the land to grow the European economies.

In the aftermath of these struggles for independence, Africans have generally existed in a political purgatory of sorts. While we may call ourselves citizens of the states that were created on the lands of South America, we were never really Colombians or Ecuadorians or Guyanese.

In Brazil where nearly a hundred million Africans live, the Portuguese colonizers cleverly and maliciously appropriated African culture, renaming themselves, the culture and the enslaved Africans, "Brazilian."

Although a consciousness of our African identity is growing throughout South America where our people are now defining themselves as Afro-Colombians, -Venezuelans, -Hondurans, etc., confusion on this question is one of the great encumbrances to be overcome. Confusion over our national identity is even greater in South America than it is in the U.S. and North America.

Despite our weaknesses and challenges, the African Socialist International is already having an impact on the politics of the African world, whether in Africa, Europe, North and South America and the Caribbean. Our organizational, political and ideological footprints can be found everywhere and the imperialists would be hard-pressed to wipe them out.

Throughout Europe and the United Kingdom, the ASI has challenged or changed the political culture in African communities. For thirty years we have waged fierce political battles in England, ripping the fabric of Pan-African and other expressions of often radical petty bourgeois political tradition. Our first big battle in England was to win the activist African community to recognize the importance of organizing struggle as Africans.

This was not only in opposition to a false national consciousness that characterized Africans as "Black Brits." It was also in opposition to the Pan-Africanists who saw the struggle in England as support for or in solidarity with our liberation movement on the Continent, as opposed to recognizing the need to build the UK Front for the same African Liberation Movement. Another contending position was one that opposed African Internationalism because it was seen as violating a strategy of "black-Asian" unity that required obfuscation of African national identity.

Over the years Party-led or -involved struggles have now been largely accepted by most African militants, with the entire political landscape having been influenced by the Party.

Today, the issue of reparations is a household word in African communities and elsewhere. Now, the black-Asian unity proponents are "more African than anyone," including those of us in the Party! We have also contributed to a greater materialist approach to political analysis within the general African movement.

Similarly, throughout Europe, the presence of the Party has challenged the status quo among African activists. The African Socialist International has given the African community the ability to fight for a future of a liberated Africa. It challenges the political implications of seeing a future trapped in a hostile Europe, while Africa, the land from which many have only recently emigrated, continues to experience shameful immiseration and oppression.

The ASI moves us from the position of having to fight for reforms in Europe, which is just another way of improving European imperialism and strengthening its hold on Africa and the world. It brings us to a position of conscious combat with imperialist Europe in order that Africa might know the development and prosperity historically expropriated by Europe at our expense.

The ASI has shown that Africa can and must be free. It provides the ability for Africans to understand that our presence in Europe represents the European Front of the African Revolution. It is not our destiny to remain permanently on the defensive, attempting to hold on to our national dignity while we are engrossed in an unending battle to win white approval to become European and to stay in Europe.

The ASI means that Africans who have been chased to Europe by conditions in Africa that were created by Europe are capable of extending the struggle for Africa's future into the heart and politics of Europe. When understood this way, African Internationalism helps to deepen the crisis of parasitic imperialism, moving us closer to the day when we can defeat it, freeing Africa and Africans everywhere from its bloody grasp.

Throughout the Caribbean, African Internationalism and the ASI are the only means through which the masses of African people can become conscious of their class interests, as they were by the thousands during the era of Garvey. They can recognize their interests in achieving real national liberation as components of the African-centered African working class-led nation of genuinely free women and men finally in charge of our own affairs and our own future. Building the Party across the Caribbean region will be one of our top goals in the upcoming period.

We must enhance our ability to build the Party throughout the world. The ASI is the organizational expression of our commitment to this task, one that every member of the Party in every country on every continent must accept as her responsibility.

We have begun the process of building the ASI. Now we must seize the time and consolidate our gains rapidly and urgently as the Final Offensive against Imperialism plays out before our eyes.

IX. What is to be done

Our Sixth Party Congress will clearly define the road that we must pursue to advance our revolution into the future of liberation, unity and socialism. All of our work subsequent to our Fifth Congress was designed to move us forward. In this upcoming period we will continue the trajectory established at that historic Congress.

The resolutions and mandates from our Congress are our bulwarks against spontaneity and opportunism. They are among the factors that distinguish our Party and contribute to the continuity that we think so important.

Some of the agenda for our Party going into our Sixth Congress can be found in the Political Report to our Fifth Congress. In that report we laid out critical mandates that our Party must address if we are to be successful in recruiting into the Party and forwarding the African Revolution. Some of these mandates were not fulfilled and must be kept on the front burner for our current strategy.

These mandates revolve around the urgent need to organize whole sectors of the African population including African students, labor, the imprisoned and women, to begin with. I will quote here the manner in which the Fifth Congress Political Report addressed some of these issues:

> *The Party has also moved to build a student wing of our organization. The African Internationalist Student Organization (AISO) is our work to win African students to a permanent place in the revolution.*
>
> *Students are not a class. However, through the imperialist vetting process of accepted imperialist-influenced definitions of success, especially among the colonized and subject masses, it is not unusual*

for African students to be burdened with deep-seated petty bourgeois aspirations.

AISO must be the weapon in the hands of the African working class to challenge African students to become revolutionary intellectuals. They must be influenced by AISO to reject the attempts of institutionalized seduction, the ongoing efforts to build a wall of contempt between the students and the African working class, in most instances their neighbors, friends and families.

African students must realize that their presence in the academic institutions is a result of concessions to the bloody battles of the working class for access to what was assumed to be an avenue for the advancement of our whole people, not the self-aggrandizement of a chosen few.

There are African student organizations on campuses throughout the U.S., many of which have existed as a consequence of the struggles of the 1960s. For the most part these students are involved in inconsequential and sometimes even decadent activities. These groups also function as "company unions" or arms of the institutional administration.

At best they involve themselves in minor reforms, often directed at improving their lot as students. Many times these students are drawn to African cultural—sometimes mystical—formations or expressions that lead nowhere. Or, they express their militancy or self-defined "blackness" by sponsoring performers, some of whom are political speakers, at their university. In almost every instance, when these students graduate or leave their campuses for other reasons their departure marks the end of their political activism.

AISO is the Party's method of winning the students to our revolution. It is our way of seizing as our base the universities, colleges and even the high schools, where thousands of African students are looking for answers to the issues confronting African people and the world. AISO is the Party's way of contesting bourgeois ideology in the very centers of production and reproduction of bourgeois colonialist ideas and their thinking representatives.

The educational system of the U.S. is one of the major weapons used to undermine the revolutionary consciousness of our people. It is a system that assumes for itself the sometimes not too subtle task of "civilizing" African students. It is a system that is based on the assumption that African students are simply empty vessels, bringing no worthy history or culture of their own to the educational process, waiting to be filled with white colonially informed "knowledge." This results in an instinctive resistance by most of the African students (especially in the middle and high schools), the criminalization of many and a process of vetting those timid and malleable souls most likely to perform future neocolonial functions against the interests of Africans and other oppressed and laboring people.

The vetting process continues during "higher" education, where students are faced with intensive ideological assaults and the results of the reversal of policies won by our movement during a higher point of resistance that opened the doors of the colleges and universities to more African and colonized students.

The key attack on the students, however, is the ever-increasing cost of tuition that serves to eliminate an even larger proportion of the African students. This leaves the possibility of colonial education being primarily open to a narrow elite element of the African population.

Obviously AISO organizers will not suffer from a dearth of issues around which to hone their fighting capacity and organize students and their parents into members and supporters of AISO and the revolution. AISO can turn the campuses into ideological and political battlegrounds that will have significance beyond the campuses. Such struggles during this period of the students' lives can serve to shape and develop a militant African Internationalist consciousness for many of them forever.

The campuses will provide our Party with a ready base of Africans whose primary endeavors are intellectually based. These are Africans who are open to new ideas and are fast developing the capacity to process and develop ideas.

By building AISO we assure the revolution a continuous flow of revolutionary recruits that are won to the ideas of the revolution and have a greater capability of improving on and transmitting those revolutionary ideas. We immediately raise the level of political discussion within our Party and the movement at large.

However, our work to consolidate AISO has left a lot to be desired and we must consider this one of the outstanding issues to be resolved.

The Fifth Congress also spoke to the need for the Party to take seriously the issue of influencing and organizing African labor, Africans in prison and African women.

These sectors contain millions of African people who need to be in organization and who are crucial to the development and leadership of the African Revolution through participation and leadership in their own revolutionary organization, the African People's Socialist Party.

Our approach to these questions also speaks to the pressing question of recruitment that continues to plague us, notwithstanding the success of the OPOPOD Campaign in institutionalizing the recruitment process, along with protocols which when adhered to result in recruitment.

With a proper approach to the issues of students, labor, prisoners and women, we can better engage in mass and what the Chinese called wave recruitment, bringing in entire organizations, neighborhoods or sectors of the population at once. This is something that should guide the National Office of Recruitment and Membership in its approach to recruitment.

Millions of Africans, mostly of the working class, many of whom are concentrated in environments that are most favorable for rapid political education, radicalization and recruitment must be brought directly into the Party or indirectly into the Party through participation in mass organizations under the leadership of the Party.

The rationale for the Party's inclusion of these issues on our agenda can be found in these words of the Fifth Congress Political Report:

Influencing and organizing African labor

Hopefully this period will also see the Party achieve a greater influence within organized labor, especially within trade unions with significant

African membership. While we recognize that within a capitalist world economy all workers are exploited at the point of production, this has different implications for workers of countries whose peoples and resources constituted the "primitive accumulation," or start up of the capitalist system itself.

This "primitive accumulation," made up of whole countries and continents and all that is produced therein; that stems from the enslavement and dispersal of Africans in Africa and globally and continues to operate through colonialism and neocolonialism, is obscured by capitalist production at the point of production.

Neither the workers nor the imperialist economists are able to recognize the relationship between the brutal extraction of coltan from war-torn Congo and the ability to have jobs in Silicon Valley in California and efficiently cheap computers throughout the U.S. and around the world.

They do not recognize the relationship of the African extraction of bauxite from mines in Guyana and Guinea-Conakry and the concomitant loss of sovereignty and freedom, to the jobs created in the U.S., Canada and elsewhere in the European world and their ability to shop at any local supermarket for aluminum goods cheaply produced at the points of production there.

Similarly, African, Mexican and other workers in the U.S., as well as internally colonized workers in other parts of the European world, while exploited at the point of production as workers, suffer the brutality of colonial domination that cannot be resolved by simply struggling to recover the loss of value stolen at the point of production. Ours is a struggle for our liberation as a people and a dispersed, captive nation, whose national homeland provides fodder for the capitalist production that feeds the capitalists and all the beneficiaries of capitalist development.

Our task is to win African workers to a consciousness of themselves as workers who never receive the value of their labor and often not even the value necessary for reproducing real life and the ability to labor.

In addition to educating the workers to this theft of value that goes to make the bourgeoisie rich at the expense of the workers, as Africans the workers must be brought to the understanding that it is our colonial oppression as a people that makes this exploitation possible; that it is our experience at the point of the bayonet that created the conditions for exploitation of workers of the oppressor nation at the point of production.

Hence, the African workers must be brought to consciousness of their task to lead the struggle against our national oppression as a strategic necessity for the emancipation of African labor and the elevation of the African working class to the position of the ruling class of a liberated, united Africa and African people worldwide.

Through the African Socialist International, the Party committed to build an international African labor union that would take on the struggle to win concessions from the bosses where laborers are employed, both in the informal and formal sectors of the economies where they work.

However, the greater task of our labor work would be to take revolutionary science to the struggles of the workers and help them to move toward defeating the existing bourgeois ruling class and overturning the capitalist state in the process of themselves, as workers, becoming the new ruling class in a socialist society.

This would be our main task working with labor here in the U.S. And, while we have a history going back many years of working intermittently with organized African labor in the U.S., it has never had strategic significance for our Party. That must change and hopefully we are on course to contribute to that change.

Incarcerated Africans must be recruited!

The Party's Fifth Congress must resolve to re-establish the African National Prison Organization (ANPO) or some other similar organizational vehicle that can intervene in this critical question of the mass incarceration of African people. In 1979 the Party did organize ANPO as a response to this nakedly brutal attack on the democratic rights and integrity of our colonized community. Internal contradictions within the Party, including a lack of capacity for consistent leadership of ANPO, allowed the organization to die an early death.

Today, with more than 2.3 million people in prisons, the U.S. has by far the largest prison population in the world, outnumbering China's prison population by nearly a million people. One of the obvious reasons for the high number of prisoners in the U.S. is the presence of Africans and other internally colonized subjects. Africans, who according to the U.S. census only make up 13 percent of the population of the U.S., account for at least half of those in prison.

Lame explanations for this rate of incarceration of our people include such inanities as dysfunctional families and pathological communities, poor economies in communities of high African concentration, inadequate job skills, and the like.

However, all these explanations fail to recognize that historically some form of incarceration has victimized our people since we were brought to the shores of the U.S. as enslaved captives. Even at the end of formal enslavement of our people, the 13th Amendment to the U.S. constitution, passed by Congress in January 1865, gave "democratic" cover for our continued enslavement through use of prison, with these words:

"Neither slavery nor involuntary servitude, except as a punishment for crime whereof the party shall have been duly convicted, shall exist within the United States, or any place subject to their jurisdiction." (Emphasis added)

The true measure of the significance of these words for Africans and prison was to be seen in the post-slavery implementation of convict leasing throughout the South. Convict leasing, characterized as "worse than slavery," was a heinous practice of leasing Africans who were convicted on contrived, sometimes designer charges, to plantations of former slave owners and major U.S. corporations and mines.

Convict leasing was considered worse than slavery because unlike the situation with despotic and vermin-like slave owners who had some stake in the preservation of their African private "property," the African convict was the property of the state and the degenerates to whom he was leased had no concern for his safety or well-being. The slogan of convict leasing was "One dies, get another."

In addition to being subjected to the most dangerous, backbreaking, dirty and dignity-crushing labor, torture was a sport that was commonly practiced against imprisoned Africans.

When the system of convict leasing was finally ended after almost a hundred years duration, special prisons that replicated the plantation system of slavery were used throughout the South to control the colonized African population and extort more slave labor from Africans. Prisons from that era, such as Atmore-Holman and Parchman in Alabama and Mississippi, and Raiford and Angola in Florida and Louisiana, became the models for the prison system throughout the U.S.

Today the prisons are cesspools of murder, rape and other forms of violence that are condoned and encouraged throughout the prison system as a means of bestializing and controlling the prisoners as well as the general African population. Special Housing Units (SHU) that utilize sensory deprivation and mind warping techniques are gratuitously used as means of torture.

While the entire prison system is a form of class oppression, it has a special character in the U.S. that is strongly influenced by its use as a tool of control of Africans, Mexicans and other colonial subjects. It is the use of prisons as a tool of colonial control—its use to control the "others"—that make *its bloody tradition and practices permissible to the oppressor nation citizens, even though whites who are imprisoned for lesser durations and with less frequency for similar "offenses," also experience a measure of prison brutality as a form of class oppression.*

We are a captive and colonized population that has never known a measure of freedom since our sojourn in the U.S. We consider all Africans imprisoned in the U.S. to be political prisoners. Because colonialism deprives a subject people of its access to self-determination, the relationship between the colonizer and the colonized is illegitimate, notwithstanding the efforts of the colonizer to paint its oppression in democratic terms.

This means that all who violate the colonial laws of the U.S. are, in fact, violating an illegitimate relationship that was imposed on a whole people at the point of a gun or through some other form of extortionary violence. It is this reality that makes political prisoners of all Africans held in U.S. prisons.

In addition to ordinary African political prisoners, who we refer to as "non-conscious" political prisoners, U.S. prisons are also filled with "conscious" political prisoners, those who have been imprisoned because of acts of resistance or who, while imprisoned were penalized further for acts of resistance. These are men and women who are rotting in prison cells in addition to all those who are imprisoned because of the frame-ups common to our experience as colonial subjects.

The use of the death penalty is another concern that we must address when dealing with the issue of Africans and prisons. It is no accident that the states with the highest incidence of death penalty cases are those with high concentrations of Africans and other colonized people.

The death penalty is another vicious tool of class oppression that expresses itself most sharply against colonial subjects, especially Africans. Opposition to the death penalty must be a defining plank in our anti-prison work.

We must build a prison organization that will take up the issues of political prisoners as well as those others who are unjustly imprisoned according to the class-based, colonial laws of the U.S.

But just as important, we have to build a prison organization that will attack the prison system in its totality as a tool of colonial oppression. Our people and the world must be brought to the understanding that U.S. prisons are despicable organizations of mass torture and brutality and that the prison system is a multi-billion dollar colonial industry that has functioned as economic stimulus for the white population for many years.

The Party's prison organization must make it clear that the real crime is America itself and not the victims of America who are rotting in the colonial prison concentration camps.

We must support all meaningful, non-opportunist efforts to reform the prison system and bring immediate relief to those who are festering in its grips. However, our main task must be to throw open the cell doors and free our people from this form of colonial terror. We must oppose the prison system with all our strength. We must ignite a hatred of the prison system in our people that will make it impossible for the colonial state to successfully maintain its effectiveness against our people and our struggle.

We must also remember that because prison is such a highly concentrated form of class warfare and national oppression, it lends to an easier achievement of revolutionary consciousness among its victims. Prisons must be recognized as critical bases for recruitment into the ranks of the revolution, and our prison organizational work must have such recruitment as its highest objective. Behind the prison walls are a stationary, highly concentrated population of potential students of revolution who must be transformed into revolutionary anti-colonial weapons of conscious African resistance.

Organizing African women as revolutionary leaders

Our Party has always believed in the equality of African men and women and held up the leadership of women in our Party and revolution. For years our position on the question of women in the Party and the world has been summed up in our platform with these words:

"We want an end to the political and social oppression and economic exploitation of African women. We believe in the absolute, unequivocal, political, social and economic equality of African women and men. We believe that a fundamental test of the progressive or revolutionary character of any organization, party, movement or society is its commitment, confirmed in practice, to the destruction of the special oppression of women and the elevation of women to the rightful place as equal partners and leaders in the forward motion of

the development of human society and as leaders, makers and shapers of human history."

Our commitment on the question of women's role in society has always been reflected in the leadership of our Party, where women have historically been well represented and sometimes in the majority. However, we have never structured our Party or our work in a manner to guarantee that concerns and issues critical to the progress and protection of women were always considered and advanced as a natural aspect of all our work.

I am not speaking here of feminism, a bourgeois philosophy that advances a biological analysis that liquidates or minimizes issues of class exploitation and national oppression. We recognize that there really is no such thing as women in general, that there is a huge distinction between the women of the slave owning oppressor nation and the women of the enslaved oppressed nation. All available social and economic data reveal that while there are contradictions between the men and women of the colonizer nation, they are contradictions that play themselves out on the pedestal of the oppression of the colonized or oppressed nation.

The truth is that the oppressor nation can and does resolve fundamental contradictions between oppressor nation men and women at the expense of the whole people of the oppressed nation. North American women do win the "right" to occupy prominent places in oppressor nation military forces that are currently murdering men, women and children all over the world, especially in the Middle East and police operations of the barrios and African domestic colonies of the U.S.

But African women, who often bear the brunt of the attacks on our whole people, are catching hell. It is they who suffer the vicious humiliation and degradation associated with the definition of all women who experience bourgeois rule. But African women also suffer the consequence of being of an oppressed nation that is defined as bestial and inhuman by the ruling class of the oppressor nation.

Additionally, as women of an oppressed nation from which value is extracted at the expense of the ability of the oppressed nation to produce and reproduce real life, African women and girls in most places find themselves reduced to beasts of burden fighting for the survival of themselves, their children and families.

African women and girls carrying massive loads on their heads while walking miles, sometimes with the firewood that they will then have to use to cook for their families, are a common sight on the Continent. Women and girls carrying pails of water balanced on the two ends of poles across their shoulders after having walked all day to procure it, are an iconic sight, consigned to inanimate mental postcard status that reduces the sense of brutality associated with such cruel labor.

The success of the white ruling class and colonial state in breaking up the colonially-imposed monogamous form of the family has resulted in huge concentrations of housing projects and other communities with households headed by single African women left to fend for themselves and their children.

Welfare and other so-called social safety nets that provide "aid" for families do so with a stipulation that there cannot be a man in the house. This "help" from the colonial state, assisted by the mass incarceration of African men, not only leads to women-headed households, but it also heaps artificial contradictions between African men and women onto an already precarious situation.

All too often African women see their children being kidnapped by direct agents of the bourgeois state in places like the U.S., where the children become commodities as foster children or juvenile prisoners. Or, there is the indirect, state-aided kidnapping of their children by white celebrities or agencies whose actions are characterized as charitable benevolence.

Men within our oppressed communities also sometimes subject African women to horrible brutality. Rapes, beatings and even murders of women are too common and are too often viewed with macho approval. These are contradictions of horizontal violence that demand a response by our Party.

They are contradictions that flow from the European-based bourgeois assumption that women are the property of men. They are contradictions that are highly influenced by the reality of bourgeois private property resting on a foundation of Africans ourselves as the primary or primitive private property that gave birth to the capitalist social system. They are contradictions that are inflamed and provoked by the imperialist disruption of African life and the substitute synthetic foundation of colonial society.

African women also find themselves locked into backward social practices that have assumed the weight of culture. Genital mutilation is one of the most obvious of such practices. While there is debate on whether this practice was introduced into Africa by Arabs or other external forces, the fact remains that genital mutilation is a brutal method used in attempt to guarantee male inheritance rights by limiting the sexual freedom of women.

Backward notions of "men's and women's work" also limit women. While some such differentiation may have been valid at one point, the fact is that technology has eliminated much of such differentiation that was often based on physical strength. Today, when work is done by computer or motorized tractor, there is little justification in attempting to prevent women from participation in much of the production process based on physical differences.

This means that in places where the technology has been denied us because of imperialist domination, we must understand that the struggle for technology is a part of the struggle for the emancipation of women. By the same token, the technology that facilitates women's expanded participation in the labor force contributes to the equalization of men and women in the participation of household labor, previously known as women's work.

Our Party must initiate serious struggle against the deplorable conditions suffered by African women. This includes the attitudes that afflict men (and women) who have bought into the notion that women are incapable of leading or that the measure of the worth of a man is his capacity to oppress women.

I am proposing that the Party's Constitution be amended to create a Women's Commission as a permanent position in the leadership of the Party. This is in addition to women who always occupy leadership in the Party in different capacities, as has been our history. This is also different from the concept of dual leadership comprised of men and women. The responsibility of the Women's Commission would be representation of the interests of African women. It would be to organize women to fulfill their roles as revolutionaries that will help to determine the future of women through their fully conscious, organized participation in defining and creating that future.

One such project for this commission would be the organization of an African National Women's Organization (ANWO). ANWO could become the powerful home to African women who are constantly under some form of assault by a myriad of contradictions peculiar to African women. ANWO would provide a mass organization for women who need to confront their oppression and exploitation. It would allow the Party to develop a reserve for the revolution through helping women to recognize the universal contradictions confronting our people and class that are located in the specific contradictions they are confronting as women.

Once again, "Recruit! Recruit! Recruit!"

These are among the important mandates raised by our Political Report or Main Resolution at the Party's Fifth Congress that still must see fulfillment by our Party.

The International People's Democratic Uhuru Movement, All African People's Development and Empowerment Project,

Black Star Industries and the various economic-related institutions under the leadership of the Office of Economic Development and Finance are among the examples of the Party's progress in building a real revolutionary capacity. They are material manifestations of the Party's theory.

The same can be said of the African People's Solidarity Committee and the general strides made in building a solidarity movement under the leadership of the Party and the African Revolution. In addition to this front of our work opening another door for entry into the ranks of our Party-led movement, the solidarity work is also a manifestation of African Internationalism at work. It is a clear example of a theory that works in the real world.

Along with the Black is Back Coalition and its European-based expression, the We are Patrice Lumumba Coalition, these organizations help the Party to provide leadership for masses of Africans at a time when revolutionary leadership is most critical. They help to provide reserve forces for the Party and revolution, and act as training grounds for recruiting and developing new members to forward our revolution.

We must make every effort to grow our ability to provide the necessary leadership and training for the cadres responsible for leading this crucial work. This is fundamental to all our recruiting efforts. This will be a key aspect of our Party-building work coming out of our Sixth Congress. This continues the understanding that influenced the Party's decision to build the One People! One Party! One Destiny! Campaign.

The Party Congress is not an event. It is a place where we lay out our understanding of the world, our place in it and what it will take to build a future of a free, united Africa and African people. The resolutions from the Congress are designed to forge the way forward. However, for the resolutions to be meaningful, they must be followed through and carried out.

One of the fundamental questions our Congress was determined to confront is the issue of recruitment. The defeat of the Black Revolution of the 1960s nearly depleted the ranks of our struggle of revolutionaries and undermined mass consciousness of the need for revolution and revolutionary organization. The Party is the only surviving revolutionary organization that has even understood that our revolution was defeated and requires rebuilding.

The work to organize a student wing of the Party through building the African Internationalist Student Organization; the significance of concentrating on the African labor front; the goal to organize the million or more African prisoners behind bars, and to bring African women fully into revolutionary political organization should inform all our recruitment efforts. This is the work that will facilitate wave and mass recruitment, recruitment that goes beyond the important work done by each Party member and organization to bring individuals into our ranks.

Since the Fifth Congress and establishment of the One People! One Party! One Destiny! Campaign, the Party has struggled to push the newly-created recruitment office, the National Office of Recruitment and Membership (NORM), to develop and implement a serious recruitment campaign.

Our Sixth Party Congress is mandating a recruitment Plan of Action that, first of all, concentrates on building and developing existing fronts of our Party. This includes APSC, InPDUM, AAPDEP, BSI and the host of related economic components of the Party.

Our cadre development work must involve ideological and organizational training for carrying out the work in these areas and becoming more proficient in using them as platforms through which we recruit growing numbers into the Party and Party-led organizations.

We must develop a greater political and ideological appreciation for our work with the Black is Back Coalition and the We are Patrice Lumumba Coalition. Our coalition work provides the Party the necessary organizational tool to extend the Party's influence within various mass movements and allows us opportunities to help them with the correct line around the pressing issues of our times.

This is especially true of the questions revolving around war and peace. These are issues usually dominated by white leftists, the loyal opposition that may protest various imperialist policies instead of opposing imperialism itself.

Also, the white Left is never able to describe the attacks on Africans, Mexicans and Indigenous people as the colonial wars that they are. Their politics usually assume legitimacy of the colonial relationship enjoyed by those who are colonized within the borders of the U.S. even if they think there are unjust aspects associated with the relationship.

Our coalition work also affords the Party our most consistent recent arena of recruitment. This is another reason the Party must develop a Plan of Action to make this work more efficient and effective and Party members must be provided the ideological, political and organizational skills to do coalition work.

Obviously I am laying out a general plan for recruitment that has been overlooked or neglected since our Fifth Congress. This is the material that our recruitment office must use as the basis of any recruitment strategy.

When added to the development of our student, prison, labor and women's work as well as all our mass organizational fronts, building our coalitions gives us a comprehensive strategy for recruitment that keeps our Party constantly involved in providing leadership for all the critical questions facing the masses today. This is a recruitment strategy that is tied to revolutionary practice.

African Internationalist Party-building is directly connected to forwarding the revolutionary process. It is not building an organization simply for the sake of doing so.

In summation, to achieve our Party's commitment to advance the African Revolution that will provide the strategic leadership for the emerging world revolution to overthrow an imperialism in crisis, our Sixth Congress must continue Party-building as our strategic thrust.

Immediately this will mean developing the existing Party committees, organizations and institutions that now comprise the basic constituent components of our Party. Namely, this includes AAPDEP, APSC, InPDUM, Black Star Industries and the related economic expressions of the Party's Office of Economic Development and Finance.

For the most part, the structures, plans and leadership are in place to develop and/or implement this aspect of our Party-building work. We must simply continue to insist that this work is carried out as mandated under the principles and protocols developed through the One People! One Party! One Destiny! Campaign. Recruitment strategies must employ the necessary plans for developing the cadres for the success of this work within each of the constituent organizations and committees.

Secondly, the National Office of Recruitment and Membership must organize a strategy to advance the areas of the work put forward in the Fifth Congress Political Report. This includes developing AISO, the African labor work, prison organizing and the consolidation of the African Women's Commission and the African National Women's Organization.

The plan from NORM will provide the coherence for that work that has been missing up to now. It will take the abstraction out of our recruitment, move us away from the elusive mission of organizing the masses in general and give us actual definable targets for recruitment and the ability to build plans for carrying out the work with specific timetables according to a specific recruitment agenda.

Become African Internationalist propagandists

Our basic organizational training mission should be geared toward building the organizational, political and ideological capacity of our members and organizations to realize this end.

Since the Party's Fifth Congress we have focused on organizational and political development, while the ideological development has lagged. We must fix that.

The Party must become an organization of propagandists with a primary mission of spreading the theory of African Internationalism. This means that we must equip the members of our Party for this task. We recognize the absolute necessity to change the political narrative. The current narrative relies on an imperialist or imperialist-influenced, European-based worldview that is incapable of defining reality from a materialist perspective.

African Internationalism represents the participation of the peoples of the Earth, made "wretched" by becoming the "primitive accumulation" upon which the foundation of the prevailing social system and its ideological manifestations depends.

This Political Report to our Sixth Congress is central to this work. All our organizations must initiate study of this Political Report. Our Party's Constitution mandates at least three months for study and discussion of the Report, but it is critical that we continue to study this document on an on-going basis. Our members must be transformed into enthusiastic African Internationalist evangelists who recognize that the promised land of African liberation and unification can only be entered when we have gained supremacy in the ideological struggle with imperialism and its representatives.

The entire APSP membership and movement must be made aware of the task history has imposed on our Party and the Africans and poor peasants of the world. Stated simply our task is to build the African People's Socialist Party, the revolutionary organization of the advanced detachment of the international African working class.

Our Party of the general staff of the African working class is the only instrument capable of leading the international African Revolution to victory over imperialism and the elevation of the African working class to the position of the ruling class in a liberated socialist Africa and African world.

While we will engage imperialism in struggle on every front and in every area of the world around a myriad of issues that will sometimes include reform; and although the various committees and organizations under the influence and leadership of the Party will continue to organize to accomplish their specific missions, the strategic work of the Party will continue to be directed at building the Party.

We must emerge from this period as the strong and accomplished instrument necessary to win the socialist liberation and unification of Africa and the dispersed African nation.

Comrades, the process of preparing this Political Report to our Sixth Congress was complicated by the blistering pace of changing events that characterize this era of the Final Offensive against Imperialism. Every day there is new evidence of crisis. Fortunately the Party's constitutionally mandated three month period for study and criticism of this Political Report requires me to end it and turn it over to you.

Undoubtedly there will be major crisis-related changes occurring in the world by the time of our Sixth Congress. The parasitic world capitalist economy is being uprooted by the formerly prostrate and subjugated mass of humanity.

Social upheaval is naturally following in the wake of the fissures in the economic base of slavery and colonialism, threatening all existing ideas and institutions. Everything of the past that was assumed to be true is being called into question by the unfolding events of history.

We are mobilized! This Congress of our Party will function to establish the African People's Socialist Party in our proper role as facilitators of history. We are the harbingers of human progress that will result in the end of misery for the world's majority and the destruction of a social system that relies on exploitation and suffering for its success.

This Congress will serve to arm every single member of our Party with the theory, confidence and organization to reclaim our history, our dignity and Our Africa.

We will win!

We are winning!

Part II

Resolutions from the Sixth Congress of the African People's Socialist Party

RESOLUTION 1

Build the African Socialist International; defeat the neocolonial AU

The ASI, as the organization of African workers, will build a single all-African union and defeat the petty bourgeois OAU/AU.

WHEREAS, the creation of the Organization of African Unity (OAU) was a reflection of the interests of international imperialism with the complicity of a sector of the African petty bourgeoisie, with the aim to maintain the status quo and the colonially imposed borders in Africa; and

WHEREAS, the OAU, which later became the African Union (AU) is an instrument of the African petty bourgeoisie for the purpose of reproducing itself as a social class within the imperialist-created artificial borders of Africa; and

WHEREAS, the imperialist-funded OAU/AU was created to stop and reverse the African Revolution that achieved its greatest momentum in the 1960s, threatening the destruction of the artificial borders separating Africans from each other and from our resources; and

WHEREAS, the African petty bourgeoisie rejects genuine African unity which will overturn imperialism; and

WHEREAS, the African petty bourgeois leaders and the imperialists of the United States, the United Kingdom and France united against Nkrumah's vision of the immediate creation of a single government of an African continental political union;

NOW, THEREFORE, BE IT RESOLVED BY THE SIXTH CONGRESS OF THE AFRICAN PEOPLE'S SOCIALIST PARTY HELD IN ST. PETERSBURG, FLORIDA, ON THE DATES DECEMBER 7-11, 2013:

SECTION ONE: That the African People's Socialist Party will launch an international struggle to overthrow parasitic capitalism and its neocolonial minions in order to achieve the unification and liberation of Africa and African people under the leadership of the African working class in a society that will, as declared by Kwame Nkrumah, "advance the triumph of the international socialist revolution and onward progress towards world communism, under which every society is ordered on the principle of—from each according to...ability, to each according to...needs."; and

SECTION TWO: That the African Socialist International (ASI), the revolutionary organization of African workers, will intensify its efforts with the objective of uniting Africa under the government of a single all-African union led by the African working class and poor peasantry; and

SECTION THREE: That the ASI will launch and lead an international struggle to reverse the betrayal of the OAU/AU, by ending petty bourgeois rule and replacing it with the rule of African workers in alliance with poor peasants; and

SECTION FOUR: That this resolution shall be in full force and effect immediately upon its adoption and approval in the manner provided by the Constitution of the African People's Socialist Party and the Rules of Procedure of this Congress.

RESOLUTION 2

Support the Mexican national liberation struggle

Maintain the strategic alliance and active collaboration between the APSP and Unión del Barrio.

WHEREAS, Unión del Barrio is a Mexican liberation organization that struggles for the socialist unification of Mexico and Latin America under political, social and economic control by Raza, Indigenous workers and peasants; and

WHEREAS, the African People's Socialist Party is an African liberation organization that struggles for the socialist unification of Africa under political, social and economic control by African workers and peasants; and

WHEREAS, Mexicans and Africans suffer under colonial violence and oppression characterized by European settler colonialism in both Africa and the Americas, including what is known today as the United States; and

WHEREAS, the economic basis of our oppression is the extraction of the value of our labor by the capitalist bosses, the usurpation of our natural resources, the dispossession of our lands and the division of our peoples; and

WHEREAS, our peoples represent the great majority of workers, the creators of all material wealth throughout the continents of Africa and the Americas and are collectively at least a third of the population within the political borders of the United States;

NOW, THEREFORE, BE IT RESOLVED BY THE SIXTH CONGRESS OF THE AFRICAN PEOPLE'S SOCIALIST

PARTY HELD IN ST. PETERSBURG, FLORIDA, ON THE DATES DECEMBER 7-11, 2013:

SECTION ONE: That the African People's Socialist Party and Unión del Barrio shall maintain a strategic alliance to raise the class consciousness of our communities to build the necessary revolutionary unity to bring Mexicans and Africans into revolutionary struggle and organization. We resolve to bring our peoples into organized struggle where we do not have organizational representation on the ground. We recognize that a strong and consolidated revolutionary party in the form of the African People's Socialist Party or Unión del Barrio is a victory for both peoples; and

SECTION TWO: That the African People's Socialist Party and Unión del Barrio shall collaborate strategically to reach as many people as possible in each of our working class communities to end the horizontal violence as a result of European imposed colonial subjectivism that distorts our perspectives as to our common enemy; and

SECTION THREE: That we will set the example for our communities by uniting to combat the efforts of the state to pit our people against each other in order to maintain the state's hegemonic political, economic and social control over our peoples; and

SECTION FOUR: That when possible we will work to bring representatives of each of our parties to gatherings to deepen our political, ideological, organizational and economic practices; and

SECTION FIVE: That this resolution shall be in full force and effect immediately upon its adoption and approval in the manner provided by the Constitution of the African People's Socialist Party and the Rules of Procedure of this Congress.

RESOLUTION 3

Build the African People's Socialist Party Bahamas

Combat the imperial and neocolonial rule of foreign capitalists and the black petty bourgeoisie by building the African People's Socialist Party as the revolutionary party of the African working class in The Bahamas.

WHEREAS, despite the fact that in the general election of May 2012, the Progressive Liberal Party and Free National Movement both campaigned on platforms promising to bring peace and prosperity to all in The Bahamas, the gap between "the haves" and "the have-nots" has increased, with the African working class still exploited and oppressed; and

WHEREAS, European imperialists and the African petty bourgeoisie in The Bahamas continue to work together to keep the African working class in social and economic misery; and

WHEREAS, the only solutions that the African petty bourgeois leadership offers to the current economic and social crisis are holidays and cultural events that promote Bahamian nationalism, which is nothing but petty bourgeois nationalism, along with European-enforced structural adjustment policies that lead to the privatization of social services and basic utilities and the further underdevelopment of the African working class in The Bahamas; and

WHEREAS, after the general election of May 2012, nothing has fundamentally changed for Africans in The Bahamas; the African working class is still being oppressed and exploited by foreign and national capitalists;

NOW, THEREFORE, BE IT RESOLVED BY THE SIXTH CONGRESS OF THE AFRICAN PEOPLE'S SOCIALIST PARTY HELD IN ST. PETERSBURG, FLORIDA, ON THE DATES DECEMBER 7-11, 2013:

SECTION ONE: The African People's Socialist Party stands in total opposition to imperial and neocolonial rule and leadership in The Bahamas and other countries where Africans are dispersed throughout the Caribbean and the world; and

SECTION TWO: The African People's Socialist Party will do all within our power to emancipate all African people and build the African nation; and

SECTION THREE: That toward this end, the African People's Socialist Party will build the Party in The Bahamas as the true voice for the African working class; and

SECTION FOUR: That this resolution shall be in full force and effect immediately upon its adoption and approval in the manner provided by the Constitution of the African People's Socialist Party and the Rules of Procedure of this Congress.

RESOLUTION 4

Organize families of police murder victims

The International People's Democratic Uhuru Movement will organize African families of victims of police murder.

WHEREAS, a statistic reveals that every 28 hours an African in the U.S. is killed by the police or civilian white vigilantes functioning as arms of the colonial state; and

WHEREAS, the police departments, courts and legal system label these assassinations legally justifiable; and

WHEREAS, in the absence of organized African working class political power, hundreds of African mothers, wives, sisters, family members and the African community in general, in addition to the burden of having lost our loved ones, are forced to live with a sense of helplessness; and

WHEREAS, this attack on African people represents a clear example of genocide by the definition in the United Nations *Convention on the Prevention and Punishment of Genocide* which speaks to "murdering members of a group;" and

WHEREAS, the African People's Socialist Party recognizes this question as an important question that must be brought under the leadership of the African Revolution, so as to mobilize masses of colonized Africans and our allies internationally to implement Point 8 of the African People's Socialist Party's 14-Point Platform which calls for the removal of the police from African communities;

NOW, THEREFORE, BE IT RESOLVED BY THE SIXTH CONGRESS OF THE AFRICAN PEOPLE'S SOCIALIST

PARTY HELD IN ST. PETERSBURG, FLORIDA, ON THE DATES DECEMBER 7-11, 2013:

SECTION ONE: That the International People's Democratic Uhuru Movement, the revolutionary mass organization of the African People's Socialist Party, uses its 2014 Convention to organize African families and the African community in general to not only implement Point 8, but also to launch the international campaign for reparations to the families of the murdered Africans; and

SECTION TWO: That this resolution shall be in full force and effect immediately upon its adoption and approval in the manner provided by the Constitution of the African People's Socialist Party and the Rules of Procedure of this Congress.

RESOLUTION 5

Establish a Know Your Rights campaign throughout the African community

Combat and document the harassment and brutalization of Africans by the police in the U.S. by establishing a Know Your Rights campaign throughout the African community.

WHEREAS, 200,000 people, mostly African and Latino, were stopped and frisked by police in 2012 in Philadelphia and millions of people, mostly African and Latino, have been stopped and frisked to date in New York City; and

WHEREAS, on a daily basis all over the U.S. the police use counterinsurgent measures of population and resource control, stopping thousands of African people in a colonial tactic similar to the pass laws used against African people colonized under Apartheid in South Africa; and

WHEREAS, the police act as the front line of the legal colonial force against African people who are colonized in the U.S.; and

WHEREAS, the rights and lives of African people are under direct threat by police counterinsurgency tactics that attack our right to organize and hold up our own leaders; and

WHEREAS, Point 8 of the African People's Socialist Party's 14-Point Platform states in part, "We want the immediate withdrawal of the U.S. police from our oppressed and exploited communities. We believe that the various U.S. police agencies which occupy our communities are arms of the U.S. colonialist state which is responsible for keeping our people enslaved and terrorized. We believe that the U.S. police agencies do not serve us, but instead represent the first line of U.S. defense against the just struggle of our people for peace, dignity and socialist democracy. Therefore, we believe the U.S. police are an illegitimate standing army, a colonial army in the African community and must withdraw immediately...";

NOW, THEREFORE, BE IT RESOLVED BY THE SIXTH CONGRESS OF THE AFRICAN PEOPLE'S SOCIALIST PARTY HELD IN ST. PETERSBURG, FLORIDA, ON THE DATES DECEMBER 7-11, 2013:

SECTION ONE: The African People's Socialist Party stands in total opposition to the harassment, brutalization and murder of African people by the police; and

SECTION TWO: The African People's Socialist Party will do all within our power to win mass participation in the Know Your Rights campaign and will build the campaign through our mass organizations. This campaign will consist of recruiting the African community to use camera phones and other recording devices to document police activity in the African community as well as reproducing "Know Your Rights" cards in mass to be distributed throughout the African community; and

SECTION THREE: That toward this end the African People's Socialist Party will help drive the Know Your Rights campaign through our mass organizations and Party members participating in those mass organizations. The Party will provide political education and leadership to the campaign; and

SECTION FOUR: The police must be driven from the African community; and

SECTION FIVE: That this resolution shall be in full force and effect immediately upon its adoption and approval in the manner provided by the Constitution of the African People's Socialist Party and the Rules of Procedure of this Congress.

RESOLUTION 6

Organize youth and families into the Uhuru Movement

Build Marcus Garvey Saturday schools and Uhuru Houses in New Jersey. Win African youth to revolutionary organization.

WHEREAS, the Chairman's Political Report speaks to the need to organize African women, workers and prisoners; we propose that organizing African youth can fundamentally reach all the targets the Chairman spoke to in the Report; and

WHEREAS, African youth (teens and young adults) are becoming African workers, they should be won to enter the work force with African Internationalism and organization; and

WHEREAS, African males make up a disproportionate percentage of prisoners in the U.S., we recognize that colonial attacks systematically target African youth—especially African males—through schools, youth correctional facilities and in other ways;

NOW, THEREFORE, BE IT RESOLVED BY THE SIXTH CONGRESS OF THE AFRICAN PEOPLE'S SOCIALIST PARTY HELD IN ST. PETERSBURG, FLORIDA, ON THE DATES DECEMBER 7-11, 2013:

SECTION ONE: To educate youth on the importance of revolutionary organization, guided by African Internationalism; and

SECTION TWO: To provide organized revolutionary activity; and

SECTION THREE: To win neighborhoods through youth and family organization; and

SECTION FOUR: To start and sustain Marcus Garvey Saturday Schools; and

SECTION FIVE: To open Uhuru Houses in Newark and Plainfield, New Jersey, as centralized havens for the African community and to organize the youth in order to control our communities; and

SECTION SIX: To enhance the ability of *The Burning Spear* newspaper and other Party organs to target African youth; and

SECTION SEVEN: That this resolution shall be in full force and effect immediately upon its adoption and approval in the manner provided by the Constitution of the African People's Socialist Party and the Rules of Procedure of this Congress.

RESOLUTION 7

Rebuild the International People's Democratic Uhuru Movement in Oakland, California

Combat the continued anti-African, anti-democratic attacks on the African community by the Oakland city government.

WHEREAS, for several months, the Oakland Uhuru House has not seen real political activity and we must, therefore, organize African workers back into revolutionary political life; and

WHEREAS, the Oakland city government, in the form of the city council and mayor Jean Quan, have intensified the police occupation of African communities throughout Oakland; and

WHEREAS, the city of Oakland has stepped up the gentrification, which continues to displace Africans into areas remote from Oakland; and

WHEREAS, the unorganized African community has remained defenseless under these and other colonial attacks;

NOW, THEREFORE, BE IT RESOLVED BY THE SIXTH CONGRESS OF THE AFRICAN PEOPLE'S SOCIALIST PARTY HELD IN ST. PETERSBURG, FLORIDA, ON THE DATES DECEMBER 7-11, 2013:

SECTION ONE: That the members of the International People's Democratic Uhuru Movement (InPDUM) in Oakland stand ready to take on these critical political questions of police occupation, gentrification and the economic stagnation of the African community caused by the colonial domination exercised by the city of Oakland; and

SECTION TWO: That the members of InPDUM in Oakland have already submitted a plan of action which focuses on the reestablishment of a Local Executive Committee, Sunday mass rallies and political actions that include the reimplementation of the monthly African Community Conventions and the call for the establishment of an African Community Farmers/Flea Market to push the question of genuine African economic self-reliance; and

SECTION THREE: That in order to forward the economic and political progress for African workers in Oakland, the African People's Socialist Party will provide political guidance for InPDUM as it establishes an African Community City Council; and

SECTION FOUR: That this resolution shall be in full force and effect immediately upon its adoption and approval in the manner provided by the Constitution of the African People's Socialist Party and the Rules of Procedure of this Congress.

RESOLUTION 8

Free Lynne Stewart now!

On December 31, 2013, a few weeks after the Congress, Lynne Stewart was released from prison following a mass campaign of intensive international pressure on the U.S. government. Comrade Stewart spent four years as a political prisoner of the U.S. government.

BE IT RESOLVED BY THE SIXTH CONGRESS OF THE AFRICAN PEOPLE'S SOCIALIST PARTY HELD IN ST. PETERSBURG, FLORIDA, ON THE DATES DECEMBER 7-11, 2013:

SECTION ONE: That the African People's Socialist Party recommits to the liberation of Lynne Stewart, who we recognize as a political prisoner of the U.S. government; and

SECTION TWO: That toward this end the Secretaries General of the African People's Socialist Party and the African Socialist International will immediately adopt the Campaign for Justice for Lynne Stewart, mobilizing our base within the U.S. and throughout the world through a phone and social media campaign targeting U.S. president Barack Hussein Obama, attorney general Eric Holder and Bureau of Prisons director Charles Samuels demanding the immediate release of Comrade Stewart to be effected during the upcoming Christmas holidays and no later than January 1, 2014; and

SECTION THREE: That this resolution shall be in full force and effect immediately upon its adoption and approval in the manner provided by the Constitution of the African People's Socialist Party and the Rules of Procedure of this Congress.

RESOLUTION 9

Combat abusive housing policies imposed on the African community of Chicago

The Uhuru Movement will organize against colonial housing policies in Chicago that separate African people from their families and force them to live in hazardous conditions.

WHEREAS, it is typical for Africans to be on so-called "bar lists," which prevent people from seeing their own families in public housing units in Chicago, and those barred from their families in public housing units include teenagers younger than 16 years old; and

WHEREAS, the African petty bourgeoisie attempts to distract Africans from our goals of self-government and independence; and

WHEREAS, the housing conditions are hazardous due to insect and rodent infestations and contain other unsafe structural conditions;

NOW, THEREFORE, BE IT RESOLVED BY THE SIXTH CONGRESS OF THE AFRICAN PEOPLE'S SOCIALIST PARTY HELD IN ST. PETERSBURG, FLORIDA, ON THE DATES DECEMBER 7-11, 2013:

SECTION ONE: That the International People's Democratic Uhuru Movement fights for African community control of housing and self-determination; and

SECTION TWO: That the African People's Socialist Party engages the masses of African people to fight for self-determination and enter political life through the International People's Democratic Uhuru Movement; and

SECTION THREE: That towards this end, the African People's Socialist Party, with the help of all appropriate Party organizations, will help drive this campaign to overturn the conditions faced by Africans in public housing units; and

SECTION FOUR: That this resolution shall be in full force and effect immediately upon its adoption and approval in the manner provided by the Constitution of the African People's Socialist Party and the Rules of Procedure of this Congress.

RESOLUTION 10

Build solidarity with the Roma people

*Stop the attacks and persecution
of the Roma people and build solidarity.*

WHEREAS, the Roma people live under political conditions of persecution and humiliation around the world and especially in Europe; and

WHEREAS, many Roma live below the poverty line in slums and suburbs in the worst conditions possible; and

WHEREAS, Roma children are segregated into ghetto schools, assumed to be incapable of achieving the very first levels of education; and

WHEREAS, hundreds of thousands of Roma families face unemployment and Roma workers are the worst paid workers in Europe; and

WHEREAS, between 1971 and 1991, the Czech Republic and Slovakia reduced the Roma population through sterilization of Roma women without their knowledge; and

WHEREAS, an estimated 500,000 Roma were slaughtered by Nazi Germany; and

WHEREAS, the Roma people have been under constant repression since their arrival in Europe 700 years ago; and

WHEREAS, representatives of the Roma people have stated that, "The only solution for Roma people is to join with other oppressed people to overthrow our financial and political domination by the white world, to stop the inhumane capitalist regime and to fight for emancipation and equal rights all over the world for all people. The only solution is the revolution of the oppressed people;"

NOW, THEREFORE, BE IT RESOLVED BY THE SIXTH CONGRESS OF THE AFRICAN PEOPLE'S SOCIALIST PARTY HELD IN ST. PETERSBURG, FLORIDA, ON THE DATES OF DECEMBER 7-11, 2013:

SECTION ONE: That the African People's Socialist Party stands in total opposition to the attacks on the Roma people by governments as well as by the white population and white nationalist vigilantes; and

SECTION TWO: That the African People's Socialist Party will do all within our power to build solidarity with the Roma people; and

SECTION THREE: That toward this end, the African People's Socialist Party will call for an international meeting of oppressed peoples, including the Roma people, to take place in Europe as part of a revolutionary trajectory promoting the movements for liberation for all those who have borne the brunt of white power colonial domination; and

SECTION FOUR: That this resolution shall be in full force and effect immediately upon its adoption and approval in the manner provided by the Constitution of the African People's Socialist Party and the Rules of Procedure of this Congress.

Part III

Solidarity Statements to the Sixth Congress of the African People's Socialist Party

Benjamin Prado

Undersecretary General, Unión del Barrio

Uhuru!

I would like to express deep appreciation and gratitude to the Central Committee of the African People's Socialist Party and to Compañero Omali Yeshitela, Chairman of the African People's Socialist Party.

To all you delegates, Compañeros y Compañeras:

On behalf of Unión del Barrio, a Mexican liberation organization founded within the political borders of the United States, based in Southern California primarily, we extend our fraternal message of solidarity. We salute this Congress for its historic character, for its significance in the liberation movements not only of African people but also of Mexican people and all oppressed peoples around the world.

Unión del Barrio was founded in 1981 after the defeat of the Chicano Power Movement of the 1960s and 1970s. It was founded by comrades and it's fitting to be here to express this message. The last person to deliver a solidarity statement on behalf of our organization was our founder and comrade Ernesto Bustillos, who addressed the Party's Fifth Congress in 2010.

It is through his example and his sacrifice that we created this alliance of nearly 30 years with the African People's Socialist Party.

It is a tremendous honor for me to be here with you. Coming into this hall, listening to the presentations both cultural and political that have just briefly begun, and to be amongst those who struggle for peace, justice, dignity and freedom is an inspiration to our movement.

It is truly an honor to participate and engage with you because it is at this Congress that the questions of organization, unity and liberation are being discussed. In no other place here in the United States is this kind of discussion taking place where the crisis of imperialism is recognized as having been caused by the people who are conscious, the people who have been dispossessed, the people who have had our labor subjected to the worst kind of exploitation as we continue to struggle to reclaim not only our labor power but also our lands; to live with justice and dignity.

So it is an honor for us to participate in this discussion here today.

It is also important for us because it is not every day that organizations like the African People's Socialist Party hold this type of gathering. This is only the Sixth Congress in the Party's entire 41-year history.

For us, the historic character of the Party congresses is of tremendous significance precisely because the congresses provide clarity, direction and most importantly the unity that is necessary to carry out the Final Offensive, which is laid out in the Party Congress documents and the Political Report.

For us, this organization represents the highest expression of commitment and struggle to overturn this terrible parasitic relationship that we have with capitalism. We cannot talk about change; we cannot talk about revolution; we cannot talk about any type of living with peace and justice if we are not part of an organized resistance to that parasitism. Unión del Barrio is an organization that fights and struggles to unify our communities and our peoples, to unify the working masses of the Méxicano, Latino Américano and Indigenous peoples of Nuestra América.

We, as an organization, believe in the historical process of the socialist unification of Mexico and of the entire continent known today as Latin America. We see ourselves intrinsically linked to and unified with the peoples and struggles of all Latino América.

As a people we recognize that our lands, our histories and our traditions are indigenous to this continent. We refuse to accept any falsification of our history or any political and economic restrictions that limit our people's ability to move freely throughout this continent.

We, as an organization, recognize that we are on stolen Indigenous lands and that U.S. imperialism and the European settler nation washed up on this continent now known as the Americas but which we have historically known and recognized as Abya Yala.

This continent has its original name and we have the historical memory to recognize that we as an indigenous people have every historical right to live on our land. We have the right to work for ourselves with the capacity to build roads, houses, bridges and all types of infrastructure. We have the right to benefit from our own labor, to feed our families, to clothe ourselves and to be able to live with justice, dignity and as human beings. We reject the slander of the U.S. and the settler population in labeling us "illegal aliens" and "criminal illegal aliens" on our own land.

The Political Report to this Congress has consistently laid out that there would be no U.S. imperialism without the theft of our lands, without the usurpation of our resources and without the parasitic relationship that capitalism has with our peoples.

That is why this type of gathering here today is of significance to the Mexican Liberation Movement. We see ourselves physically linked and connected to the rest of humanity, and the rest of humanity is the majority of the people in this world who are suffering the same oppression, the same attacks, the same assaults by our common enemy known as capitalism, imperialism and colonialism.

As a people who struggle for our very liberation, we unite with the African People's Socialist Party in celebrating this historic event. Our solidarity goes beyond the fraternal relationships that we've had. It goes deeper than a strategic alliance to put that final nail in the coffin of a dying imperialism and a dying colonialism.

Finally, I would like to express that the liberation movements taking place in all of Latin America, with the historic example of revolutionary Cuba, are now expanding. We see today a movement throughout Latin America that links us to a strategic battle in the struggle to reclaim our natural resources. The examples of revolutionary Cuba, of revolutionary Venezuela, of Bolivia and Ecuador make it clear that the time has come for the masses of the world and oppressed people to reclaim our rightful place in history and move forward a revolutionary process that will defeat our common enemy.

In our historic alliance as part of a historic continental liberation movement, as we struggle to unify an entire continent, we envision a world without borders. Just as Africa has been divided by the colonizers, so has Nuestra América—Latin America—been divided by the imperial powers.

Today, we see our struggle intrinsically linked to that unifying process that is happening throughout Nuestra América. Our historical reference can never be defined by what happens in Washington or Sacramento or any state capital, but by what is defined within the movements of Nuestra América and even of Africa.

We are part of the struggles of the peoples of the world to create an economy that is fundamentally based on working people, based on the fact that we as working people who produce the wealth of society must be able to be the main benefactors of the fruit of our labor.

What is being expressed today is that strategy to build the necessary organization, the necessary unity and the necessary ideological clarity that will move that process forward.

We are proud and we are honored to share this historic moment with you. We extend to you our most heartfelt congratulations for this event. We look forward to engaging in the debates and the struggles that will lend clarity because it's not only clarity for the African Liberation Movement; it's also clarity for us as a liberation movement that struggles to reclaim our lands and resources. We understand and recognize that at some point our movements and our struggles are one movement and one struggle!

The necessary unity that is being debated and discussed here today is one that we will bring back to our organization because throughout our nearly 30-year history of unity and alliance we have learned tremendously from the example of the African People's Socialist Party.

We continue to uphold the African People's Socialist Party's unconditional right to determine its destiny and we will continue to be alongside you in struggle, in alliance to form the necessary organization and unity that will carry forward our struggle for freedom and liberation.

¡Hasta la victoria siempre!

¡Venceremos!

Nkwame Cedile

Organizer, Enkangala Kwantu Embo,
Occupied Azania

Dear comrades, let me greet you in the name of my community based organization Enkangala Kwantu Embo, which envisages a world where Africans occupy our rightful place among all nations of the world as respected human beings and not just as objects of Arabic, Chinese and white parasitic capitalism.

The Sixth Congress of the African People's Socialist Party comes at a time when Africans the world over seem to be under siege, whether it is the majority of black South Africans in Occupied Azania, the Marikana massacre, the attack on the original Libyans after the fall of the Qaddafi government by the racist Arabs, or the attack on Africans in Saudi Arabia, again by the racist Arabs. The attacks on Africans in America have not stopped after the killing of Trayvon Martin and we see the attacks on Africans and the people of Occupied Palestine by the racist government of Israel.

Comrades, as has been said by the great African giants such as Marcus Garvey, Malcolm X and Patrice Lumumba, it is upon us now as we are the ones we have been waiting for.

Izwe Lethu i Afrika!

Filiz Demirova and Georgel Caldararu

Roma activists based in Germany

Uhuru!

We would like to express our profound appreciation for having the chance to give our statement to the Sixth Congress of the African People's Socialist Party.

We believe that this Congress is a very important gathering and we are thankful to have this great opportunity to speak about the situation of the Romani people without any censorship.

We believe that this is a strong sign of solidarity and therefore we send you our appreciation and our solidarity together with our statement.

The foundation of Europe is based on the enslavement, oppression and exploitation of African, Asian and other peoples. The economic development, financial supremacy and political power of the European states have their origins in hundreds of years of robbery, wars and extermination of millions of innocent people.

As Chairman Omali Yeshitela says, slavery as a process created a political economy that is parasitic. It is an economy that must suck the blood of Africa and of African and oppressed peoples of the world in order to survive.

Roma are located in between borders in a bureaucratic, political and social no-man's land where they are persecuted and humiliated. They live below the poverty line in slums, suburbs and in the worst conditions possible, having no access to resources, being forced to feed their families from the garbage and being victims of disease provoked by the worst living conditions, hunger and lack of healthcare.

Roma children are segregated into ghetto schools, assumed incapable of achieving the very first levels of education and very often treated as animals. They are stigmatized and have no prospects from the very beginning of their lives. Many of them live on the streets, exposed to drugs, child prostitution and human trafficking. They never gain the chance to live in better conditions, to have their needs met, to receive basic respect as human beings.

The unemployment rate in our communities is intolerably high, touching hundreds of thousands of families. As a consequence, the majority of those families have a very low income that makes Roma the worst paid workers in Europe.

The teenagers are victims of marginalization and racist assaults. They are eliminated from public life because they are considered criminals. They are targeted for violence and hatred on a daily basis. Their presence is not wanted and they're seen as foreigners even if they are born in the land in which they live.

Roma women suffer all kinds of prejudices. They are exposed to the worst experiences possible, forced into prostitution and the lowest paid jobs that can be found.

Between 1971 and 1991 in Czechoslovakia, now the Czech Republic and Slovakia, the Roma population was reduced through surgical sterilization, performed without the knowledge of the women themselves. It was a widespread government practice. The life of the Roma is a long road of humiliation, permanent fear and isolation.

The majority of our people have a very low income. They have no access to medical assistance and in the very few cases they do, they are treated poorly. Very often they are sent home to die when their lives can still be saved. Many have no resources to pay their debts and remain homeless. They are ignored by the institutions and not protected by any law.

After the Second World War, Roma were forced to keep silent about Nazi era persecution in which hundreds of thousands of Romani people were slaughtered. At the same time, the USA and western European states were more interested in supporting Germany, which was and is responsible for the murder of millions of people and the disaster of Europe. Instead of helping the Roma victims, the situation of Roma people was ignored for more than 50 years.

After the reunification of Germany in 1992, it became the most important political and economic power in Europe. At the same time, there was no solidarity or reparations given to Roma people. Conditions in many Roma communities have not changed since the end of the Second World War. There has been no interest in supporting these communities or to fight the racism and discrimination they face.

Actually, the persecution of the Roma never ended since the arrival of our people over 700 years ago. There is no period of time when Roma were treated equally. For 700 years, Roma life has meant fear of murder, fear of brutality, abuses of discrimination of all kinds, deportations and isolation.

In 2005, at the initiative of George Soros, governments of 12 European states signed the agreement known as the Decade of Roma Inclusion. What was meant to be a sign of solidarity ended as an explosion of resentment and hate.

Any political campaign is a threat to Roma life. Corrupt and irresponsible politicians misused the Roma's situation and the lack of representation at the official level to propagate populist anti-Roma measures. These are euphemistically known as struggles against criminality, when actually the real criminals are sitting in the parliaments and governments.

Human rights abuses are a common practice. Roma can be deported from one country to another within Europe, even if they are European citizens or are victims of racial persecution in the countries from which they came.

In the present day, they use the same accusations as in the National Socialist [Nazi] era in order to justify anti-Roma measures.

In July 2013 two French males confronted a group of around 100 Roma who were camping in a field, saying, "Hitler didn't kill enough of you."

A Hungarian nationalist, Zsolt Bayer, said in an interview, without suffering any consequences, "Most gypsies are not suitable for cohabitation. They are not suitable for being among people. Most are animals and behave like animals. They shouldn't be tolerated or understood, but stamped out. Animals should not exist, in no way."

The financial resources allocated to Roma communities for combating poverty are misused by corrupt people and centralized structures dominated by non-Roma, who are themselves often very racist. These resources never come to the families in need, but to the corrupt officials and mafia-like organizations protected by the states.

On the other hand, some Roma representatives misuse the political work and resources for their own interests and damage the struggle for emancipation.

Roma activists and artists like Marika Schmidt have been censored and accused of racism when they tried to fight against the anti-Roma status quo.

All over Europe, mass media reports are falsified in discriminatory ways that often negatively influence public opinion. Newspapers and television publish racist, anti-Roma statements in order to protect the privilege of non-Roma. They protect the racist structures against the Roma. There are no laws to forbid the anti-Romaists, but there are laws that give no chance to our people.

We consider that the Roma are in a very dangerous situation and racism and anti-Romaism are manifesting at all levels of society. We do consider that there's no solidarity from white Europeans. We consider the situation of our people to be a result of the racist policies which began when the Roma arrived in Europe and which have never ended.

We consider that Roma have no right to decide their own lives and that the murders and inhumane measures against our people will continue because white people are in an undeclared war with us.

Even the activists and artists who claim to be on our side and in solidarity with us act mostly to protect their own interests. They are taking the few jobs destined for Roma. They are manipulating the resources and they wreck the Roma communities with nonpolitical projects that nobody needs.

The only solution for Roma people is to join with other oppressed people, to overthrow the financial and political domination of the white world, to stop the inhumane capitalist regime and to fight for emancipation and equal rights all over the world for all people. The only solution is the revolution of the oppressed people.

As long as Europe has programs against the Roma, there is no democracy in Europe!

As long as racism exists in Europe, there's no civilization in Europe!

As long as deportation practices and elimination practices exist in Europe, there is no respect for human rights in Europe!

In solidarity, all power to the people!
Uhuru!

Ralph Poynter

Activist and leader of the committee for
Justice for Lynne Stewart, a political prisoner in the U.S.,
who was released December 31, 2013

Thank you so much for having me here representing Lynne Stewart. Lynne Stewart is in prison and she's in prison because of her words. We know from Edward Snowden's report that there were no secrets. Everybody knows what we believed. The proof is there, but Lynne is suffering in jail. And because of her words, the statement that she has prepared from prison is having difficulty getting out. You could call that bureaucracy. We call it pure censorship.

She said to be sure to remind everyone here that she is aware that when the moment of oppression became very personal for her, she knew who stepped forward first.

She said to tell the people that this is very important because the people here understand those first steps that must be taken in a journey of a thousand miles.

Lynne extends her solidarity with the message of the African People's Socialist Party. She will continue to work in that vein to make this a better world.

I will report back to Lynne when we get that seven minute phone call this evening as to what happened today. Thank you, Chairman. Thank all of you for the support because this is what keeps people alive in our death camps, as Lynne says. Let us not be confused about where our brothers and sisters are.

So many of our people have fought over the years—in the struggles of the '60s and the '30s; the Civil Rights struggle; the Human Rights struggle; the historical struggle of all people to change this oppressive nation.

We support all that is expressed here today by the people who have joined the African People's Socialist Party movement.

Uhuru!

Letter from Lynne Stewart, addressing the African People's Socialist Party:

First, I want to praise the concept of African socialism. Millenniums before Karl Marx, Africans lived socialistically and were successful and content, artistic and cultural. It was the coming of imperialism, including slavery, that destroyed this precious harmony, which has yet to be restored to both mother Africa and those who have found themselves in the diaspora.

Indeed, the rape and the looting of the Continent has been accelerated. Nevertheless, facing a fierce power in the industrial capitalistic enemy, your organization has adopted a newer socialism and embarked ambitiously in establishing beachheads and developing cadre to expose this ancient and most correct doctrine worldwide. Long live the APSP!

I also want to mention that your method of organization is very impressive. To me, who has seen movements come and go since I was a bright-eyed young thing 50 years ago, the crucial difference I note is in the work. The membership is involved in running businesses that not only serve the community but also serve this socialist organization. Baking pies and collecting and displaying collectibles are two activities that I must admit are close to my personal heart. Just ask Ralph.

This work not only lends itself to unity but builds collectivism and love among the members and raises much-needed revenue. The radio programming and The Burning Spear newspaper are exemplary efforts with the real content not mired in doctrines long since discarded and unworkable. In this past issue, I appreciated your wonderful obituary of Vietnamese General Giap. It wasn't what The New York Times wrote and I know because I read both. Long live the APSP!

Finally, I need to once again ask your assistance in forcing the Bureau of Prisons to grant my compassionate release that they have been stonewalling now since August 5. My life expectancy as per my cancer doctor is down to 12 months. They know I am fully qualified to be released. There are 40,000 people who have signed up to force them to do the right thing, which is to let me go home to my family and receive advanced care in New York City, my home.

They have refused to act, and it is entirely within the range of their politics and their cruelty to hold political prisoners until we have days to live before releasing us. Witness Herman Wallace of the Angola Three and Marilyn Buck. We are fighting against this and mobilizing for a big push. Email, mail and telephone Obama, the Gutless Wonder; and attorney general Eric Holder, Big Speech, No

Action; and the Bureau of Prisons on December 10, 11 and 12. Bring Lynne home for the holidays. We are many. They are few.

A few final thoughts: First, Ralph needs to know the dates of the APSP weightlifting competition so he can challenge your finest with his own 79-year-old prowess.

Lastly, as you discuss political prisoners, remember that I am a virtual newcomer, having just finished four years inside. Not far from here in Coleman, Florida, at the Federal Bureau of Prisons there is a heroic defender of the people, Leonard Peltier. He is as far from his nation, the Turtle Mountain Band in North Dakota, as is possible.

Everybody home! Free Leonard!

Free all political prisoners!

Long live the African People's Socialist Party!

Amaru Pachacutec

Member of the Tawantinsuyu Nation

Greetings from the belly of the European world beast.

I write this message from the cold island of Britain. I am forced to write to you from the land of my oppressor, and you are forced to read this letter on the land taken from my people 500 years ago by our common oppressor. This is the land where your ancestors were taken as captives, enslaved and treated like the worst sorts of animals.

You must all know the story all too well. We must never tire of repeating and reminding ourselves about the terrible conditions the Europeans have made our people go through. We must also remind ourselves that we had a great history before the Europeans came and stole it all away from us, not only by force but in a most dishonorable and inhumane way.

The other day I was speaking to a fellow captured brother from my part of the world, and he told me to forget about slavery and move on with what we have today. Our sight has been tampered with, Brothers and Sisters. We are enslaved to the core, yet we have been programmed into not seeing it and blaming our social problems on ourselves. Our eyes have carefully been trained to not see the external enemy who is the cause of all our social, economic and political problems.

An Indigenous man like me should not have to be here living off the scraps of the whites. I should be back in my homeland enjoying the vast riches of my land, in the company of my fellow race. I am here because the white settlers, the anchor babies of the first settlers, still have power over us. They control the production of goods and commodities. They control the market. They control the political arena and the laws of my land. They control the education system. They control the media and the arts. In other words, the European parasites have refined their oppression to an extent that we are on the periphery of their white power, their white dominion.

My people sometimes talk about neocolonialism and neo-liberalism as if they somehow halted and started again—as if what we are experiencing today is NEW. There is nothing new in the oppression of our colonized people. They haven't let go of our damn necks for the last 500 years. For too long these pale skins have had us acting like fools in poverty and in sickness and pain. All evidence points to the irrefutable fact that white people are still shitting over humanity and getting away with it.

We must end this period in our respective histories as Nican Tlaca Indigenous and African people. We must end with their poisons of weed, alcohol, hard drugs as well as the incessant need for clubbing, shopping and other non-productive activities that dominate our society today. We must end the gang violence and the incessant hatred toward ourselves. We must strive to look deep within ourselves and find the courage to end this infinite cycle of self-destruction. They put all this shit on our plates and we eat from it, because they have trained us to normalize the terrible conditions they have placed us in.

The most important part of all this is our willingness to challenge the white supremacist, colonialist power structure. We must confront it by educating ourselves on our history that has been distorted to help them keep us trapped as their subordinates. We must challenge them by refusing to be part of the gangs and violence that destroy our own people and help keep them in positions of authority and power. We must join the Uhuru Movement and fight back all aspects of our modern oppression—that same oppression that has been ongoing for so many centuries now. Onward to a future where our people enjoy political, economic and social freedom.

To all of the members and supporters of the Uhuru Movement: you are all an inspiration to all colonized and oppressed people around the world.

I look forward to meeting you all in the very near future.

Uhuru! Qispi Kai! Freedom!

Emma Khadija Jones

Activist mother of Malik E. Jones, murdered by police in East Haven, Connecticut in 1997, when he was 21 years old

Revolutionary Greetings!

I deeply appreciate your invitation to honor me at the Congress of the African People's Socialist Party.

I regret that circumstances prevented me from physically being present at this historic Congress. However, I continue to hold my firm, united position with the Party in the liberation struggle, as I absolutely have no other choice but to resist when the government aggressively sponsors the savage brutalization and murder of our children and loved ones without consequences.

I direct your attention to April 14, 1997, when a white East Haven police officer, Robert Flodquist, followed Malik from East Haven into New Haven and brutally gunned him down, KKK-lynching style, as Malik sat unarmed and boxed-in inside a car.

Malik lies in a grave on the allegation of a motor vehicle infraction, which the officer did not see nor did anyone else. This horrific, unspeakable, wicked attack led to over 16 years of rigorous struggle for meaningful solutions.

Two separate juries and a federal court awarded $2.5 million in punitive damages; $900,000 plus costs and expenses in compensatory damages. The courts held that the officer violated Malik's rights under the U.S. constitution and further decided that the East Haven Police Department and the officer violated Malik's and other oppressed people's rights by engaging in the discriminatory practice, pattern and custom of border patrols and racial profiling.

The officer was granted qualified immunity. The town was held liable. However, the entire case has been overturned strictly on a narrow legal technicality. The police chief claimed that he didn't know what was going on with respect to racial profiling. The second circuit court of appeals left the murder of Malik to stand as illegal, but with no remedy or consequences. This is totally outrageous and insane.

Despite the widespread, vicious attacks upon me, my family and the people, I have never fainted, lost sight, focus or hope.

In summation, I need to be in the same room and environment with my brothers, sisters and allies from Africa, the U.S. and throughout the world, to feel that spirit and witness the faces of those who clearly understand that freedom and liberation are not for sprinters or cowards, but for the long distance runner.

After all is said and done, without any doubt whatsoever, 40 years of struggle on the front lines of freedom, justice and liberation speaks volumes for the long distance mountain climbers and the awesome power and will of our people.

African workers and peasants of the world unite!
Peace!

Marcos Garcia

Labor Attaché, Venezuelan Embassy, Washington, DC

African People's Socialist Party:

Dear Brothers and Sisters,

As most of you know, I had the opportunity to attend your Fifth Congress in Washington, DC. I also accepted a kind invitation to a reception at your headquarters in St. Petersburg, Florida. So I have a clear understanding of your efforts to build a revolutionary alternative for the people of African descent. This Sixth Congress is another step on that way.

The topics for discussion during the Congress are very relevant today, and especially for those who struggle on behalf of the poor and who one day hope to free themselves from the chains of oppression that have hindered our peoples for so many centuries.

As you well know, such noble objectives for social justice face strong opposition at the national and international levels from sectors that profit from poverty, malnutrition, hunger and lack of health services. Opposition comes from those who use the mass media's power to justify aggression and violence without consideration for any basic regulation of peaceful coexistence among nations, in their effort to retain the current system of exclusion and oppression that only benefits an extreme minority.

This reality raises the urgent task of encouraging international solidarity with the struggles of the peoples for their right to sovereignty and basic human rights. Ultimately, a strong collective effort to support the just causes of our peoples before the threat of barbarity that shows us its most aggressive face, should be made by progressive, socialist and revolutionary sectors from various countries.

We wish a great success to the Sixth Congress of the African People's Socialist Party. We are sure that the discussions will be deep and the decisions adopted will allow you to continue advancing in the ways of peace, progress and organizing for social justice and liberation.

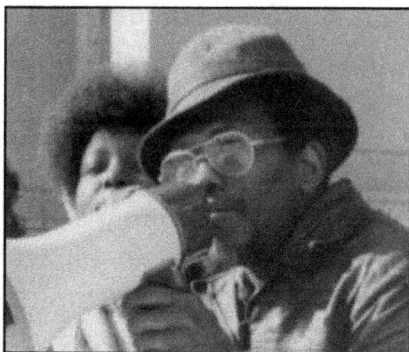

Richard Mafundi Lake

*African political prisoner and long-time Party supporter
held in Alabama*

Congratulations and solidarity greetings from the bowels of the Alabama prison system. It is with love, humility and great respect that I greet the African People's Socialist Party and the righteous strugglers who are in attendance for the APSP's Sixth Congress.

You have been consistent and persistent in this struggle for freedom, justice and human dignity. Over the last 40 years, the African People's Socialist Party has done a herculean job of serving the people! It has provided a sterling example of revolutionary leadership, fortitude and courage for African people and other oppressed people throughout the world.

I feel honored to have worked closely with the APSP and to have served as the National Coordinator of the African National Prisoner Organization (ANPO), one of the many outstanding and effective organizations created by the African People's Socialist Party.

I would be greatly remiss if I did not acknowledge the presence of my wife, Carolyn Weyni Njeri Lake, my children and members of my support committee, who have steadfastly demonstrated their love, loyalty and support for me in over 30 years of my incarceration.

Perhaps by now you have had the pleasure of being blessed by the beautiful and melodious voice of my wife, and I think she deserves an ovation from those in attendance for her remarkable example of an African woman standing in the gap for over 30 years of my incarceration without flinching. I love you, baby!

I also want to acknowledge all of my friends and supporters from around the world who learned of my plight from reading *The Burning Spear* newspaper.

Finally, I want to acknowledge and salute the African People's Socialist Party for over 40 years of love, support and friendship. Thanks APSP for all you have done for me, my family and for the people of the world. Please stand and take a bow!

Unbroken and Unbreakable!

Carolyn Weyni Njeri Lake

Richard Mafundi Lake Support Committee

Uhuru!

How humbled, grateful and excited we are to extend our greetings, congratulations and solidarity to the African People's Socialist Party for your Sixth Congress. We greet those in attendance as well.

On behalf of Richard Mafundi Lake, his family and support committee, we would like to express our gratitude to the Party for all the unselfish work and support given to us in our fight to free Mafundi over the past 30-plus years. Though Mafundi is unable to be here with you physically, his spirit is here.

Mafundi Lake is a black political prisoner who was reared in Birmingham, Alabama, a city that even Dr. Martin Luther King, Jr. called "the most segregated city in America!" Mafundi, like tens of thousands of political activists, known and unknown, has been targeted by COINTELPRO and other government agencies for his principled and uncompromising quest for freedom, justice and human dignity for all oppressed people.

It is not necessary to remind those here of the devastation that corrupt government agencies have had on families, communities and the lives of individual political activists across the country. These nefarious government agencies have wrought havoc and misery through the employment of informants and collaborators who give false testimony and provide manufactured evidence with the collusion of the judges and the courts. Hundreds of prisoners have been exonerated of false convictions. Thousands more languish in jails and prisons today fighting fraudulent convictions and draconian sentences.

We know that the American judicial system is gravely flawed, but are we building effective organizations to fight the injustice that targets political activists who dissent in our communities? This is the injustice that creates widows, orphans and single parents in our communities, the injustice that creates poverty and foments crime in our communities. How can we depend upon law officers to prevent crime in our communities when most of them are criminals?

I am sick and tired of being sick and tired!

Power to the People!

Larry Adams

Vice Chair, External Affairs,
People's Organization for Progress

To the Sixth Congress of the African People's Socialist Party:

Sisters and Brothers; Comrades in Struggle of the African People's Socialist Party:

The People's Organization for Progress (P.O.P.) extends warm and sincere feelings of solidarity to you on the occasion of your Sixth Congress!

You have politically and organizationally consolidated step by step, year by year, through a process that reflects five congresses of growth and development of advanced forces in the struggle for the liberation of African people and the defeat of the system of world imperialism, led by U.S. imperialism.

You have thereby contributed to the emancipation of all humankind from our history of exploitation and oppression. This is a testament to the serious consistency and commitment of APSP leadership, cadre and followers to forge a weapon of liberation. Your experience provides an inspirational example for emulation by P.O.P. and forces for black liberation and the defeat of imperialism.

The current situation of imperialist crisis is characterized by the intensification of attacks on, and oppression and exploitation of oppressed peoples and the international working class; as well as the politics of impoverishment and disempowerment of the masses of the sons and daughters of Africa and our allies, along with wars for plunder of material resources and the enslavement of our labor. Therefore, the historic task of the day is the organization of struggle and resistance.

You recognize the situation and are rising to the task. We join you in this endeavor. We too are committed through struggle to developing the consciousness and organization of our people for day-to-day struggle and ultimate liberation.

We have unity on our particular responsibility, as oppressed daughters and sons of tormented Africa in the belly of the beast that leads world oppression and exploitation, to expose, struggle against and defeat "our own" ruling class. We must stand with denigrated black humanity and the peoples of the world, who struggle for freedom and full realization of our potential.

Together we will oppose the enemies of black people and all creators of wealth, regardless of the color or ethnicity of the servants of imperialism. We will not let anything distract us from our march to liberation. We will judge political actors by their deeds and substance, not by words and appearances.

Comrades, march on! We march with you on the long road to freedom and justice!

Uhuru Sasa!! Pamoja tutashinda!!

Deloyd T. Parker

*Executive Director, S.H.A.P.E. Community Center,
Houston, TX*

To the Sixth Congress of the African People's Socialist Party:

Greetings of solidarity and peace to our Brothers and Sisters of the African People's Socialist Party.

We at S.H.A.P.E. Community Center want to acknowledge the African People's Socialist Party's Sixth Congress and the work your esteemed organization has done for over 40 years.

We wish you continued strength and success in your vital cause to improve the living conditions and nurture the development of relationships with Africa and Africans worldwide.

Here at S.H.A.P.E. we now and forever applaud the grueling and inspirational work that gives a resounding voice to our African brothers and sisters who have been dispersed and displaced throughout the world while affording them the opportunity to make informed decisions through education.

Through this unbreakable bond, we share in your tireless efforts to continue the imperative and necessary reforms for the betterment of our people.

Your vigilant Brother in the cause.

The struggle continues!

Chokwe Lumumba

Mayor of Jackson, MS

To all those combating structural racism, classism and imperialism:

We the New Afrikan People's Organization and the Malcolm X Grassroots Movement stand in solidarity with the African People's Socialist Party.

Capitalist Adam Smith's invisible hand theory consists of maximizing profits while exploiting others. The economic system that governs this country is fundamentally flawed. Martyrs of Adam Smith's conceptualization can attest to the fact that a profit-over-all ideology is counterintuitive to human values.

The African People's Socialist Party, founded in the 1970s, continues to be on the front lines for social justice and liberation. Raising the consciousness of the masses is a key step in being victorious in this fight for liberation. This movement has worldwide significance.

Imperialism relentlessly permeates our society. United States foreign policy consists of targeted executions, isolation and fragmentation. We therefore salute the African People's

Socialist Party and their commitment to establishing steps towards a liberated African people.

Free the Land!

Mayor Lumumba passed away February 25, 2014

Fenty Tholley

*Chairman, African People's Socialist Party,
Sierra Leone, West Africa*

Uhuru!

The African People's Socialist Party Sierra Leone salutes the African People's Socialist Party USA for their hard work to make the Sixth Congress a remarkable event of 2013.

Special thanks and recognition goes to the leadership of the African People's Socialist Party, Chairman Omali Yeshitela for his tremendous and courageous work and for providing a reliable leadership for the liberation and unification of Africa and its masses from the brutal colonial capitalist and imperialist relationship that exists between the oppressor nation and the oppressed nation.

Bravo to the Deputy Chairwoman Ona Zené Yeshitela who exemplifies the true value of what African women are capable of doing. May you live long, until the end of the struggle!

I say bravo to the National Central Committee of the African People's Socialist Party for your brave fight. You are indeed great warriors of Africa and a force for good. You are worth more than a thousand soldiers at war with our greatest enemies. Keep the fight going!

The APSP Sierra Leone would not hesitate to climb mountains and to swim across oceans to stand by you at all times in the struggle.

Long live Africa!

Long live the APSP!

Touch one! Touch all!

Uhuru!

Part IV

Photos from the Sixth Congress of the African People's Socialist Party

1. Tammy Harris opens the Congress. 2. Ron Bobb-Semple brings Marcus Garvey to life. 3. African People's Socialist Party (APSP) Secretary General Gaida Kambon leads the National Central Committee (NCC) flag procession. 4. APSP Chairman Omali Yeshitela stands with members of the NCC. 5. Carolyn Lake asks the question in song, "What does it mean to be free?" 6. Ralph Poynter speaks from the Lynne Stewart Defense Committee. 7. Unión del Barrio delegation brings solidarity from the Mexican liberation movement. 8. People's Vanguard performs. 9. Deputy Chair Ona Zené and Chairman Omali Yeshitela at the One Africa! One Nation! Freedom Ball.

1. Chairman Omali Yeshitela presents the Political Report. 2. Deputy Chair Ona Zené Yeshitela leads the economic development workshop. 3. Charo Walker-Morley (l) and Tammy Harris unveil the Party's travel agency. 4. Glen Ford presents on the history of U.S. surveillance of the African community. 5. Tiffany Murphy brings gifts to Party supporters. 6. Panel on Party history. From l: Omowale Kefing, National Office of Recruitment and Membership Director Chimurenga Waller and Secretary General Gaida Kambon. 7. ASI Secretary General Luwezi Kinshasa presents a resolution on building a united Africa. 8. Alex Morley, APSP Bahamas. 9. Nyabinga Dzimbahwe promotes *The Burning Spear*. 10. Kazoots performs.

1. Standing, l to r: Charo Walker-Morley, Aisha Fields, Fosiya Aqli, Sabrin Ibrahim, Waleeah Brooks, Makda Yohannes. Seated: Zenobia Spencer, Ka Meritah, Yejide Orunmila. **2.** Secretary General Gaida Kambon. **3.** ASI Secretary General Luwezi Kinshasa and Patricia Lumumba. **4.** Deputy Chair Ona Zené Yeshitela and Vanessa Childs. **5.** From l: Charles Oliver, Jennifer Madden, Agit-Prop Director Dedan Sankara. **6.** Chairman Omali Yeshitela (center) with Ron Bobb-Semple (l) and Alex Jordann Darby. **7.** Chairman Omali Yeshitela speaks at the One Africa! One Nation! Freedom Ball. **8.** Penny Hess, Chair, African People's Solidarity Committee. **9.** L to r: Cara Locke, Stephanie Midler, Wendy Craig, Uhuru Solidarity Movement.

1. Security forces at the Congress. 2. Congress participants prepare to raise the African flag outside the Uhuru House. 3. John Thomas, Manager and Personal Trainer, TyRon Lewis Community Gym. 4. Dr. Aisha Fields, Director, All African People's Development and Empowerment Project. 5. APSP member from Chicago, Wil Lockett. 6. Waleeah Brooks, InPDUM President. 7. Fenty Tholley, APSP Sierra Leone. 8. Party members vote. 9. Newly elected APSP NCC, from left: Dedan Sankara, Luwezi Kinshasa, Gaida Kambon, Dr. Aisha Fields, Chairman Omali Yeshitela, Deputy Chair Ona Zené Yeshitela, Chimurenga Waller, (Not pictured: Ushindi Watu, Kobina Bantushango, Waleeah Brooks). **See more Congress photos at apspuhuru.org.**

Bibliography

Berger, Dan. *The Hidden 1970s: Histories of Radicalism.* New Brunswick, N.J.: Rutgers University Press, 2010.

Brzezinski, Zbigniew. *Second Chance: Three Presidents and the Crisis of American Superpower.* New York: Basic Books, 2008.

Buchanan, Patrick J. *Day of Reckoning: How Hubris, Ideology, and Greed Are Tearing America Apart.* New York: Thomas Dunne Books/St. Martin's Press, 2007.

Buchanan, Patrick J. *Suicide of a Superpower: Will America Survive to 2025?* New York: Thomas Dunne Books, 2011.

Cannadine, David. *The Undivided Past: Humanity Beyond Our Differences.* New York: Alfred A. Knopf, 2013.

Diop, Cheikh Anta. *The Cultural Unity of Black Africa: The Domains of Patriarchy and of Matriarchy in Classical Antiquity.* Chicago: Third World Press, 1978.

Engelhardt, Tom. "Debacle! How Two Wars in the Greater Middle East Revealed the Weakness of the Global Superpower." *TomDispatch.com,* January 3, 2012.

Fukuyama, Francis. "The Future of History: Can Liberal Democracy Survive the Decline of the Middle Class?" *Foreign Affairs,* January/February 2012.

Huntington, Samuel P. *Who Are We? The Challenges to America's National Identity.* New York: Simon and Schuster, 2004.

Jaffe, Hosea. *A History of Africa.* London: Zed Books, 1986.

Johnson, Walter. "King Cotton's Long Shadow." *The New York Times,* March 30, 2013.

Kadalie, Modibo M. *Internationalism, Pan-Africanism and the Struggle of Social Classes: Raw Writings from the Notebook *of an Early Nineteen Seventies African-American Radical Activist.* Savannah, Georgia: One Quest Press, 2000.

Ki-Zerbo, Joseph. *"African Personality and the New African Society."* From: *Gideon-Cyrus Makau Mutiso and S. W. Rohio, Readings in African Political Thought.* London: Heinemann, 1975.

Lenin, Vladimir Ilych. *Imperialism and the Split in Socialism.* Moscow: Foreign Languages Publishing House, 1954.

Mao Zedong. *Win the Masses in Their Millions for the Anti-Japanese National United Front:* (May 7, 1937). Beijing: Foreign Languages Press, 1968.

Marx, Karl. *The Poverty of Philosophy.* Chicago: Charles H. Kerr & Company, 1920.

Marx, Karl. *Capital.* London: J.M. Dent & Sons, 1934.

Padmore, George. *The Life and Struggles of Negro Toilers.* Hollywood: Sun Dance Press, 1971.

Padmore, George. *Pan-Africanism or Communism.* Doubleday Anchor, 1972,

"The 1928 and 1930 Comintern Resolutions on the Black National Question in the United States." Washington, DC: The Revolutionary Review Press, 1975. Online at: *http://www.marx2mao.com/Other/CR75.html.*

Yeshitela, Omali. *A New Beginning: The Road to Black Freedom and Socialism: the main resolution, constitution and program adopted at the First Congress of the African People's Socialist Party.* St. Petersburg, FL: African People's Socialist Party, 1982.

Yeshitela, Omali. *Black Power Since the Sixties: The Struggle against Opportunism within the U.S. Front of the Black Liberation Movement.* St. Petersburg, FL: Burning Spear Publications, 1991.

Yeshitela, Omali. *"Build and Consolidate the African People's Socialist Party."* Oakland: Marcus Garvey Club, 1986.

Yeshitela, Omali. *Izwe lethu i Afrika! (Africa is our land): the era of the worldwide African revolution and socialist unification of Africa and African people under the leadership of the African working class and poor peasants.* Burning Spear Publications, 1990.

Yeshitela, Omali. *Omali Yeshitela Speaks.* St. Petersburg, FL: Burning Spear Uhuru Publications, 2005.

Yeshitela, Omali. *One Africa! One Nation! The African Socialist International and the Movement to Unite and Liberate Africa and African People Worldwide.* St. Petersburg, FL: Burning Spear Uhuru Publications, 2006.

Yeshitela, Omali. *One People! One Party! One Destiny! The Political Report to the Fifth Congress of the African People's Socialist Party USA.* St. Petersburg, FL: Burning Spear Uhuru Publications, 2010.

Yeshitela, Omali. *Reparations Now! Abbreviated Report of the International Tribunal on Reparations for African People in the U.S.* African People's Socialist Party, 1983.

Yeshitela, Omali. *Stolen Black Labor: The Political Economy of Domestic Colonialism.* Oakland: Burning Spear Publications, 1983.

Yeshitela, Omali. "Tactics and Strategy for Black Liberation in the U.S.: The Political Aspects of Building a Mass Movement." Oakland: African People's Socialist Party, 1979.

www.ingramcontent.com/pod-product-compliance
Lightning Source LLC
Chambersburg PA
CBHW020332270326
41926CB00007B/149